Where the

ASHLAND -MEDFORD AND BEYOND

How to find nearly 150 recreation trails located in or around the Rogue River Valley, or on nearby public lands. The geographical area covered in this book extends from near the California-Oregon border, north to the Diamond Lake vicinity. Historical and map information is included.

Cover design and art work by Bob Sisson

Independent Printing Co. - 640 Tolman Cr. Road - Ashland, OR

LATE PRESS-TRAIL PARK PASSES ARE REQUIRED AT SOME NATIONAL FOREST TRAILHEADS- PLEASE SEE PAGE 182 FOR DETAILS!

ACKNOWLEDGEMENTS

This book became reality due to the contributions of many persons and agencies including:

U.S. FOREST SERVICE: Rogue River, Winema,and Umpqua National Forest Ranger District personnel. The forest recreation map at the rear of the book and many historical notes were reproduced from Rogue River National Forest information.

OTHER SOURCES INCLUDE: U.S. Bureau of Land Management, U.S. Army Corps of Engineers, Boise Cascade Timber and Wood Products Group, Crater Lake National Park Staff, Jackson County & Medford Parks and Recreation Departments, The Nature Conservancy and Oregon Fish and Wildlife personnel.

AUDREY WILLIAMS: "Over the shoulder advice"
IVAN COLLVER, Ashland computer programmer, helpful guidance.

PLEASE NOTE: The emphasis of this book is to DESCRIBE HOW TO GET TO THE TRAILS AND WHAT EQUIPMENT TO BRING. Although known precautions are listed, the author cannot be responsible for trails that may be hard to follow due to reduced maintenance, abandonment, new roads,logging operations or any other unforeseen conditions. Check with the applicable agencies for the latest trail status.

 ISBN: 0-9622114-5-1

TABLE OF CONTENTS

CHAPTER 14 PACIFIC CREST TRAIL-ROAD ACCESS Page

Collings Mountain Trail

Bill says, "Leave things as you found them for others to enjoy."

INTRODUCTION

Southern Oregon is a paradise for outdoor enthusiasts! It provides year-round opportunities for hiking and backpacking, horseback riding, and a variety of winter sports! Southern Oregon has less rain than does most parts of the State, and if a person is careful in choosing where and when to go, it is possible to find trails where rain is at a minimum. It is also possible to locate areas above the fog and into the sunshine!

DURING THE WINTER MONTHS, the Applegate Valley and vicinity provide spectacular outdoor experiences! This is a great place to soak up some sunshine and enjoy the open views of the surrounding mountains, or to travel the trails along the Applegate River or Applegate Lake area.

Other favorite winter trails are those at Lost Creek Lake, Table Rocks, Roxy Ann Peak, or the beautiful Lower Rogue River Trail. Ashland generally lifts its head above the Rogue Valley winter fog, and the trails are less muddy due to granite soil.

Mt. Ashland is a favorite for winter sports and is complete with a ski lodge, ski rental facilities, rope tows, chair lifts and trails for cross-country skiing. Contact a Forest Ranger Station for locations of other cross-country ski trails in the Cascade Range.

IN LATE SPRING OR SUMMER, the trails at high elevations begin to open up, but above 7000 feet elevation the snow might not be gone until mid-July. The Pacific Crest National Scenic Trail in this area travels 31 miles through Crater Lake National Park before it continues south another 75 miles along the Cascade Range, crest of the Siskiyou Mountains and on to the Klamath River. This is but a portion of the Pacific Crest National Scenic Trail that extends 2500 miles from Canada to Mexico.

In addition to Crater Lake National Park, southern Oregon boasts several Wilderness Areas: The Rogue-Umpqua Divide, Sky Lakes, Mountain Lakes and Red Buttes. The summit of Mt. McLoughlin at 9495' elevation, is the highest point one can reach in the area covered by this book.

The author has hiked many of these trails during outings conducted by the Oregon-Idaho Conference of the United Methodist Church or by the Rogue Chapter of the Sierra Club. While along on these trips, it became obvious that a book was needed to help find the trailhead locations, because many road junction signs were damaged or missing. Maps are sometimes hard to follow or may need revision, and so an effort is made to present a fairly simple access description to the trailheads, giving directions from nearest mileposts. Every effort will be made to keep this book up-to-date, but changes beyond our control can rapidly happen!

HOW TO USE THIS BOOK

It is very important to BRING MAPS listed in each hike description, and a COMPASS to help you find your way. The U.S. Forest Service has a very excellent leaflet entitled "MAP AND COMPASS." It contains work sheets with practice drills that are easy to understand. It takes the confusion out of using a compass and may save your life!

The U. S. Geological Survey publishes TOPOGRAPHIC MAPS (Topos) that are available from libraries, sporting goods stores, stationary or book stores, and some office suppliers. They can be ordered directly from U. S. Geological Survey, Distribution Section, Federal Center, Denver Colorado 80225. The maps cover every section of the United States in minute detail. An "Index To Topographic Maps of Oregon" is also available from the USGS.

U.S. Forest Service maps are often printed in TOPO form. For the area covered by this book, the Pacific Crest National Scenic Trail, Mountain Lakes Wilderness and Sky Lakes Area maps are all topographic. TOPO MAPS are also available from the Applegate, Ashland, Butte Falls, Prospect, Tiller and Diamond Lake RANGER DISTRICTS.

TOPO MAPS have contour lines that determine elevation and the altitude of peaks, valleys and other landmarks. They also indicate roads, trails, rivers, streams, railroad tracks and other details. MOST ELEVATION DATA IN THIS BOOK WAS ESTIMATED FROM TOPO MAPS AND SHOULD NOT BE CONSIDERED ACCURATE NOR OFFICIAL.

EQUIPMENT NEEDED: In addition to MAPS and COMPASS, the following items are important:

- BOOTS OR STURDY SHOES: Waterproof, well fitted with warm socks.
- CLOTHING that can be layered, preferably wool.
- RAINGEAR. Rainsuits have more wind protection than do ponchos.
- EMERGENCY SUPPLIES: First aid,matches,flashlight,bug repellant.
- CANTEEN - WATER PURIFICATION: There is no guarantee that any water in the woods is free from Giardia, or other harmful bacteria. The only sure way to avoid sickness is to BRING WATER FROM HOME or to have absolute resolve not to drink any water in the woods unless it has been treated. Water purification tablets are not quite 100% effective. The safest way is to boil the water for at least 10 minutes, or to bring a water filter, available from suppliers of recreation equipment.

The wood tick is much smaller than this but they can be easily seen if they get on you. They are in area all year long.

RULES TO CONSIDER.

SAFETY: Before you leave home, let others know where you are going and stick with the plan! When in the woods, stay with your group, as you may need to rely on each other in case of emergencies! Do not run on the trails or take needless chances. Help may be far away! Drive safely on forest roads and be alert for logging vehicles or other traffic.

OBEY FIRE REGULATIONS. Build fires only where allowed, and make sure they are COMPLETELY OUT before leaving camp. No smoking while traveling, except in vehicles on roads.

OBTAIN PERMITS. Before hiking in the woods, check with the appropriate agencies for fire or wilderness entry permits. TRAILHEAD PARKING PERMITS REQUIRED ON DESIGNATED TRAILS-SEE PAGE 182.

PACK OUT ALL TRASH. Don't bury it. Leave campgrounds cleaner than you found them! Remove litter encountered on the trail.

DO NOT POLLUTE. Keep soaps and other pollutants out of rivers and streams. Bury human waste away from streams or lakes.

PRIVATE PROPERTY. Respect posted signs, stay on the trail.

DON'T CUT ACROSS SWITCHBACKS. This can cause erosion and severe damage to the trails.

LISTEN TO THE WILDERNESS! Leave radios and tape players at home.

ALWAYS BE PREPARED. Bring the equipment listed on the previous page. CARRY DRINKING WATER ON EVERY OUTING!

HAZARDS TO AVOID. Poison oak, deer ticks or an occasional rattlesnake may be encountered while hiking in southern Oregon. Using caution can help minimize these hazards.

POISON OAK is generally found in the lower elevation hills (below 6000 feet) in the Applegate and Rogue River Valleys. Learn to identify this noxious plant. Its shiny green leaves are in groups of threes turning to red in late summer. Oils from the plant can cause an itching rash or blisters. The treatment methods include scrubbing the skin with naptha or alkaline soap, or by cleansing with rubbing alcohol. Calamine or other skin lotion may be beneficial if the rash is mild. It may be necessary to seek medical advice in severe cases.

TICKS can carry Lyme disease,or recently reported cases of H.G.E. (Human granulocytic ehrlichiosis) and Babesiosis. THESE DISEASES CAN BE DISABLING OR FATAL IF NOT DIAGNOSED AND TREATED. SEEK THE LATEST MEDICAL ADVICE.

PREVENTING BITES: Wear long sleeves and pants tucked into boots. Avoid trail margins, brush and grassy areas when in tick country. Use tick repellant on clothes and shoes. White clothes help make ticks visible. Check yourself and pets carefully for ticks.
TREATMENT: Remove attatched tick at once with fine-jaw tweezers, grasping the tick's mouth-parts as close to the skin as possible, slowly and gently pulling straight out. AUTHORITIES ADVISE not to squeeze tick or spray it with oil as it may inject fluid into you. Wash bite area, hands and apply antiseptic. GET MEDICAL TREATMENT IF ANY PARTS ARE LEFT IN THE SKIN OR IF COMPLICATIONS DEVELOP.

RATTLESNAKES. This is not a common problem in southern Oregon, but an occasional snake may be spotted at lower elevations. During summer months, look for them in shaded areas especially during early morning or late afternoon. In case of snake bite, the best treatment is to get the victim to a doctor or a hospital as soon as possible. Apply cold compresses if available. Loose constricting bands may be placed above the bite, but not so tight as to stop blood circulation.

WHERE TO GET INFORMATION AND PERMITS.

ROGUE RIVER NATIONAL FOREST.

-Forest Supervisor, P.O. Box 520, 333 W. 8th St., Medford, Or. 97501 Phone (541)858-2200

-District Ranger, Ashland Ranger Station, 645 Washington St., Ashland, Oregon 97520 Phone (541)482-3333

-District Ranger, Butte Falls Ranger Station, P.O. Box 227, Butte Falls, Oregon 97522 Phone (541)865-2700

-District Ranger, Prospect Ranger Station, Prospect, Oregon, 97536 Phone (541)560-3400

-District Ranger, Star Ranger Station, 6941 Upper Applegate Road, Jacksonville, Oregon 97530 Phone (541)899-1812

WINEMA NATIONAL FOREST.

-Forest Supervisor, 2819 Dahlia St., Klamath Falls, Oregon, 97601 Phone (541)883-6714

-Klamath District Ranger, 1936 California Ave., Klamath Falls, Oregon 97601 Phone (541)885-3400

UMPQUA NATIONAL FOREST.

-Forest Supervisor, P.O. Box 1008, Roseburg, Or. 97470 Phone (541)672-6601

-Diamond Lake Ranger District, Toketee Route Box 101, Idleyld Park, Oregon 97447 Phone (541)498-2531

-Tiller Ranger District, Route 2 Box 1, Tiller, Oregon 97484 Phone (541)825-3201

SISKIYOU NATIONAL FOREST.-Supervisor, 200 N.E. Greenfield Road, Grants Pass, Oregon 97526. Phone (541)471-6500

KLAMATH NATIONAL FOREST. -Supervisor, 1312 Fairlane Road, Yreka, California,96097. Phone (916)842-6131

-BUREAU OF LAND MANAGEMENT
3040 Biddle Road, Medford, Or.. 97504. Phone (541)770-2200
1465 N.E. 7th St., Grant Pass, Or. 97526. Phone (541)479-7244

-MEDFORD PARKS AND RECREATION DEPT., Medford City Hall, Rm. 140, Medford, Oregon 97501 Phone (541)770-4586

-THE NATURE CONSERVANCY, 1205 N.W. 25th Ave., Portland, Oregon, 97210 Phone (541)228-9561

-OREGON DEPT. OF FORESTRY, 5286 Table Rock Rd., Central Point,Or. 97502 Phone (541)664-3328

-OREGON DEPARTMENT OF FISH AND WILDLIFE, 1495 Gregory Road, White City Oregon.
-PORTLAND DISTRICT, U.S. ARMY CORPS OF ENGINEERS, Lost Creek Project, Trail, Oregon, 97541.
-GEOLOGICAL INFORMATION: BLM staff, 3040 Biddle Road, Medford. USFS Supervisor's Office, 333 West 8th St., Medford, Oregon. Southern Oregon State College, Ashland, Oregon.
-BOTANICAL, BIOLOGICAL INFORMATION: BLM staff, Medford office. USFS Supervisor's Office, 333 West 8th St., Medford, Oregon.

HELPFUL ORGANIZATIONS: Several Rogue Valley organizations have scheduled meetings and field trips. Up-to-date information can be obtained from their chapter newsletters or from the local news media. Chambers of Commerce of the area may also have some listings. The organizations include:

FRIENDS OF THE GREENSPRINGS
MOUNT MAZAMA MUSHROOM ASSOCIATION
NATIVE PLANT SOCIETY OF OREGON
ROGUE VALLEY AUDUBON SOCIETY
ROGUE GROUP SIERRA CLUB
SODA MOUNTAIN WILDERNESS COUNCIL

WHY NOT ADOPT A TRAIL? Outstanding TRAIL MAINTENANCE has been provided by VOLUNTEER GROUPS in our area! Credits to them will be noted as you read through this book. Without their help some of our trails may not have that special "Well-groomed" look, and it is a very rewarding experience to those doing the work! It does make a difference...ask anyone using the trails! To become a part of this vital program, please contact personnel of the USFS Ranger Districts or their Supervisor's office; Bureau of Land Management offices or other agencies listed in this book.

BIKES ARE PERMITTED ON THE FOLLOWING TRAILS:

NOTE: Bikes are not permitted on: Pacific Crest Trail, Wilderness area trails, National Recreation Trails,

*NOTE MOTOR BIKES ALSO ALLOWED WHEN INDICATED BY *

CONTACT LOCAL AGENCIES FOR UPDATED INFORMATION!

CHAPTER 1 - ASHLAND AREA

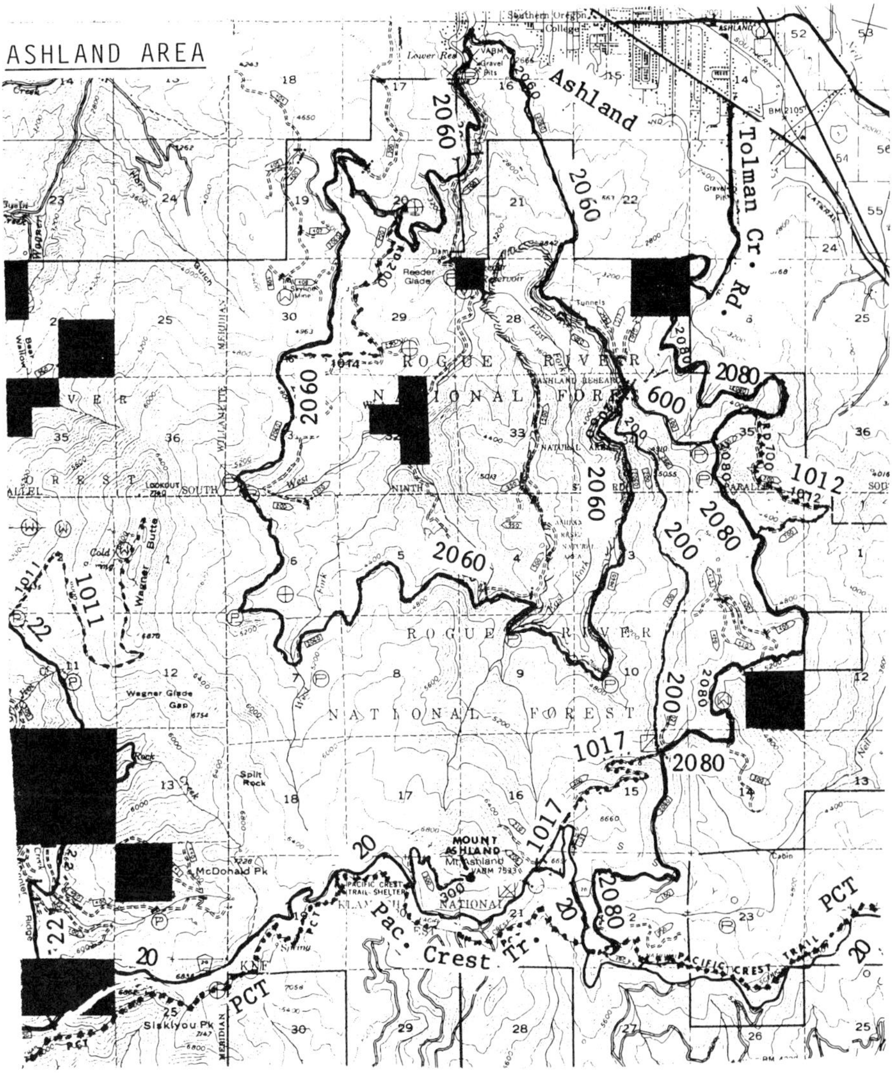

ASHLAND'S LITHIA PARK HIKING TRAILS.

PARK ENTRANCE: Adjacent to downtown Ashland Plaza, just below the Oregon Shakespeare Festival Theaters.
SEASON: All year, EASY TRAILS for hikers or joggers. Bicycles, animals and overnight sleeping prohibited. The park is closed from 11:30 pm to 5:30 am.

FEATURES: Hiking in Ashland's Lithia Park is a very relaxing and educational experience! From the park entrance, the trails extend about one mi. to the far end of the park along both sides of Ashland Creek. Foot-bridges inter-connect, allowing the visitor to create an individualized experience. Picnic and restroom facilities are located throughout the park.

From the upper park boundary, hikers often extend their outing by going 0.2 mi. further south on Granite St. to a newly constructed "Reservoir Trail" leading about 1/4 mile to a park setting along Ashland Creek. This area is used by picnickers and swimmers, and is located at the junction of Granite St. and Glenview Dr....that are often used for more hiking/jogging adventures!

The one mile LITHIA PARK WOODLAND TRAIL also begins from the park entrance and extends past 99 numbered interpretive posts located at various trees and shrubs that have been imported from all over the world. An excellent guide-booklet is available at a very minimal cost from Ashland Parks and Recreation Dept. (located in the park), or from Ashland Chamber of Commerce. A companion booklet entitled "Lithia Park", by Marjorie O'Harra, provides information on the history of Lithia Park and is available from the above locations.

Lithia Park is a very special place that provides various recreational activities for many visitors. Because of its professional landscaping design and maintenance,Lithia Park is included in the National Register of Historic Places.

ENJOY!

BEAR CREEK GREENWAY (See map on page 27)

NORTH ASHLAND TO TALENT SECTION: 3.7 mi. CLOSED DUE TO '97 FLOOD. (REPAIRS SCHEDULED IN 1998)

FROM INTERSTATE HIGHWAY 5, NORTH ASHLAND EXIT 19, (South Valley View Road), travel toward Ashland, 0.4 mile to the junction with Highway 99. Turn RIGHT and go 0.7 mile to a road leading RIGHT to a parking area. When repaired the path will lead north to Oregon RV Roundup, immediately west of Interstate Hwy. 5, Talent Exit 21 off-ramps.

A new section of trail will lead south from North Valley View Rd. to Nevada Sreet in Ashland (Scheduled completion date 1998).

IN MEDFORD, a 3.75 mi. section is paved from Barnett Road to Pine St. in Central Point. The trail may be impassible in North Medford due to work in progress at the Highway 62 interchange. Fundraising is underway to extend the path from Barnett Road to Suncrest Road in Talent.

"The Bear Creek Greenway is a corridor stretching 30 miles from Emigrant Lake to the Rogue River. When completed, this project will provide a natural greenbelt through the heart of the most populated land in Jackson County and will link the cities of Ashland, Talent, Phoenix, Medford and Central Point by a trail system. Eventually, the Greenway will include land along the Rogue River and Little Butte Creek to connect Eagle Point. The Greenway will provide a wide range of close-to-home recreation opportunities including bicycling, horseback riding, hiking, jogging and picnicking. The Greenway will protect wildlife habitat throughout the Bear Creek Basin." (Quote: Jackson County Parks)

GRIZZLY PEAK TRAIL

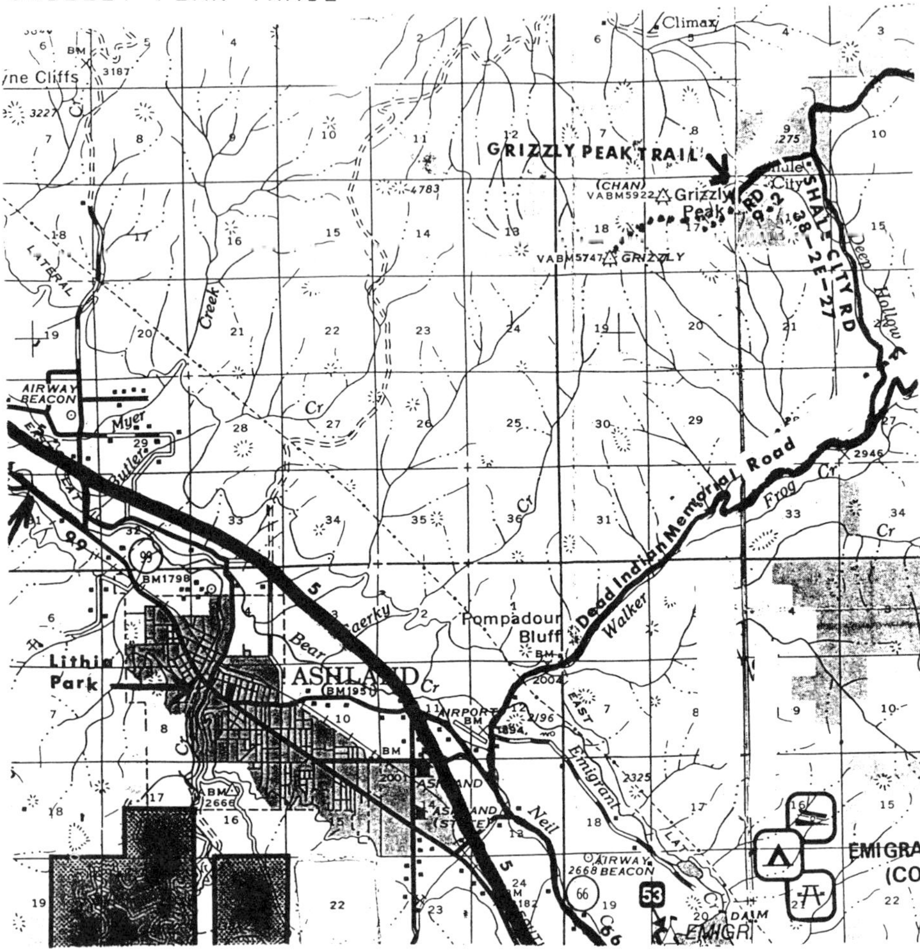

July 2000
~ 6 miles, pretty arduous for 60+ crowd
Nicely kept trail. Ate onions/strawberries

GRIZZLY PEAK. (The peak northeast of Ashland that looms over the city) (See maps 21 and 22)

TRAIL BEGINS:	-BLM Road 38-2E-9.2	ELEV. 5200'
TRAIL ENDS:	-Scenic overlook.	ELEV. 5800'
DISTANCE:	-1.5 miles, Moderately easy. Carry water!	
USE:	-Hikers, horses, mountain bikes.	
SEASON:	-Spring to fall, trail can be very muddy just after the snow has melted.	
BRING MAPS:	-Local BLM information.	

ACCESS: From Interstate Hwy. 5, Ashland-Klamath Falls Exit 14, travel 0.6 miles east on State Hwy. 66 to the junction with Dead Indian Memorial Road. Turn left (northeast) onto this road and follow mileposts to mile 6.6 at the junction with Shale City Road (BLM Road 38-2E-27). Turn left onto 38-2E-27 and go 2.9 mi. to the junction with BLM Road 38-2E-9.2 Turn left onto 38-2E-9.2 and go 3/4 mile to a 3-way road junction. Road 38-2E-9.2 continues straight ahead uphill 0.9 miles to a parking area on the left.

FEATURES: The trail begins its 1.5 mile journey through the forest and some meadows, before it reaches a trail junction. Keep straight ahead, a short distance to the overlook that affords views of Mt. Shasta, Black Butte, Mt. Ashland and of the I-5 freeway making its way over Siskiyou Pass.

Backing up to the above trail junction, work has begun to extend the trail about one mile south along the rim-top to "Grizzly",Elevation 5747'. From this rocky viewpoint, there are good views of Ashland and of the mountains to the south. A future loop trail back to the trailhead is planned.

The BLM advises that "fire danger is high during late summer, refrain from building fires or smoking".

This is one of the more outstanding trails in southern Oregon. It has been reported that because of the altitude, poison oak, ticks or snakes are not in the area. The trail was envisioned by John Ifft, a retired BLM trail planner. With BLM approval,the work was completed in 1991 by Ifft and his crew ot 30-40 volunteers.

PACIFIC CREST TRAIL-GROUSE GAP TO FOREST BOUNDARY.

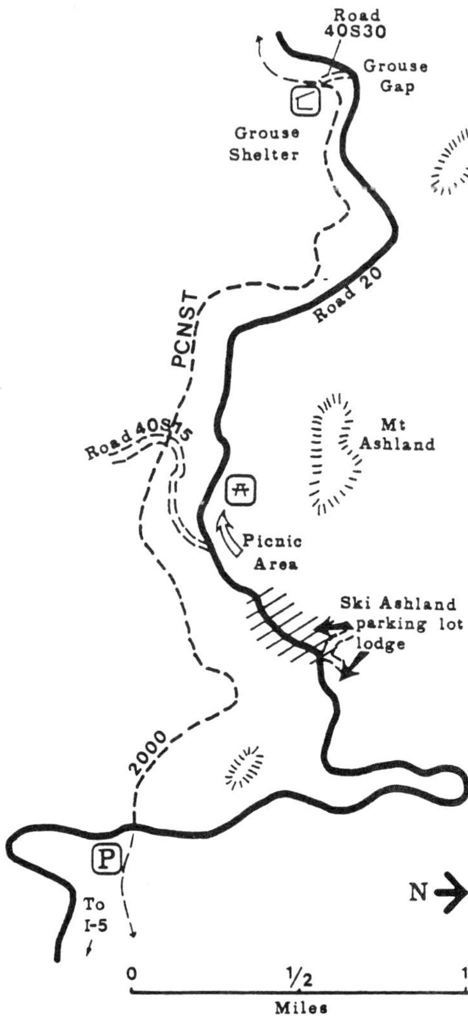

PACIFIC CREST NATIONAL SCENIC TRAIL-GROUSE GAP TO FOREST BOUNDARY.

(See map 28)

TRAIL BEGINS: -Forest Route 20-Grouse Gap. ELEV. 6400'
TRAIL ENDS: -Forest Route 20-Forest Boundary. ELEV. 6200'
DISTANCE: -3.5 miles (one way), EASY. USE: hikers/horses.
SEASON: -June through October.
BRING MAPS: -USFS Pacific Crest Trail-Oregon Southern Portion.
-USFS Ashland Ranger Dist.-Rogue River Ntl.Forest.
-USFS Recreation Opportunity Guide.

ACCESS From Ashland Exit 14, drive south on Interstate 5, 9.0 miles to Mt. Ashland Exit 6. Turn right and go 1/4 mi.to Mt. Ashland Access Road (later becoming Forest Route 20). Follow this road 7.2 miles to the NATIONAL FOREST BOUNDARY SIGN. The Pacific Crest Tr. crosses the road at this point. Look along the left side of the road for the trail leading to Grouse Gap. If making a car shuttle, leave one car here and drive to Access #2.

ACCESS # 2
Continue 4 mi. on the same road (from this point posted as Forest Route 20) to Grouse Gap near milepost 11, at the junction of Road 40S30. The Pacific Crest Trail crosses Road 40S30 at this point, proceed east along the trail to Access #1.

FEATURES: Beginning at Access #2, the Pacific Crest Trail follows along the southern flanks of Mount Ashland through a mixed conifer forest, granite rock formations and small mountain meadows. Mid-summer wildflowers include columbine, scarlet gilia, Indian paintbrush, mountain gentians and lupine. A selection of views would include Mt. Shasta, Marble Mountains and the Trinity Alps. Water from several springs along the trail has not been tested and may be unsafe to drink.

PACIFIC CREST NATIONAL SCENIC TRAIL -WRANGLE GAP TO SISKIYOU GAP.

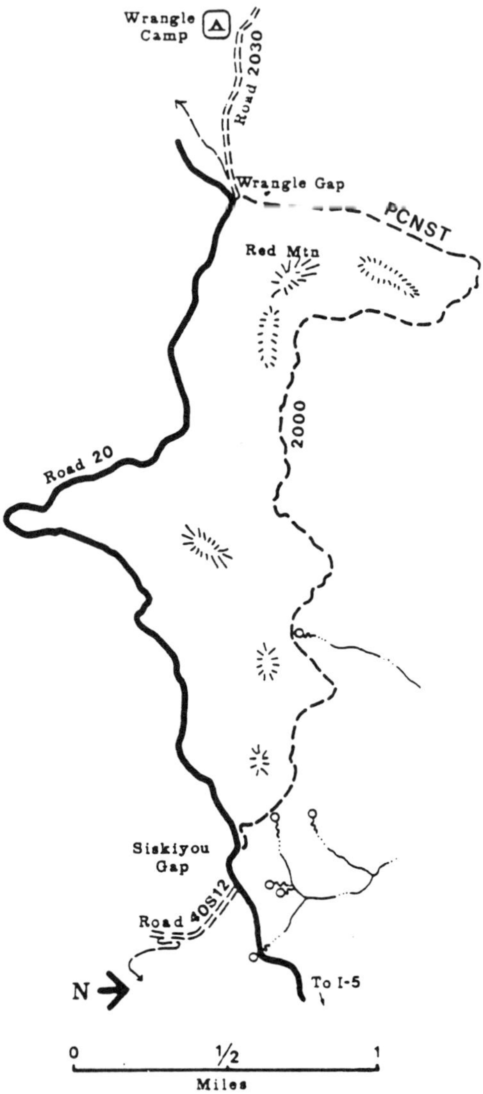

PACIFIC CREST NATIONAL SCENIC TRAIL -WRANGLE GAP TO SISKIYOU GAP. (See maps 27 and 28)

TRAIL BEGINS: -Forest Road 20 at Wrangle Gap. ELEV. 6496'
TRAIL ENDS: -Forest Road 20 at Siskiyou Gap. ELEV. 5879'
DISTANCE: -3.8 miles (one-way)-MODERATE.
SEASON: -June through October. USE: hikers/horses.
BRING MAPS: -USFS Pacific Crest Trail-Oregon Southern Portion.
-USFS Ashland Ranger Dist.-Rogue River Ntl. Forest.
-USFS Recreation Opportunity Guide.

ACCESS #1 From Ashland Exit 14,drive south on Interstate 5, 9.0 miles to Mt. Ashland Exit 6. Turn right and go 1/4 mile to Mt. Ashland Access Road(later becoming Forest Road 20). Follow this road 17 miles (1.0 mile beyond the junction with Road 22),to where the Pacific Crest Trail crosses Road 20 at Siskiyou Gap. If making a car shuttle, leave one car here and drive to Access #2.

ACCESS #2 Continue 3.0 miles further on Road 20 to the junction with Road 2030 at Wrangle Gap. Park along Road 20 and hike 150' down Road 2030. The Pacific Crest Trail leads right (northeast) to return to Siskiyou Gap (Access #1).

FEATURES: Beginning at Wrangle Gap,the trail contours along the flanks of Red Mtn. through a forest of Shasta red fir and mountain hemlock, and continues to contour the ridgeline with vistas of Mt. McLoughlin, the Crater Lake Rim, Dutchman Peak Lookout, Brown Mountain and the rim of Mountain Lakes Wilderness. The trail contours above Monogram Lakes before beginning its moderate descent to Siskiyou Gap. CARRY WATER,there are no water sources along the trail.

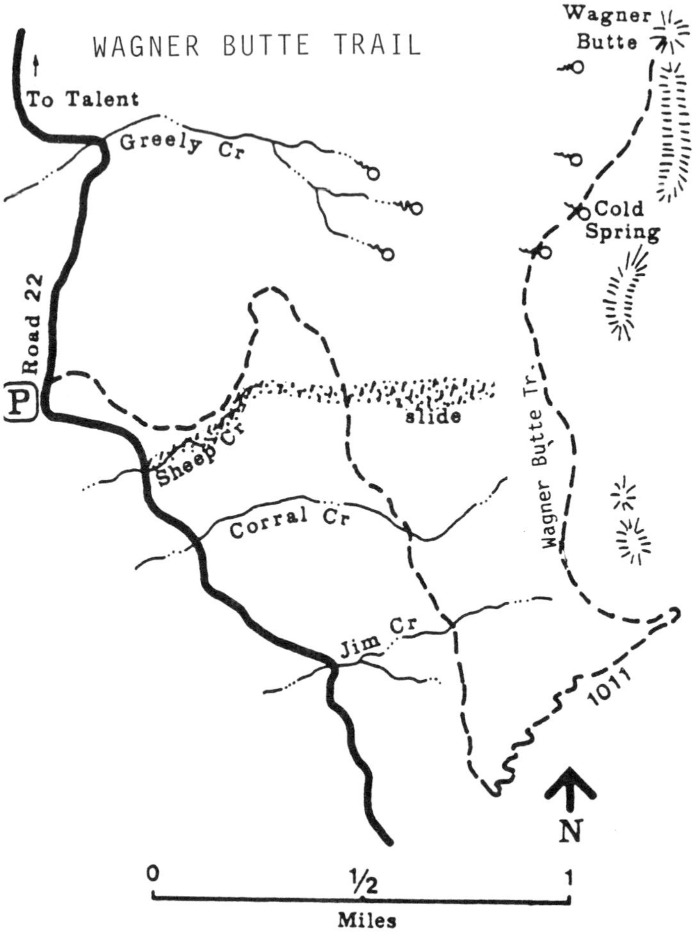
WAGNER BUTTE TRAIL
To Talent
Greely Cr
Road 22
P
Sheep Cr
slide
Corral Cr
Jim Cr
Wagner Butte
Cold Spring
Wagner Butte Tr.
1011
N
0
½
1
Miles

WAGNER BUTTE TRAIL #1011. (Old #972) (Maps 20 and 21)

TRAIL BEGINS: -Forest Route 22 beyond milepost 10. ELEV. 4960'
TRAIL ENDS: -Wagner Butte Lookout (former site). ELEV. 7140'
DISTANCE: -5.2 miles, time up 4 to 5 hours. USE: hiker only.
DIFFICULTY: -Difficult, steep 15% grade in first .65 mile.
SEASON: -June through October, wildflowers all summer.
BRING MAPS: -USFS Ashland Ranger Dist.-Rogue River Ntl. Forest.
-USFS Recreation Opportunity Guide-Wagner Butte Tr.

ACCESS: From Talent, Oregon, at the intersection of Talent Ave. and Main St., travel south on Main Street for 0.4 mile after which Main Street becomes Wagner Creek Road. Continue south on Wagner Creek Road, which veers left at a junction beyond milepost 7, and continues 2 miles to a three-way junction. Keep left onto Forest Road 22 and go 2.0 miles to a large parking area on the right. The Wagner Butte Trailhead is on the opposite (east) side of the road, look for a sign nailed to a tree. WATCH CAREFULLY FOR TRAFFIC-ROADS ARE NARROW,STEEP WITH MANY CURVES.

Hike the trail 0.3 mi.to an old road. Turn right and go about 0.6 mile to the northern edge of a meadow. Look for a "Trail" sign. It is about 2.3 mi. further to Wagner Glade Gap. Portions of the trail were hard to follow through hillside meadows or at a large landslide, but conditions improved after a 1987 trail reconstruction project. From Wagner Glade Gap, turn left at a sign indicating Wagner Butte 2 miles. The trail skirts the western slopes of Wagner Butte and ends at the base of the former Wagner Butte Lookout site. Find your way to the top by following old blazes or cairns.

TREES/PLANTS: Noble, white and Douglas-firs, mountain mahogany, quaking aspen, golden chinquapin, sage, serviceberry, ceanothus, manzanita and snowbrush. Wildflowers are abundant.

HISTORY: "WAGNER BUTTE: Named for Jacob Wagner, settler in the present area of Talent, Oregon, who later operated the flour mill near the Ashland Plaza." (USFS quote)

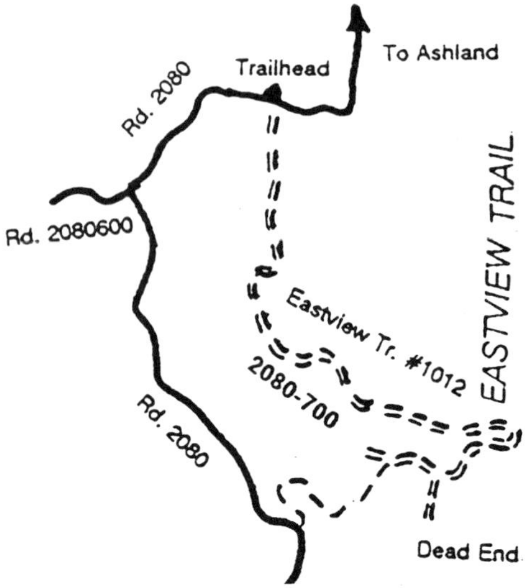

EASTVIEW TRAIL

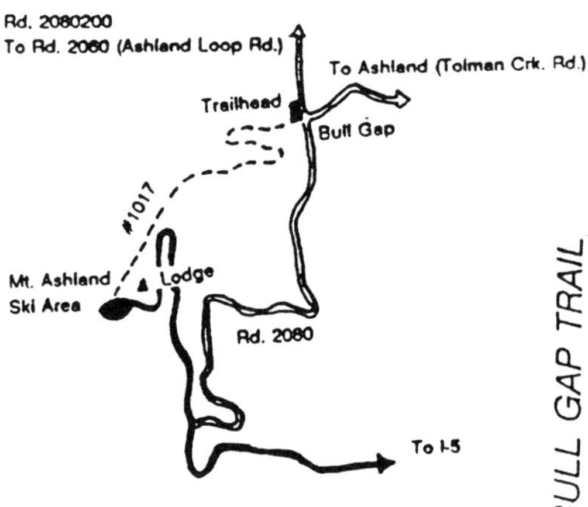

BULL GAP TRAIL

EASTVIEW MOUNTAIN BIKE TRAIL #1012. (See map 21)

TRAIL BEGINS: -Lower Trailhead, Road 2080. ELEV. 4320'
TRAIL ENDS: -Upper Trailhead, Road 2080. ELEV. 4720'
DISTANCE: -2.5 miles.
USE: -Mountain bikes, hikers.
DIFFICULTY: -More difficult.
SEASON: -June thru October.
BRING MAPS: -USFS Recreation Opportunity Guide (this trail).
-USFS Ashland Ranger Dist.-Rogue River Ntl.Forest.

ACCESS: From Interstate Hwy 5, Ashland-Klamath Falls Exit 14, travel west on Hwy 66 (Ashland St.) one block to Tolman Creek Road traffic light. Turn left and follow Tolman Creek Road 1 mi. before crossing Siskiyou Blvd. Continue up Tolman Creek Road (later becoming Forest Road 2080), 6.5 mi. to the lower trailhead on the left. Ample parking is available in the landing located on the opposite side of Road 2080. Please do not park in front of the gate at the trailhead on Road 2080700. THE UPPER TRAILHEAD IS LOCATED 1.5 mile further up Road 2080.

FEATURES: From the lower trailhead on Forest Road 2080 the first 2.0 miles of Eastview Trail wind up Forest Road 2080700 (closed to motorized use), with panoramic views of the upper Bear Creek Valley and Emigrant Lake. At 2.0 miles the road forks and the route continues to the right another 0.1 mile before leaving the road. The singletrack trail heads uphill on the left and meanders another 0.4 miles to meet Road 2080 at the upper trail terminus. Along the way you'll pass beneath some huge old sugar pine sentinels.

ROAD 2080 receives a fair amount of vehicle traffic.Bikers should control their speed when descending this road and be watchful for oncoming cars or trucks. USFS advises to carry water and a snack or lunch.

-Excerpts USFS Recreation Opportunity Guide.

BULL GAP TRAIL #1017. (See map 28)

TRAIL BEGINS:	-Mt. Ashland Ski Area.	ELEV. 6620'
TRAIL ENDS:	-Bull Gap, Forest Road 2080.	ELEV. 5520'
DISTANCE:	-2.5 miles.	
USE:	-Mountain bikes, hikers.	
DIFFICULTY:	-More difficult.	
SEASON:	-June thru October.	
BRING MAPS:	-USFS Recreation Opportunity Guide (this trail).	
	-USFS Ashland Ranger Dist. Rogue River Ntl.Forest.	

ACCESS: From Ashland Exit 14, continue southeast on Interstate Highway 5, nine miles to Mt. Ashland Exit 6. This exit leads to the junction with Old Hwy.99 South. Keep right at this junction and go 0.7 mile to Mt. Ashland Access Road. Turn onto the Mt. Ashland Access Road and go 7.0 miles to the junction with Forest Road 2080.

LOWER TRAILHEAD at Bull Gap: Turn right onto Road 2080 and go 3.2 miles to Bull Gap, Trailhead parking with picnic table.
UPPER TRAILHEAD: located near the closed gate at the parking area between the Mt. Ashland Ski Lodge and the Rental Shop.

FEATURES: Follow the dirt road with blue diamond nordic ski trailblazers, and traverse just below the lodge to the north. Stay on the road: bikes are prohibited on the ski area slopes! The blazers leave off when entering the forest just below the ski area boundary, and the trail is easily followed to Bull Gap.

CAUTION: The trail is located within the Ashland Watershed, which is the source of the city's water supply. It is important to give special consideration to its protection. No camping or campfires allowed. Bicycles must stay on the trail,and their use is not recommended in rainy weather when soils are wet. When fire danger is high, the Ashland Watershed may be closed to all entry but the Bull Gap Trail will remain open. However,Road 2080200 to the north will be closed; so if you are descending the 15.6 miles to town, use Tolman Creek (2080) Road to the east.(Excerpts USFS Recreation Opportunity Guide).

HOBART BLUFF-Via Pacific Crest National Scenic Trail. (Map 29)

TRAIL BEGINS:-Soda Mountain Road. ELEV. 5300'
TRAIL ENDS: -Hobart Bluff Overlook. ELEV. 5502'
SEASON: -Usually snow-free late May through October. Wildflowers abundant May to July.
BRING MAPS: -USFS Pacific Crest Trail-Oregon Southern Portion.
-BLM Transportation Map -Medford District -Klamath Resource Area.
-BLM Medford District-Pacific Crest Trail Log.
USE: CLOSED TO MOTORIZED/MECHANICAL VEHICLES, INCLUDING BICYCLES.

ACCESS: From Interstate Hwy. 5, Ashland Exit 14, follow the mileposts east on State Hwy. 66, 15.7 miles to the highway summit at Soda Mtn. Road. Turn right onto Soda Mountain Road and go 4.0 miles to a large meadow on the left, with a parking area and overhead power lines. Look just beyond, along the road, to where the Pacific Crest Trail leads left, uphill through the meadow on its 1.0 mile journey to the junction with Hobart Bluff Viewpoint Trail.

FEATURES: The trail begins with great views of the Greensprings area and of Mt. Shasta. Wildflowers are plentiful early in the season. After about 1.0 mile, look left for the junction of the Hobart Trail leading about 1/2 mile to the viewpoint, where there are outstanding views of Ashland, Medford and of the Rogue Valley.

To return to the parking area, it will be necessary to take the trails in the reverse direction.

HISTORY: "State Highway 66.......Known locally as the Greensprings Highway, this road parallels the 'Old Applegate Trail' which was used during the 1840's by pioneers who branched off the main Oregon Trail at Fort Hall Idaho and crossed the sagebrush desert of northern Nevada." (USFS quote)

SISKIYOU CREST MOUNTAIN BIKE ROUTE. (See maps 27 and 28)

ROUTE BEGINS: -Mt. Ashland Ski Area Parking Lot. ELEV. 6600'
DISTANCE: -15 miles (one way). HIGH POINT ELEV. 7418'
USE: -Mountain bikes.
DIFFICULTY: -Moderate (Rd 20) to More Difficult (Rd 800).
SEASON: -July thru October.
BRING MAPS: -USFS Recreation Opportunity Guide (this route).
-USFS Ashland Ranger Dist.-Rogue River Ntl.Forest.

ACCESS: -From Ashland Exit 14, continue 9 mi. south on Interstate Hwy.5 to Mt. Ashland Exit 6. Follow the signs 0.7 mile to the Mt. Ashland Access Road. Turn right onto Mt. Ashland Road and continue 9 mi. to Ski Ashland Parking Lot.

FEATURES: Beginning from the Mt. Ashland Ski Area Parking Lot,the route follows Forest Road 20 for 14 miles along the crest of the Siskiyou Mountains to Jackson Gap. From the Gap, Road 800 ascends on the right 1.5 miles to the summit of Dutchman Peak. Road 20 is a decomposed granite surface, is maintained each year but may be rutted or rockfall in places. Road 800 to Dutchman Peak is more primitive, and requires some technical ability.

ALONG THE WAY: There is a picnic area and campground 1/2 mi. from the ski area parking lot. Another 1/2 mi. further out is Road 300 to the right, affording a side trip to the summit of Mt. Ashland (Elev. 7533'). Back on Road 20 again at about the 2 mi. point, a short road to the left leads to Grouse Gap Shelter. About 11 mi. out is Wrangle Gap; here Road 2030 goes downhill to the right 1/2 mi. to Wrangle Camp,a good lunch spot with picnic tables, shelter and vault toilet. At the top of Dutchman Peak is one of the very few "cupola style"fire lookouts left in the Pacific Northwest.The lookout was built in 1927.A brochure entitled "The Siskiyou Loop" is available at the Ashland Ranger Station for $1.00. Designed as as an auto tour guide, bikers will find it useful and very interesting.

Please note that the Pacific Crest Trail, which parallels Forest Road 20 most of the route,is closed to bicycles. Bicycles are not allowed on the ski slopes at Mt. Ashland. (Excerpts USFS Recreational Guide).

PILOT ROCK CLIMB -From Pacific Crest National Scenic Trail. (See map 29)

SEASON: -Usually snow-free June through October.

BRING MAPS: -USFS Pacific Crest Trail-Oregon Southern Portion.
-BLM Transportation Map -Medford District, Klamath Resource Area.
-BLM Medford District-Pacific Crest Trail Log.

CLIMB BEGINS: -Pacific Crest Trail below Pilot Rock. ELEV. 5120'

CLIMB ENDS: -Pilot Rock summit. ELEV. 5910'

TIME UP: -Approx. 1 hour.

DIFFICULTY: -Easy route through west gully. Careful selection of hand and footholds required in two places in the middle of the route. Hard hats are suggested in case of falling rock from above. CARRY WATER!

ACCESS: From Ashland Exit 14, travel southeast on Interstate Hwy. 5, 9 miles to Mt. Ashland Exit 6. The off-ramp leads to a junction with Old Highway 99S. Keep right at this junction, and continue under the freeway overpass, and go a total of 1.9 miles to Pilot Rock Road 40-2E-33, just beyond the crest of Old Highway 99S. Turn left onto Pilot Rock Road and at:

Mile 2.0 -Turn right onto Road 41-2E-3.
Mile 2.7 -Keep right at an unsigned road junction.
Mile 2.9 -Ridge crest, the Pacific Crest Trail crosses the road, look for trail signs on trees. It is best to park here and hike about 900' east on the Pacific Crest Trail, then follow the uphill road track on the right that leads steeply to the base of Pilot Rock. After reaching the end of the old road, follow the route on the left leading to the mouth of an obvious gully rising to the summit.

After climbing two 6 foot ledges, it is safest to stay along the left wall of the gully for best footing. Several persons have been seriously injured by slipping from the exposed slopes on the right. Views from the summit include just about all of southern Oregon and northern California!

CHAPTER 2 - MEDFORD AREA

BEAR CREEK GREENWAY (See map on page 27)

MEDFORD TO CENTRAL POINT SECTION: 5.75 MILES.
INTERSTATE HIGHWAY 5, EXIT 27, BARNETT ROAD, SOUTH MEDFORD. The bike path begins from the north side of Barnett Road, less than 0.1 mile east of the freeway interchange, continues through Bear Creek, Hawthorne and Railroad Parks (all with restrooms), before terminating at Pine St. in Central Point, immediately east of the INTERSTATE HWY. 5 EXIT 32 northbound off ramp.

The city of Medford has repaired '97 flood damage within its borders, but a section is interrupted until completion of ODOT work at the north Medford interchange. Because of heavy traffic in the area,officials don't recommend a bicycle detour to Railroad Park, where the trail continues north.

The section from Ashland's South Valley View Road north to Oregon RV Roundup in Talent was heavily damaged and scheduled for repair in 1998. In the same year, a new section is scheduled between South Valley View Road to Nevada Street in Ashland.

Fundraising is underway to extend the path from Barnett Road in Medford to Suncrest Road in Talent. This, along with other repairs and new sections, could take approximately 6 years.

"The Bear Creek Greenway is a corridor stretching 30 miles from Emigrant Lake to the Rogue River. When completed, this project will provide a natural greenbelt through the heart of the most populated land in Jackson County and will link the cities of Ashland, Talent, Phoenix, Medford and Central Point by a trail system. Eventually, the Greenway will include land along the Rogue River and Little Butte Creek to connect Eagle Point. The Greenway will provide a wide range of close-to-home recreation opportunities including bicycling, horseback riding, hiking, jogging and picnicking. The Greenway will protect wildlife habitat throughout the Bear Creek Basin." (Quote: Jackson County Parks)

BEAR CREEK GREENWAY

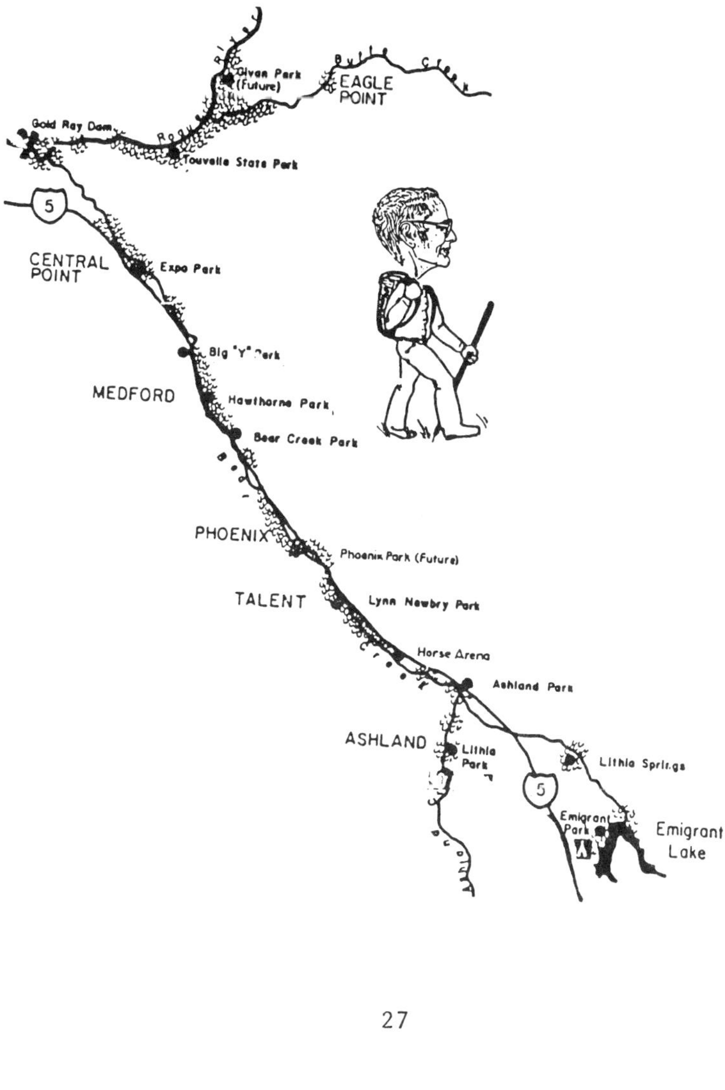

ROXY ANN TRAILS

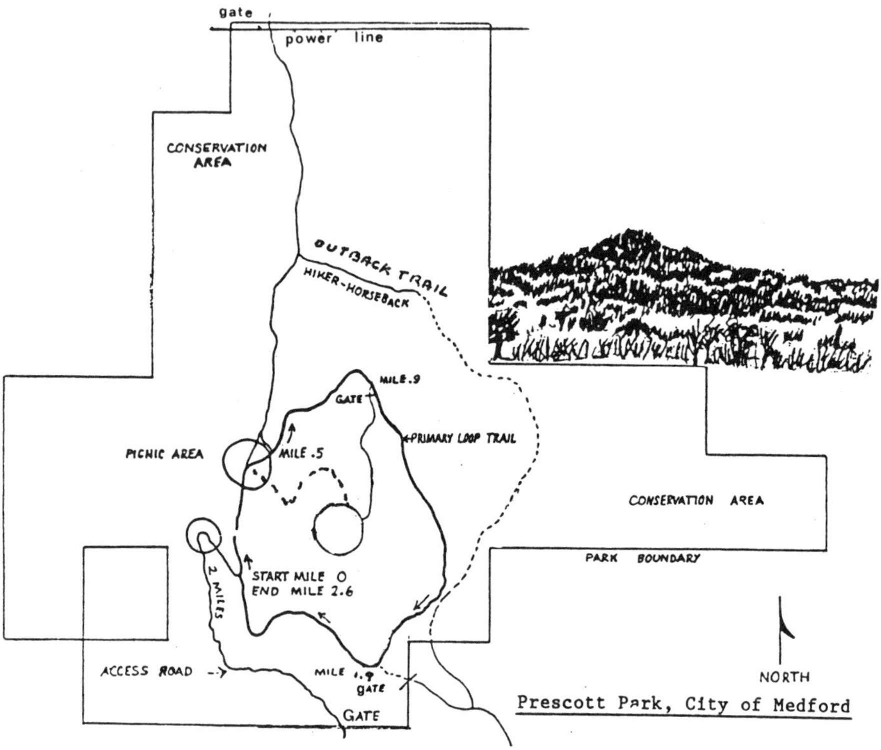

ROXY ANN PEAK HIKING TRAILS-Prescott Park) (Map 13)

SEASON: -Open 6:00 am to 1030 pm for hikers/equestrians/picnickers. Wildflowers late spring to early summer. Watch for poison oak or an occassional rattlesnake.

BRING MAPS: -See next page.For more information, contact Medford Parks and Recreation Department, Medford City Hall.

ACCESS: From Interstate Highway 5, South Medford Exit 27 (Barnett Road), travel east on Barnett Road 1.1 mi. to the junction with Black Oak Drive. Turn left onto Black Oak Drive and continue 1 mile to the intersection of Hillcrest Road. Turn right onto Hillcrest Road and go 3 1/4 miles to the junction with Roxy Ann Access Road. Turn left onto the access road and go 1.3 mile to a road gate. PARK SO AS NOT TO OBSTRUCT THE GATE,keep open for emergency vehicles.

ROAD DISTANCE FROM GATE:

Mile 0.1 Madrone Trail to Madrone Ledge picnic area on left.
Mile 0.9 Junction with PRIMARY LOOP TRAIL. Mileage points LEFT (Clockwise) on the loop trail are:
Mile 0.5 Roxy Ann Picnic Area. Just beyond to the left of the loop road is a road track leading north to the OUTBACK TRAIL or further to the park boundary.
Mile 0.9 -Private road on right.
Mile 1.9 -Keep right at a road junction.
Mile 2.4 -Madrone Ledge picnic area. Upper end Madrone Trail.
Mile 2.6 -Back to the beginning of the Primary Loop Trail. The access road leads downhill to the left.

Activities also include nature education, historic site restoration and wildlife protection. The area is closed to hunting,firearms, off-road vehicles, alcohol, narcotics, camping and building of fires. No motor vehicle access-fire season thru winter.

The picnic area and many of the trails were built by the Civilian Conservation Corps in the 1930s. More recent paths have been constructed by "Lutheran Evergreens" of Medford.

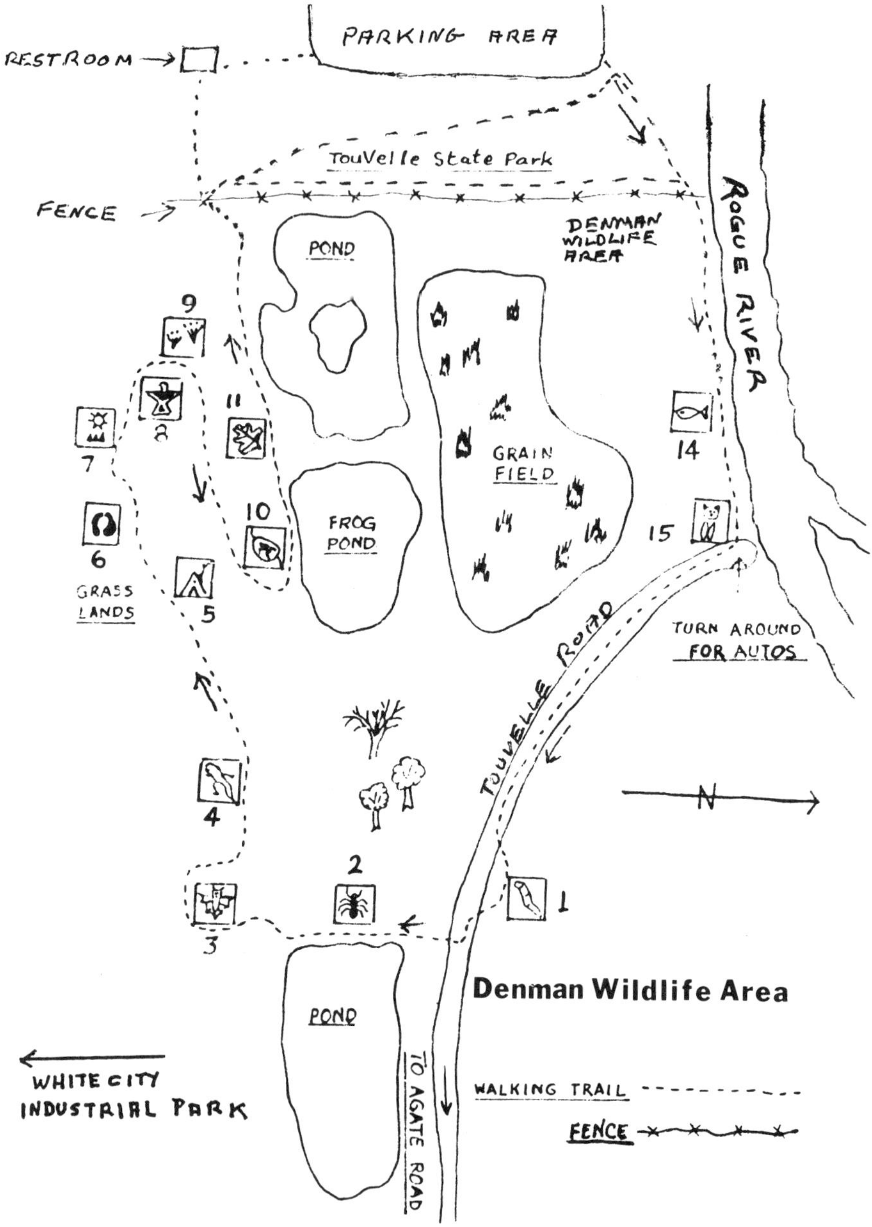
PARKING AREA
RESTROOM
TouVelle State Park
FENCE
DENMAN WILDLIFE AREA
ROGUE RIVER
POND
GRAIN FIELD
FROG POND
GRASS LANDS
9
8
7
11
10
6
5
4
3
2
1
14
15
TURN AROUND FOR AUTOS
TOUVELLE ROAD
N
Denman Wildlife Area
POND
TO AGATE ROAD
WHITE CITY INDUSTRIAL PARK
WALKING TRAIL
FENCE

TOUVELLE STATE PARK DAY USE AREA and DENMAN WILDLIFE AREA. Map 13
(DAY USE FEES APPLY AT TOUVELLE STATE PARK).

TRAILS BEGIN: -Touvelle State Park. ELEV.1222'
SEASON: -Open all year. Hunting is conducted during the fall and early winter season in the Denman Wildlife Area, check schedules.
REFERENCE: -Denman Interpretive Trail Guide.

ACCESS: From Interstate Highway 5, Central Point Exit 32, travel east one mile to the traffic light on Table Rock Road. Turn left (north) onto Table Rock Road and follow mileposts to mile 6.5 to the entrance of TOUVELLE STATE PARK. Turn right to enter the park and continue to the parking area at the end of the road.

FROM THE PARKING AREA THERE ARE TWO GOOD HIKING CHOICES:
(1) 1.5 MILE LOOP HIKE THROUGH THE DENMAN WILDLIFE AREA.
Commence upstream along the banks of the Rogue River a short distance to the fenced boundary of the DENMAN WILDLIFE AREA and hike along the river to Touvelle Road. Turn right and follow the road 0.3 mi.just before reaching a pond. A low metal sign on the right indicates the beginning of the Denman Interpretive Trail leading back to Touvelle State Park. This trail begins along the edge of a large pond before climbing to a grassy plateau that offers open views. It then drops to skirt the edges of two more ponds before reaching the State Park fenced boundary and beyond to the parking area. See the map and list of interpretive stations on the following pages.

(2)The 1.5 mile loop hike could be broken down into two meaningful hikes that would not involve Touvelle Road: Hiking upstream along the Rogue River banks to Touvelle Road and return, OR begin near the parking area restrooms, and hike east to a kiosk at the fenced boundary of the Denman Wildlife Area. Bark chips mark the route passing two ponds, climbing a grassy plateau, before dropping to Touvelle Road.

Although this trail is partially covered with bark chips, it may be obscure in a few places. It is advisable to stay on the trail to prevent contacting poison oak and destroying the vegetation. BE AWARE THAT HUNTING IS CONDUCTED IN THE DENMAN WILDLIFE AREA DURING THE FALL AND EARLY WINTER MONTHS for deer, pheasant, quail and water fowl. Otherwise, no firearms are permitted in the area.

<u>FEATURES</u>: 15 interpretive stations are located along the trail and are marked by posts with carved symbols resembling Indian petrographs. They number from Touvelle Road in the clockwise direction:

1. "Earthworm" (The Agate Desert Soil)
2. "Spider" (Woodrat Nest)
3. "The Bat" (Artificial Wildlife Nest Boxes)
4. "Lizard" (Wedgeleaf Habitat)
5. "Dwelling" (Urban Valley Development)
6. "Deer Track" (Rogue Valley Geology)
7. "Grasslands" (Grassland Habitat)
8. "The Bird" (Woodpecker Tree)
9. "Rodent Track" (Ground Burrows)
10. "Frog Pond" (The Pond)
11. "Oak Tree" (Oak Trees)
12. "Waterfowl" (Farming For Wildlife)
13. "Bird Tracks" (The Blackberry Habitat)
14. "The Fish" (The Rogue River Habitat)
15. "The Owl" (Vandalism and Litter)

<u>HISTORY</u>: The Denman Interpretive Trail, located on the Kenneth Denman Wildlife Management Area, is under the control and management for enhancement of wildlife habitat by the Oregon Department of Fish and Wildlife. Except for 160 acres surrounding the management area's office and shop structure, the 1760 acres came under the General Services Administration control after Camp White Military Reservation was disbanded following World War Two.

Credit has been given to John Ifft, U.S. Bureau of Land Management, for initial trail concept and station post materials. The BLM's Young Adult Conservation Corps crew constructed the trail with coordinating/planning by Oregon Dept. Fish and Wildlife.

Respect the rights of private property owners!

Table Rocks Location Map

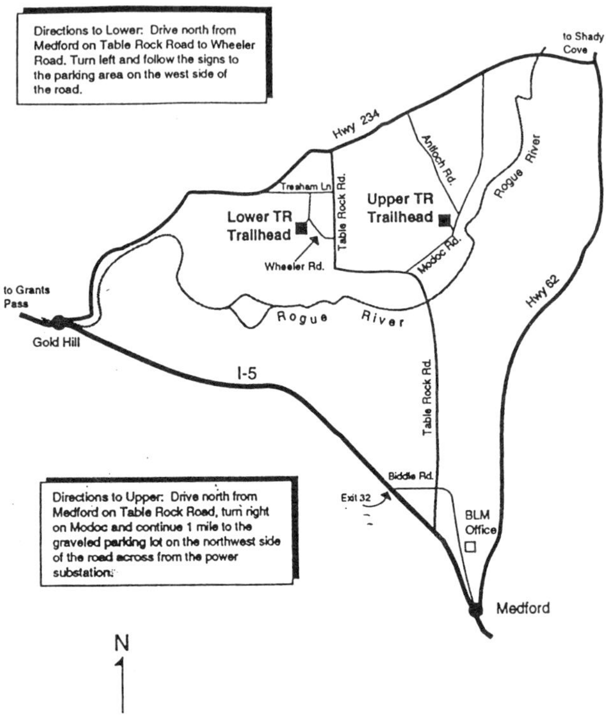

UPPER TABLE ROCK. (See map 13)

TRAIL BEGINS: -Modoc Road between mileposts 1 and 2. ELEV.1294'
TRAIL ENDS: -Top of Upper Table Rock. ELEV.2036'
DISTANCE: -1.25 mi., moderate, hiker only, day use only.
SEASON: -All year. High use in spring/limited parking. Low off-season use. Toilet facilities April and May only.
BROCHURE/MAP: -U.S. Bureau of Land Management -Recreation Opportunity Guide. Brochure available.

ACCESS: From Interstate Highway 5, Central Point Exit 32, travel east one mile to the traffic light on Table Rock Road. Turn left (north) onto Table Rock Road and follow mileposts to mile 7.5 at the junction with Modoc Road. Turn right (northeast) onto Modoc Road and go 1.5 mile to the parking area on the left side of the road.

FEATURES: Scenic panorama of the Rogue Valley. Many species of flowers blooming Feb. through May. Unique geologic origin and features. Vernal pools with pacific tree frogs.
HAZARDS: Abundant poison oak, ticks, rattlesnakes, high cliffs.

BLM ADVICE: "No potable water. Please do not pick the wildflowers. Stay on the main trails and out of the sensitive vernal pools". DOGS NOT ALLOWED.

HISTORICAL: Long ago volcanic lava covered the Rogue Valley. Millions of years have eroded most of the lava and much of the underlying sandstone sediment leaving Upper and Lower Table Rocks......Table Rock was once a sanctuary and symbol for the Rogue River Indians; a site for many important meetings. In the early 1850's, settlers and gold prospectors invaded the valley. The Table Rocks afforded the Indians choice places for hiding, ambush, attack, and Indian councils during the years of resistance and war that followed. The trail was built in 1981 by the Young Adult Conservation Corps.

NOTE: UPPER TABLE ROCK is designated an Outstanding Natural Area. This designation is more oriented toward public use than is Lower Table Rock.

Lost Creek Lake

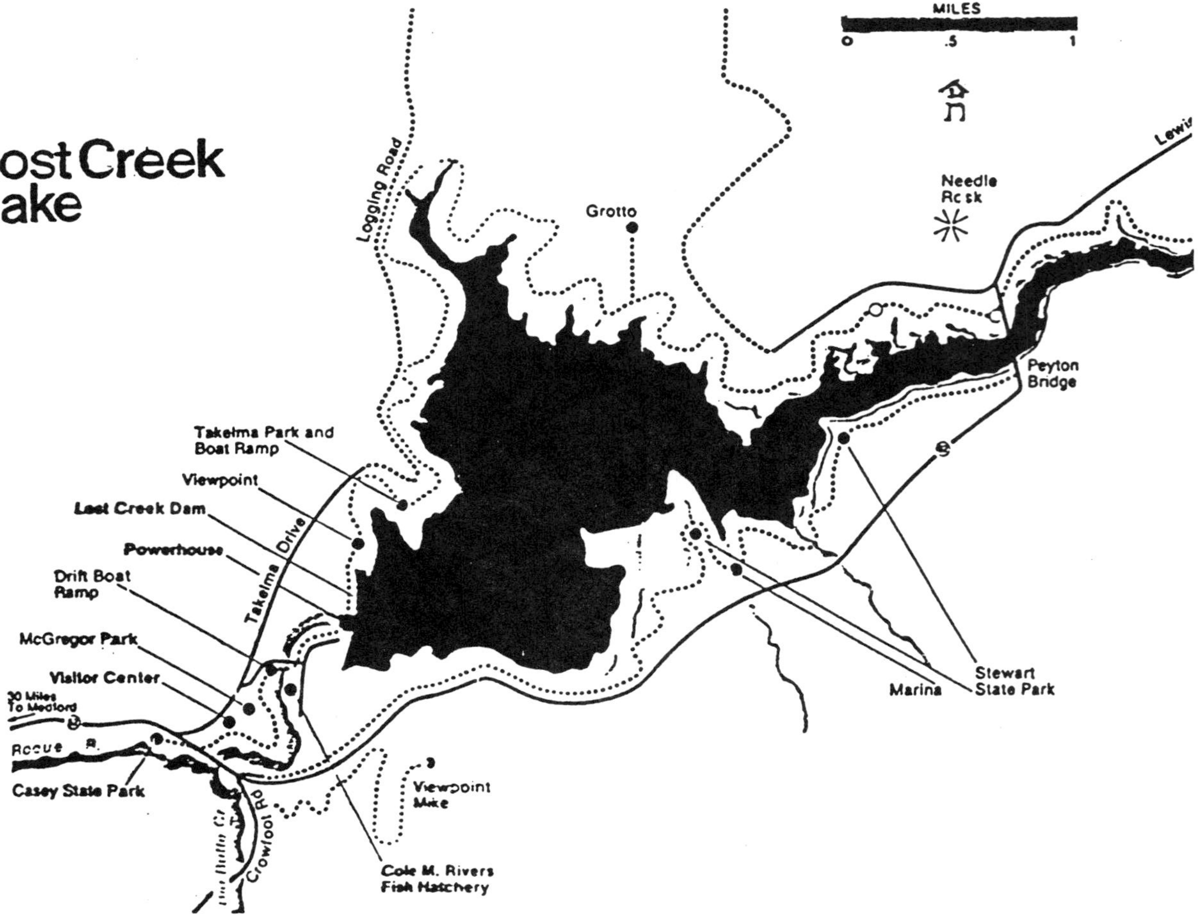

CHAPTER 3 - LOST CREEK LAKE AREA

LOST CREEK LAKE-NORTH SHORE TRAIL. (See map 9)

TRAIL BEGINS: -Casey State Park, State Highway 62. ELEV. 1538'
TRAIL ENDS: -Boundary of U.S. Army Corps of Engineers land, 4.5 miles northeast of Peyton Bridge Trailhead.
DISTANCE: -16.5 miles with access points. Easy grades.
SEASON: -Open all year.
USE: -HIKERS on all trails. MOUNTAIN BIKES on all trails except on Stewart Park hiker only trails.
BRING MAPS: -LOST CREEK LAKE HIKING TRAILS -U.S. Army Corps of Engineers.
-See also local road and forest maps.

ACCESS: From Medford, Oregon, travel north and east on Highway 62 to milepost 29 at Casey State Park.

DESCRIPTION: Condensed from "LOST CREEK LAKE HIKING TRAILS" brochure, U.S. Army Corps of Engineers.

From the east end of Casey State Park, follow the paved trail to the first junction. North shore hikers should take the right fork and pass under McLeod Bridge. The trail follows the river to McGregor Park and the Visitor Center. Hike through McGregor Park on to the Hatchery/Powerhouse Road and follow painted "paw prints" on the pavement, then cross the fish diversion dam for a possible visit at Cole M. Rivers Fish Hatchery.

The trail begins again in an open field north of the hatchery and then passes through River's Edge Park to the powerhouse. Pass between the two buildings and follow painted "paw prints" to the trail at the base of the dam. The trail then climbs gradually to the top of the dam. Please stay on the developed trail, as this area has restricted access. Follow the painted "paw prints" to Takelma Park. The trail continues 4.3 miles further to where a long arm of the lake reaches the inlet of Lost Creek. (There are two "Lost Creeks" on the lake; the other one is on the south shore.) FROM THIS LOST CREEK TRAILHEAD, THE 5.8 MILE SECTION OF TRAIL TO LEWIS ROAD TRAILHEAD IS TEMPORARILY CLOSED DUE TO THE 1997 STORM DAMAGE.

LOST CREEK LAKE-NORTH SHORE TRAIL, continued.

DISREGARD THIS NEXT PARAGRAPH UNTIL STORM DAMAGE BETWEEN LOST CR. TRAILHEAD AND LEWIS ROAD TRAILHEAD IS REPAIRED.
From Lost Creek, the trail leads south, then east 3.5 miles to a short spur trail leading to the Grotto, where rock cliffs form the walls of a small canyon. Following heavy rains, a waterfall may be spotted cascading down the far wall. 2.3 miles further along the lakeshore, the trail comes out at the Lewis Road Trailhead and follows the road east for one mile to the Peyton Bridge Trailhead.

Follow the trail under Peyton Bridge to where it enters the Rogue River Gorge. A rest area at the boundary of Corps of Engineers land marks the end of Lost Creek Lake North Shore Trail.

FOR SHORTER HIKES: From Highway 62, the North Shore Trail can be accessed by driving on TAKELMA DRIVE to the following points:

Mile 0.3 -McGregor Park and Visitor Center.
Mile 0.6 -Cole M. Rivers Fish Hatchery.
Mile 2.0 -Lost Creek Dam Viewpoint.
Mile 2.3 -Takelma Park, pavement ends, becoming Road 33-1E-27.
Mile 3.6 -Junction Road 33-1E-23, turn right for trail access.
Mile 5.0 -Rogue River Trail sign on right side of 33-1E-27.
Mile 5.8 -Lost Creek Trailhead, a parking area is on the right.

PEYTON BRIDGE TRAILHEAD is located on Highway 62 near milepost 36 at the north end of Peyton Bridge and the junction of Lewis Road. LEWIS ROAD TRAILHEAD is 1 mile west of Peyton Bridge Trailhead.

NOTES: CARRY DRINKING WATER on long hikes or in warm weather. Camping is permitted only at designated campsites. Check local fire conditions with the Oregon State Dept.of Forestry in Central Point. Phone (541) 664-3328.

LOST CREEK LAKE-SOUTH SHORE TRAIL. (See map 9)

TRAIL BEGINS: -Casey State Park, State Hwy. 62. ELEV. 1538'
TRAIL ENDS: -Peyton Bridge. ELEV. 2000'
DISTANCE: -6.3 miles, gentle grades.
SEASON: -Open all year.
USE: -HIKERS on all trails. MOUNTAIN BIKES on all trails except Stewart Park hiker only trails.
BRING MAPS: -LOST CREEK LAKE HIKING TRAILS -U.S. Army Corps of Engineers.
-See also local road or forest maps.

ACCESS: From Medford, Oregon, travel north and east on State Hwy. 62 to milepost 29 (Casey State Park).

DESCRIPTION: Condensed from "LOST CREEK LAKE HIKING TRAILS" brochure, U.S. Army Corps of Engineers.

From Casey State Park, follow the paved trail to the first junction. Take the LEFT fork, cross McLeod Bridge, then turn right to where the trail drops down and passes back under the bridge. Here the trail merges with a gravel road and follows the river. The trail resumes from the end of the road, and after 0.5 mi. ascends to a point above the dam's spillway gates. Further on is a junction with a trail cutting downhill to the left. This trail leads to the spillway gates and service road on top of the dam. (You may hike the 0.8 mi. length of the dam to reach the intake tower or North Shore Trail.)

The South Shore Trail drops down and remains near the lake's high waterline, and around the bend is a small waterfall where Rumley Creek tumbles to the lake. In another 2.4 miles the trail enters Stewart State Park day use area. To stay on the South Shore Trail, keep to the three-foot wide trail through the park. Pass the swimming beach and picnic area, then cross the inlet of Lost Creek. There are two "Lost Creeks" draining into the lake; the other one is on the north shore.

LOST CREEK LAKE-SOUTH SHORE TRAIL, continued.

Cross the pavement at the boat ramp. The trail parallels the lake shore and crosses Floras Creek. At the junction beyond the creek, the main trail bears to the left; a spur trail to the right leads to Stewart State Park Campground.

The trail passes between the lake shore and the edge of the campground. Where it joins the bike path, hikers should bear to the left and cross Taggarts Creek. The South Shore Trail ends at Peyton Bridge. Hiking across the bridge (0.3 mi.) brings you to the North Shore Trail at Peyton Bridge Trailhead.

For shorter hikes, the South Shore Trail can be accessed by driving to Stewart State Park, either at the picnic area or at the campground. Carry drinking water on long hikes or in warm weather.

VIEWPOINT MIKE- LOST CREEK LAKE. (See map 9)

TRAIL BEGINS: -Big Butte Park, Crowfoot Road. ELEV. 1550'
TRAIL ENDS: -Viewpoint Mike. ELEV. 2550'
DISTANCE: -2.5 miles, moderate grades.
SEASON: Open all year.
USE: Hiker, horse, mountain bikes. Motor vehicles not allowed.
BRING MAPS: -LOST CREEK LAKE HIKING TRAILS -U.S. Army Corps of Engineers brochure.
-See also local road and forest maps.

ACCESS: From Medford, Oregon, travel north and east on State Highway 62 to milepost 29 at Casey State Park. Continue 0.2 mi. on 62, crossing McLeod Bridge, to Crowfoot Road. Turn right onto Crowfoot Road, and go 0.2 mi. to Big Butte Park. The Viewpoint Mike Trailhead is directly across the road.

DESCRIPTION: Condensed from "LOST CREEK LAKE HIKING TRAILS" brochure, U.S. Army Corps of Engineers.

The trail to Viewpoint Mike begins across the road from Big Butte Park and climbs for 2.5 miles to a point overlooking the entire Lost Creek Lake area. The trail begins with switchbacks through an oak woodland. It gains elevation above Hwy. 62, providing an excellent view of the river and fish hatchery below. The trail ends at the viewpoint where you can rest and enjoy the view.

The panorama from this height includes views of the lake, the dam and intake tower. Massive Flounce Rock, weathered by the ages to a reddish color, rises above the north shore of the lake. Toward the northeast, you can see the rim of Crater Lake. CARRY DRINKING WATER as none is available along the trail.

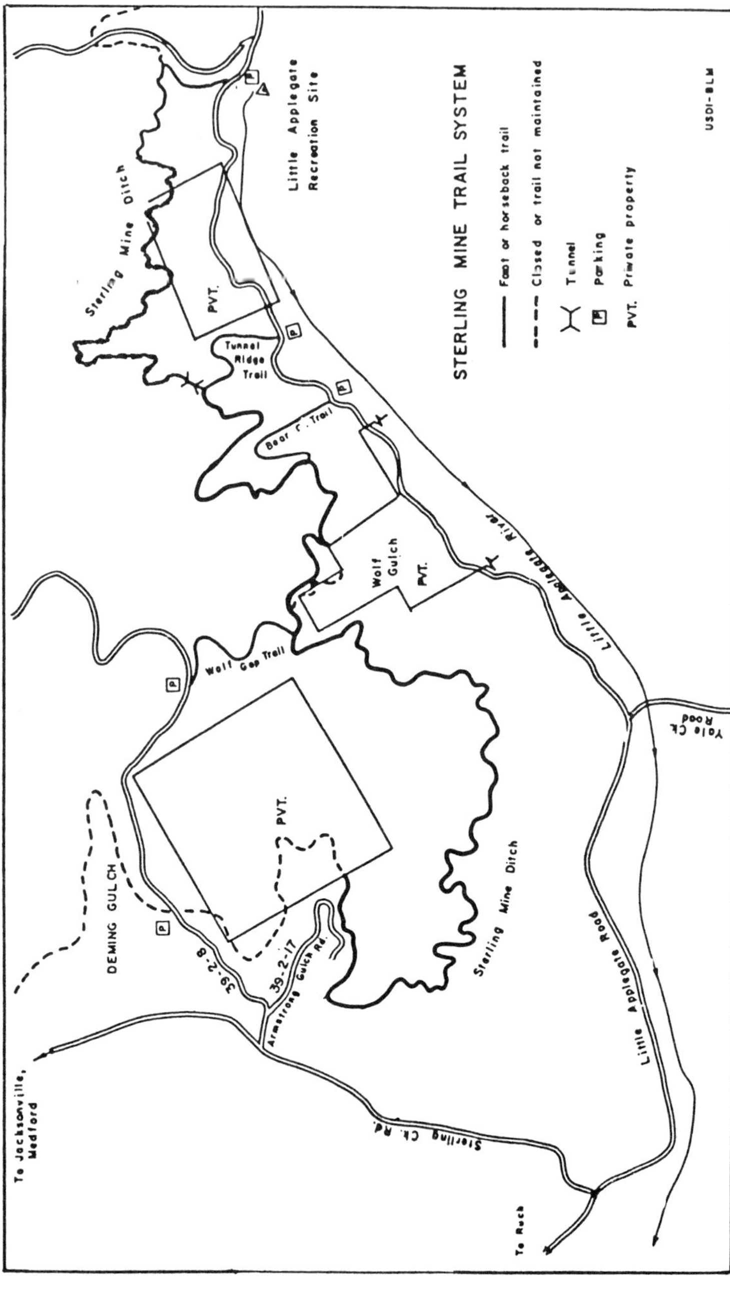
STERLING MINE TRAIL SYSTEM
Foot or horseback trail
Closed or trail not maintained
Tunnel
Parking
PVT. Private property
USDI-BLM
Little Applegate Recreation Site
Sterling Mine Ditch
PVT.
Tunnel Ridge Trail
Wolf Gulch
Wolf Gap Trail
Little Applegate River
Yale Ck. Road
Little Applegate Road
DEMING GULCH
39-2-8
39-2-17
Armstrong Gulch Rd.
Sterling Ck. Rd.
To Jacksonville, Medford
To Ruch

CHAPTER 4 - JACKSONVILLE/RUCH AREA

STERLING MINE TRAIL SYSTEM.

"The Sterling Mine Ditch, about 20.0 miles long and 3 feet deep, was started and completed in 1877 by nearly 400 workers, many of them being Chinese laborers. The ditch carried water from Little Applegate River to operate hydraulic jets for the Sterling Mine Company at the town of Sterlingville. The ditch continued to be used for gold mining through the 1930's." (BLM quote)

THE LITTLE APPLEGATE RIVER was once known by local settlers as Applegate Creek. The name was officially changed to the present form after the year 1900, in order to avoid confusion with the Applegate Creek of the South Umpqua River. (USFS information)

A trail system follows the route of the ditch, and the U.S. Bureau of Land Management advises to "Carry drinking water at all times of the year, please observe Oregon Department of Forestry fire regulations (telephone 664-3328) and respect property rights on adjoining private lands." The lower 2 mi. of trail below Deming Gulch are not open for public use.

See the text on the following pages for trailheads that provide access to the ditch:
1. Little Applegate Trailhead, Little Applegate Road.
2. Deming Gulch Trailhead, Deming Gulch Road.
3. Tunnel Ridge Trailhead, Little Applegate Road.
4. Bear Gulch Trailhead, Little Applegate Road.
5. Wolf Gap Trailhead-TEMPORARILY ABANDONED, no reconstruction date given.

SEASON: -All year. Ideal during late winter or early spring before poison oak leafs out. It is hard to avoid.
USE: -Hiker/horse, mountain bikes, no motorized vehicles.
-Moderate grades.
BRING MAPS: -BLM brochure and map STERLING MINE TRAIL SYSTEM.
-BLM Medford District Transportation Map, Jacksonville Resource Area.
-(This area is not on National Forest land, but is shown on USFS Rogue River National Forest maps.)

DEMING GULCH-STERLING MINE DITCH ACCESS. (See maps 19 & 20)

ROUTE BEGINS: -Road 39-2-8 (at Deming Gulch).
DISTANCE: -About 16 miles to Little Applegate Trail.
USE: -Hiker/horse/mountain bike. WATCH FOR POISON OAK.

ACCESS: From Jacksonville, travel southwest on Hwy. 238, 2.9 miles and turn left on Cady Road. Continue 1/2 mile on Cady Road to the junction with Sterling Creek Road. Turn right onto Sterling Creek Road and go 8.7 miles to Armstrong Gulch Road 39-2-17. Turn left onto Armstrong Gulch Road and go 0.3 mi. to the junction with Road 39-2-8 on the left. Take 39-2-8 0.6 miles, and look closely along the RIGHT side of the road for the Sterling Mine Ditch. There may be no signs.

FEATURES: Estimated distances along the ditch as it heads southwest from Road 39-2-8 are:

Milepoint	
1.5	-Ditch crosses Armstrong Gulch Road. 39-2-17.
8.0	-WOLF GAP TRAIL leading uphill left to Wolf Gap. TEMPORARILY ABANDONED.
9.0	BEAR GULCH TRAIL leads right 1 mile to Little Applegate Road.
11.0	TUNNEL RIDGE TRAIL leads right 1 mile to Little Applegate Road.
16.0	LITTLE APPLEGATE TRAIL leads right, one mile to Little Applegate Road.

Poison oak is found along trails up to about 5000 ft. altitude.

BEAR GULCH TRAIL, Sterling Mine Ditch. (See map 19 and 20)

TRAIL BEGINS: -Little Applegate Road.
TRAIL ENDS: -Sterling Mine Ditch.
DISTANCE: -1 mile, moderately uphill.
USE: hiker/horse/mountain bikes. WATCH FOR POISON OAK.

ACCESS: From the town of Ruch, Oregon, travel 2.8 miles south on Upper Applegate Road to the junction of Little Applegate Road. Turn left on Little Applegate Road and go 9.1 miles to a parking area on the left at Bear Gulch Trailhead. It is about 1 mile from the trailhead to Sterling Mine Ditch.

FEATURES: After reaching the ditch, two options are available; (1). By TURNING RIGHT, a loop trip is possible by going about 2.0 miles to the Tunnel Ridge Trail leading 1.0 mile to Little Applegate Road. At the road, turn right (west) and go 0.6 mile back to the starting point at Bear Gulch Trailhead. The total loop distance is 5 miles and requires 3 to 4 hrs.

(2). TURNING LEFT from the Bear Gulch Trail,it is about 1.0 mile along the ditch to the Wolf Gap Trail (TEMPORARILY ABANDONED) and about 8 miles further to the Deming Gulch Trailhead on Rd. 39-2-8.

TUNNEL RIDGE TRAILHEAD, Sterling Mine Ditch. (See map 19 and 20)

TRAIL BEGINS: -Little Applegate Road.
TRAIL ENDS: -Sterling Mine Ditch.
DISTANCE: -1 mile. Moderate uphill grades.
USE: hiker/horse/mountain bike.
WATCH FOR POISON OAK.

ACCESS: From Ruch, Oregon, take the Upper Applegate Road 2.8 miles to Little Applegate Road. Follow this road 9.8 miles to a parking area on the right, at a former picnic ground. The Tunnel Ridge Trailhead is directly across the road.

FEATURES: The trail continues to the ridge, providing many interesting views. Where the trail reaches the ditch, there is a tunnel dug by Chinese laborers to divert water through the hillside. A loop trip is possible by turning left (west) along the ditch, nearly 2.0 miles to the Bear Gulch Trail, and following it about 1.0 mile to Little Applegate Road. Turn left (east) and follow the road 0.6 mile back to the Tunnel Ridge parking area.

Another loop trip is possible by TURNING RIGHT at the tunnel and traveling about 5 miles east to the Little Applegate Trailhead. A portion of this trail climbs high above the ditch to avoid private property and later rejoins and follows the ditch to a signed junction of a trail leading 1.0 mi.to the Little Applegate Trailhead on Little Applegate Road. Turn right (west) along the road and go about 1.7 miles back to the Tunnel Ridge Trailhead.

Not very often do you see these things but when you do just give them room and they will move out of your way.

LITTLE APPLEGATE TRAILHEAD, Sterling Mine Ditch. (See map 19,20)

TRAIL BEGINS: -Little Applegate Road.
TRAIL ENDS: -Sterling Mine Ditch.
DISTANCE: -1.0 mile, gentle uphill grade.
USE: hiker/horse/mountain bike.

ACCESS: From the town of Ruch, Oregon, go 2.8 miles south on the Upper Applegate Road to the junction with Little Applegate Road. Turn onto Little Applegate Road and follow the mileposts to mile 11.6, at the Little Applegate Trailhead on the left side of the road. Parking is available at the Little Applegate Picnic Ground, about 100 yards further.

FEATURES: This is the eastern-most BLM public access to the Sterling Mine Ditch. It is about 1.0 mile to the ditch. To reach Tunnel Ridge, TURN LEFT (WEST) at the ditch and go about 5.0 miles. A portion of the trail rises above the ditch to avoid private property.

A loop trip is possible by taking the Tunnel Ridge Trail one mile down to Little Applegate Road. Turn left (east) on this road and go 1.7 miles back to Little Applegate Trailhead.

A left-over from the old days.
A gold seeker's "SLUICE BOX".

GIN LIN TRAIL #917. (See map 19)

TRAIL BEGINS: -Flumet Flat Campground. ELEV. 1700'
TRAIL ENDS: -Flumet Flat Campground.
DISTANCE: -3/4 mile interpretive loop trail. Easy, hikers only. Trail open all year.

REFERENCES: USFS interpretive brochure "Gin Lin Trail." USFS "Rogue River National Forest" map. Both publications available at Star Ranger Station or the USFS Supervisor's Office in Medford.

ACCESS: From the town of Ruch, Oregon, travel south on Upper Applegate Road and follow mileposts to mile 8.6 at the junction with Palmer Creek Road. Turn right onto Palmer Creek Road and continue 0.8 mile just beyond the entrance to Flumet Flat Campground. Turn right to the parking area and trailhead.

FEATURES The Gin Lin Trail has 14 numbered "stations" that are keyed to the information and diagrams of the brochure, available at the Star Ranger Station or the USFS Supervisor's Office in Medford. You will see evidence of mining ditches, dug more than 100 years ago by Chinese laborers, to divert water from Palmer Creek to a mining site where hydraulic pressure was used to loosen gravel and cobbles from nearby slopes. Sluice boxes were used to separate the materials washed down from the hillside, with the resulting collection of gold dust and mine tailings. WATCH FOR POISON OAK or an occasional rattlesnake.

HISTORICAL Gin Lin was a Chinese mining boss who purchased mining claims along Palmer Creek in 1881 after being successful in other local mining operations. More than a million dollars worth of gold dust were deposited by him in the Jacksonville Bank. The actual fate of Gin Lin is uncertain.
(Condensed from USFS interpretive brochure)

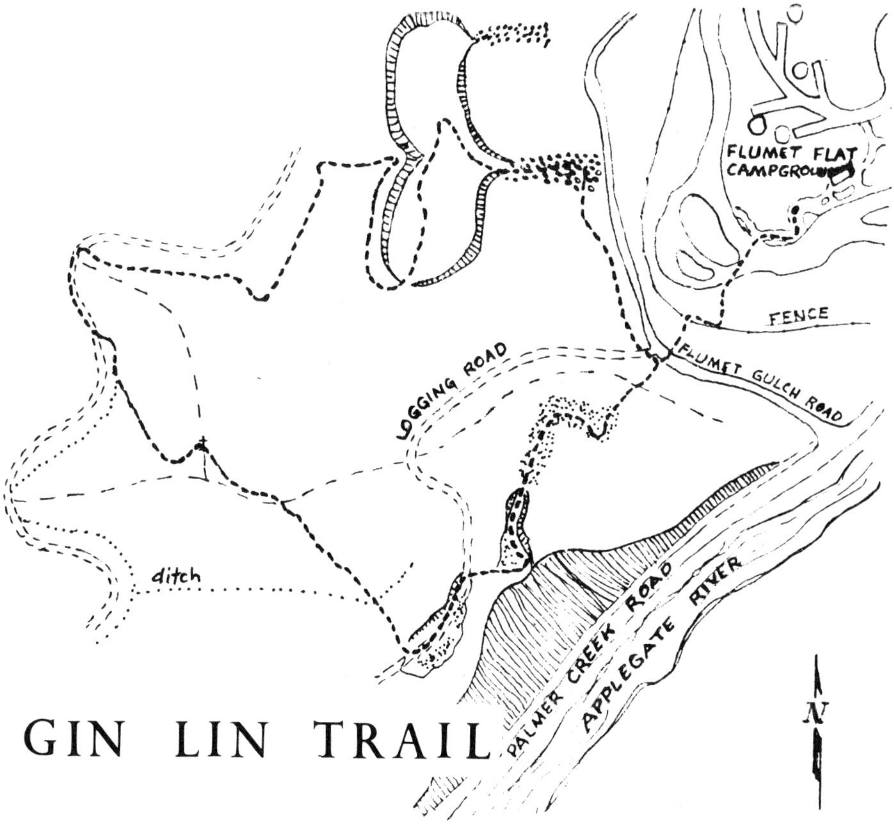

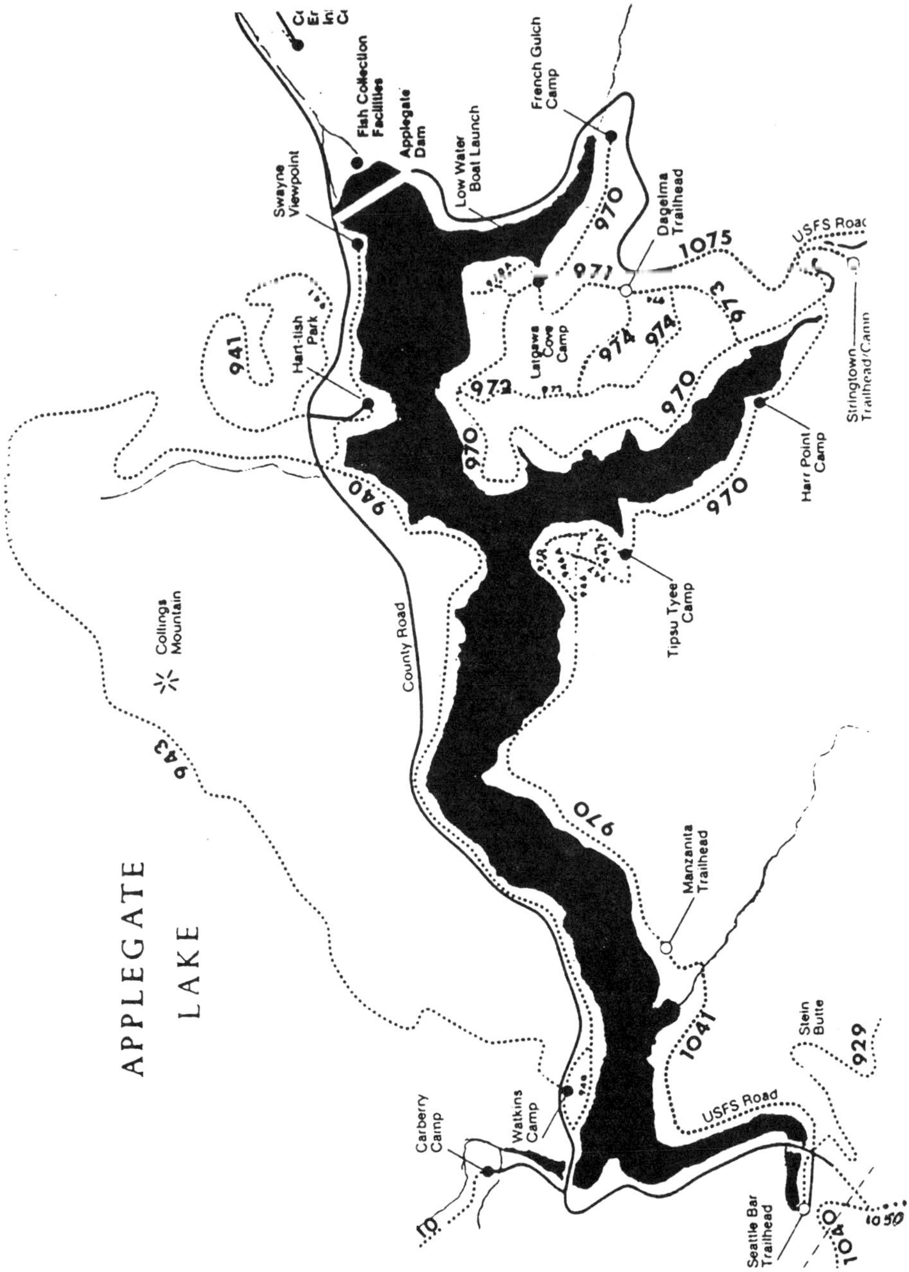
APPLEGATE LAKE
Swayne Viewpoint
Fish Collection Facilities
Applegate Dam
Low Water Boat Launch
French Gulch Camp
Dagelma Trailhead
1075
USFS Road
970
971
972
973
974
Latgawa Cove Camp
Hart-tish Park
941
940
Collings Mountain
943
County Road
Tipsu Tyee Camp
Hart Point Camp
Stringtown Trailhead/Camp
Manzanita Trailhead
1041
Stein Butte
929
USFS Road
Watkins Camp
Carberry Camp
Seattle Bar Trailhead
1040
1050
10

CHAPTER 5 - APPLEGATE AREA (see map 26)

APPLEGATE LAKE TRAILS

SEASON:	-Open all year.
CAMPS:	-ROAD ACCESS: Carberry, French Gulch, Stringtown, Watkins. HIKE-IN: Harr Point, Latgawa, Tipsu-Tyee. Schedule/facility info at Star Ranger Sta.
MAPS:	-AVAILABLE AT STAR RANGER STATION, 6941 Upper Applegate Road. -U.S. Army Corps of Engineers brochure "APPLEGATE LAKE." -Applegate Ranger Dist. -Rogue River Ntl. Forest. -USFS Recreation Opportunity Guides.
TRAIL USAGE:	-HIKERS on all trails. HORSES on Stein Butte Trail but not recommended on Collings Mountain or Dakubetede Trails. MOUNTAIN BIKES on all trails. MOTOR BIKES on Stein Butte Trail.

TRAILHEADS:

SWAYNE VIEWPOINT. Near milepost 15, Upper Applegate Road. Drinking water, restrooms, interpretive viewpoint. DAKUBETEDE TRAIL 940 begins here.

HART-TISH PARK. Near milepost 16 on Upper Applegate Road. Check with Star Ranger Sta. for park schedules/facilities. DAKUBETEDE TRAIL 940, GROUSE LOOP TRAIL 941, and the north end of COLLINGS MOUNTAIN TRAIL 943 can be accessed from this park.

WATKINS PICNIC GROUND. Just beyond milepost 18 on Upper Applegate Road. Check with Star Ranger Station for park schedules and facilities. DAKUBETEDE TRAIL 940, and the south end of COLLINGS MTN. TRAIL 941 begin here.

SEATTLE BAR. Beyond milepost 18 on Upper Applegate Road, turn left at the junction with Carberry Creek Road and continue to milepost 20 at Seattle Bar. Check with Star Ranger Station for schedules/facilities. STEIN BUTTE TRAIL 929 begins here.

MANZANITA: From Seattle Bar Trailhead drive 2 miles north on Manzanita Creek Road. No facilities. PAYETTE TRAIL 970 begins here.

FRENCH GULCH: From Swayne Viewpoint, cross over Applegate Dam on Squaw Creek Road 1075 to the trailhead just beyond milepost 1. Check with the Star Ranger Station for camp schedules/facilities. PAYETTE TRAIL 970 begins here.

DAGELMA: From Swayne Viewpoint, cross over Applegate Dam and continue on Squaw Cr. Road 1075, 2.2 miles to the trailhead parking area on the right. No facilities. CALSH TRAIL 971, SINNS BAR TRAIL 972, OSPREY TRAIL 973 and PROSPECTORS LOOP TRAIL 974 begin here.

STRINGTOWN: From Dagelma Trailhead, continue on Squaw Cr. Road just beyond milepost 3. The trailhead is on the right. This is an access point for the PAYETTE TRAIL. Check with Star Ranger Station for camp schedules/facilities.

HIKING TRAIL DESCRIPTIONS.

Detailed "USFS Recreation Opportunity Guides" are available from Star Ranger Station or from Forest Supervisor's Office in Medford.

DAKUBETEDE TRAIL 940. 4.8 miles, moderately easy. Hiker/horse/mountain bike. From SWAYNE VIEWPOINT, the trail begins just behind the restrooms and continues southwest along the lakeshore to HART-TISH PARK COPPER BOAT RAMP and ends at WATKINS PICNIC GROUND. Horses not recommended at this time (1998)Check Star Ranger Sta. CARRY WATER.

An 18 mile mountain bike loop can be made: starting at the Swayne Viewpoint and using the Dakubetede and Payette Trails.

GROUSE LOOP TRAIL 941.
2.8 MILES. Moderate for hikers, difficult for mountain bikes. At HART-TISH-PARK, the trailhead is at the upper end of the picnic area. Cross the highway to the trail beginning. The clockwise direction is suggested for ease of travel. There are good views of Applegate Lake, Elliott Creek Ridge and the Red Buttes to the south. CARRY WATER.

COLLINGS MOUNTAIN TRAIL 943.
7 mi., difficult, ELEV. GAIN 1040'. Hiker/horse/mountain bike. Horses not recommended at this time (1998) Check Star Ranger Sta. The northern end of the trail begins from the upper end of the Hart-tish Park picnic area. The trail crosses the highway to the edge of a guardrail then continues 1/2 mile to a miner's cabin, an inactive "Bigfoot trap", a mine adit and then climbs to the crest of a ridge. About 2 miles south along the ridge, the trail passes along the west slopes of Collings Mtn. and then drops down to Watkins Picnic Ground (the southern end of the trail), passing through a wildlife foraging area and the site of a 1981 forest fire burn. A 3 mile hike back to Hart-tish Park can be made via the Dakubetede Trail 940. CARRY WATER. (You may wish to start at Watkins Picnic Ground for ease of travel).

The "Bigfoot" trap was installed by a Eugene-based wildlife research organization in 1974 for the unsuccessful efforts in capturing the elusive "Bigfoot." The use of the trap was discontinued in 1976.

STEIN BUTTE TRAIL 929. 5.0 mile plus 2.5 mile on New London Trail to Road 1050 if you are doing a shuttle arrangement. Difficult for hiker, horse and mountain bikes. Moderate for motor bikes. From SEATTLE BAR, the trail climbs up the west end of Elliott Cr. Ridge, passing a 19th Century water diversion ditch that was used by the Seattle Mining Company. It then follows an old haul road past a marble deposit before reaching the top of Elliott Creek Ridge. The trail then follows the ridge to a point just north of Stein Butte summit, look for rock cairns and a faint trail on the right for a side-trip to the summit. A lookout tower existed at this location between the years 1936 and 1968. ELEVATION 4400'.

After returning to the main trail, proceed 0.5 mile to a saddle just east of Stein Butte at the junction with New London Tr. 928 and Elliott Ridge Tr. 969.

The New London Trail, formerly a continuation of the Stein Butte Trail, leads 2.5 miles downhill (south), passing two 20th Century mine adits before reaching Elliott Creek Road.

Stein Butte,Elliott Ridge and New London Trails are maintained by Motorcycle Riders Assn.

PAYETTE TRAIL 970. Easy trail, hikers/mountain bikes.
9.2 MILES.....From FRENCH GULCH TRAILHEAD TO MANZANITA TRAILHEAD. The distance can be shortened by using the Stringtown Trailhead access. Hiker campgrounds are located at Latgawa Cove, Harr Point and at Tipsu Tyee. Squaw Creek crossing damaged in 1997 flood, repairs hopefully in spring of 1998.

Latgawa Cove Camp is .7 mile from French Gulch Trailhead. Just beyond, Calsh Trail 971 leads left to the Dagelma Trailhead, and Viewpoint Trail 970A Leads RIGHT to a viewpoint. Payette Trail 970 follows the lakeshore to the Squaw Creek Arm of the lake and on beyond Tipsu Tyee Campground. Near the mouth of the lake's Squaw Arm, CUTOFF TRAIL 946 is a short cut to the Payette Trail that ends at Manzanita Trailhead. Midway along the Cutoff Trail, SQUAW POINT TRAIL 946A leads to a viewpoint.

HARR RIDGE TRAIL 947 runs from Tipsu Tyee Campground to the midpoint of the Cutoff Trail. Culy Trail 947A branches off from the Harr Ridge Trail and leads to a viewpoint overlooking Tipsu Tyee Campground and the Squaw Creek Arm of the lake.

OUTDOOR STUDY AREA TRAILS FROM DAGELMA TRAILHEAD. Hiker/mtn. bike,
CALSH TRAIL 971: Leads .7 mi. to Payette Trail near Latgawa Camp.
SINNS BAR TRAIL 972: .8 mile long, links the Prospectors Loop and Payette Trails. (RATED EASY)
OSPREY TRAIL 973: Leads .6 mile to the Payette Trail. (EASY)
PROSPECTORS LOOP TRAIL 974: 1.6 miles long, begins and ends at Dagelma Trailhead.

WHERE THE NAMES CAME FROM: Excerpts from USFS Applegate Ranger District Recreation Opportunity Guides.

HART-TISH: Chief Hart-tish was the leader of the Dakubetede Indians that inhabited the Applegate Valley and resisted the influx of miners into their territory following the discovery of gold in southern Oregon.

COPPER VISITOR CENTER: Commemorates the Copper Store built in the 1920's near the mouth of Carberry Creek before construction of the dam. The site of the store is now under water.

COLLINGS MOUNTAIN: Named for two prospectors, the Collings brothers, who mined in the Applegate Dam vicinity.

WATKINS: The name of a prospector who mined near the mouth of Carberry Creek in the 1850's. A small community post office and schoolhouse were named for Watkins.

SEATTLE BAR: Commmemorates the Seattle Mining Co. (of Washington) which conducted hydraulic mining operations above the confluence of Carberry Creek and Applegate River during the 1890's.

DAKUBETEDE: A band of Indians that lived in the Applegate Valley.

TIPSU TYEE: A bearded Shasta Indian Chief.

STEIN BUTTE: Believed to be named for a prospector who mined in this vicinity during the early gold rush years.

DAGELMA: Named for "Dagelma" or "River Takelma" Indians.

CULY: Named for the family of George and Pamelia Culy, settlers in the mining community of Steamboat in the 1880's.

SINNS BAR: Named for a Chinese prospector who mined the gravel bars along the Applegate River during the early gold rush years.

BOUNDARY NATIONAL RECREATION TRAIL #1207 -AND CONNECTING TRAILS.

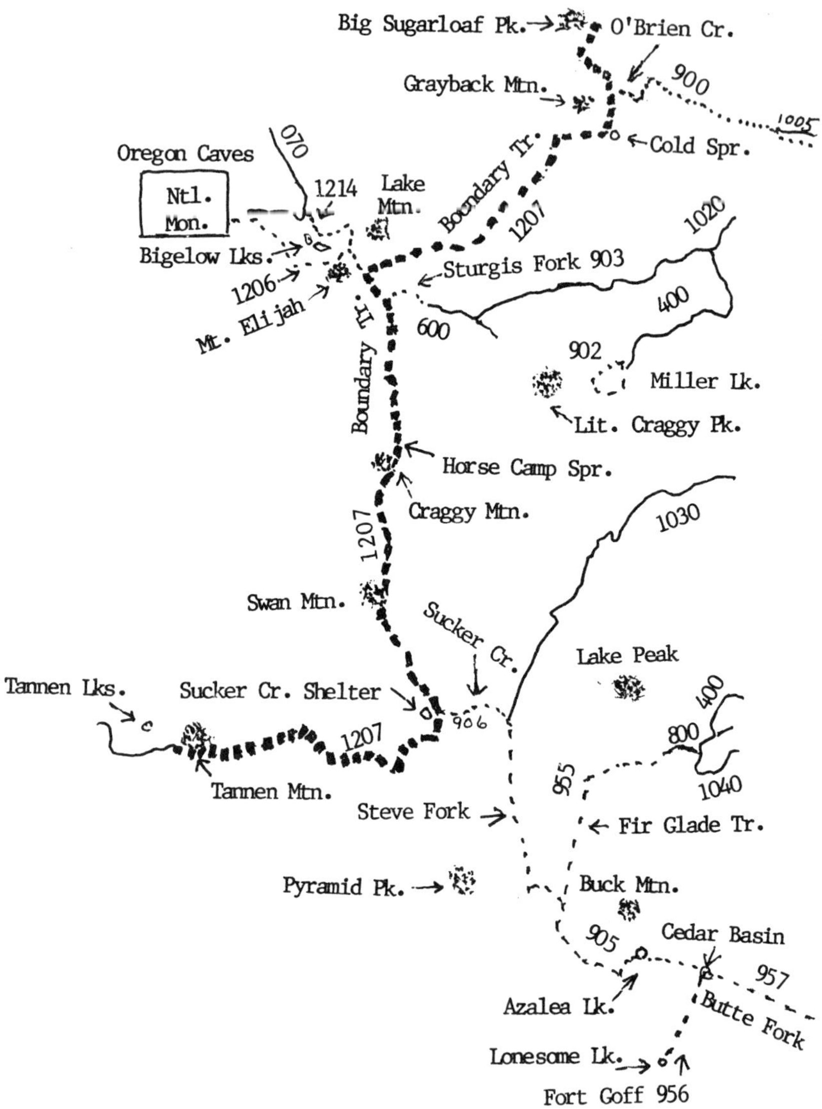

O'BRIEN CREEK TRAIL #900. (See map 18)

TRAIL BEGINS: -Forest Road 1005,near mileposts 2 & 4 ELEV. 4080'
TRAIL ENDS: -Boundary Trail 1207. ELEV. 6240'
DISTANCE: -About 3.3 mi, difficult.
SEASON: -Usually snow-free July through September.
USE: -Hiker/horse/mountain and motor bikes.
1997 STORM DAMAGE-HORSES/MOTOR BIKES NOT RECOMMENDED (Check Star Ranger Station for updates).
CONNECTING TR. -Boundary National Recreation Trail 1207.
BRING MAPS: -Applegate Ranger Dist.-Rogue River Ntl. Forest.

ACCESS: From the town of Ruch, Oregon, travel west on Hwy. 238, 7 miles to the town of Applegate. Cross the bridge and turn left onto Thompson Creek Road, which later becomes Forest Road 10. Follow this road 12 miles to the junction with Forest Roads 10 and 1005. Turn right onto 1005 and travel 2.1 miles to the junction with Forest Road 300 where a one mile extension of trail 900 offers a trailhead with trailer turnaround not available at the upper milepost 4 trailhead.

FEATURES: About 2 miles from the lower trailhead at a junction, keep right to bypass Grayback Snow Shelter and Krause Cabin where Grayback Meadows is undergoing vegetation repair for soil stabilization. (No unauthorized horse use). From the above junction, it is 1.2 mi. to BOUNDARY NATIONAL RECREATION TRAIL 1207 at the base of Grayback Mountain. The Boundary Trail is a popular route to Oregon Caves or for sidetrips to Windy Gap or Sugarloaf Peak. CARRY WATER! Treatment of water is essential since many cattle graze in the area.

HISTORY: "Grayback Snow Shelter was built for winter-time Forest Service snow surveyors who measured the water content of snowpacks for irrigation supply projections (built ca. 1944). Krause Cabin was built by a local cattleman as a round-up time 'line shack.' It was completed in August (V-J Day) 1945. 'Graybacks' were the lice that so plagued the early miners! They gave this name to a number of features." (USFS quote)

MILLER LAKE TRAIL #902. (See map 25)

TRAIL BEGINS: -End of Road 1020/400. ELEV. 4834'
TRAIL ENDS: -Miller Lake.
DISTANCE: -0.6 mile to lake, about 2 mile loop around lake. Moderate grades. USE: hiker/horse. Highpoint ELEV. about 5200'
SEASON: -Usually snow-free June thru October.
BRING MAPS: -Applegate Ranger District-Rogue River Ntl. Forest.

ACCESS: From the town of Ruch, Oregon, travel west on Hwy. 238 for 7 miles to the town of Applegate. Cross the bridge and turn left onto Thompson Creek Road which later becomes Forest Road 10. Continue southwest on Thompson Creek Road, 12 miles to the junction with Forest Road 1020. Follow Road 1020 4.4 miles to the junction with Road 1020/400. Keep left onto Road 400 and go about 2.5 mi. to where the road washed out in the 1997 flood. It may be necessary to hike 1/2 mile more to the trailhead at the end of the road.

FEATURES: From the parking area, the trail climbs, crossing an old road (also leading to the lake). Upon reaching lakeshore, a 2 mi. botanical path known as the Oliver Matthews Trail circles the lake. From the lake in a clockwise direction, the trail goes east to the top of a ridge for some outstanding views before it begins its descent, passing a small pond and ending back at the beginning of the loop.

Miller Lake was deepened and dammed to provide irrigation water to the Thompson Creek Ditch. It is stocked with trout. The lake is quite noted for its botanical interest. Rhododendrons are in bloom usually around June first.

HISTORY: "MILLER LAKE: Named for Walter Miller, a 19th century Applegate Valley rancher who made his annual hunting camp at the lake." (USFS quote)

STURGIS FORK TRAIL #903. (See map 25)

TRAIL BEGINS: -End of Forest Road 1020/600. ELEV. 5040'
TRAIL ENDS: -Boundary Trail 1207. ELEV. 5600'
DISTANCE: -0.8 mi.-moderate/hiker: difficult for mountain bikes, motor bikes not recommended.
SEASON: -Usually snow-free July through September.
CONNECTING TR.-Boundary National Recreation Trail 1207.
BRING MAPS: -Applegate Ranger Dist.-Rogue River Ntl. Forest.

ACCESS: From the town of Ruch, Oregon, travel west on Hwy. 238 for 7 miles to the town of Applegate. Cross the bridge and turn left onto Thompson Creek Road which later becomes Forest Route 10. Continue southwest on Thompson Creek Road, 12 miles to the junction with Forest Road 1020. Continue south and west on Rd. 1020, 8.1 mi. to the junction with Road 1020/600. Turn right onto Road 600 and go about 1/2 mile to the trailhead.

FEATURES: The trail criss-crosses streams of the Sturgis Fork thru a virgin stand of timber within Craggy Mountain Scenic Area and joins the Boundary National Recreation Trail 1207. This is an easy access to Lake Mtn. Trail 1206 that leads to Oregon Caves National Monument. Treatment of water is important due to cattle grazing.

HISTORY: "STURGIS FORK: Named for Albert Sturgis, a local miner who, during the early 20th century, developed several large hydraulic mines, including one on Forest Creek, southwest of Jacksonville." (USFS quote)

STEVE FORK TRAIL #905 (See map 25)

TRAIL BEGINS:	-Forest Road 1030 near milepost 11.	ELEV. 4400'
TRAIL ENDS:	-Fir Glade Trail 955.	ELEV. 5200'
DISTANCE:	-3.0 miles. Moderate, hiker/horse.	
SEASON:	-Usually snow-free July to October.	
CONNECTING TR.	-Fir Glade Trail 955.	
BRING MAPS:	-USFS Applegate Ranger Dist. -Rogue River N.F. -USFS Red Buttes Wilderness brochure.	

ACCESS: From the town of Ruch, Oregon, travel south on Upper Applegate Road, and go 18.8 miles to Carberry Creek Road (County Road 777). Turn right onto Road 777 and follow mileposts to mile 6.9 at the junction with Steve Fork Road 1030. Go left onto Road 1030 and continue 11.1 miles to a parking area and trailhead on the right. From the trailhead, it is about 1 mi. to the Steve Fork and Sucker Creek Gap Trail junction. The Steve Fork Trail bears left at this location. THE STEVE CREEK CROSSING SUSTAINED 1997 FLOOD DAMAGE-CHECK WITH USFS APPLEGATE RANGER DIST. FOR REPAIR STATUS.

FEATURES: The trail traverses the upper Steve Fork Valley, swings to the east, crosses a ridge and joins the Fir Glade Trail 955, about one mile southwest of Fir Glade. Turn right (south) onto 955 if continuing to Azalea Lake. MOTOR VEHICLES ARE NOT ALLOWED.

HISTORY: "STEVE PEAK, FORK: Named for Stephen Oster, a solitary prospector of the area during the 1860s and 1870s. Sometimes mapped as Steve's Fork, and shown on some ca. 1900 maps as Steamboat Creek." (USFS quote)

SUCKER CREEK GAP TRAIL #906. (See map 25)

TRAIL BEGINS: -Near milepost 11, Road 1030. ELEV. 4400'
TRAIL ENDS: -Boundary Ntl. Recreation Trail 1207. ELEV. 5200'
DISTANCE: -2.0 miles. Moderate.
USE: -Hiker, horse. MOTORIZED VEHICLES NOT ALLOWED.
SEASON: -Usually snow-free July to October.
CONNECTING TR: -Boundary National Recreation Trail 1207.
BRING MAPS: -USFS Applegate Ranger District-Rogue River N.F.
-USFS Red Buttes Wilderness brochure.

ACCESS: From the town of Ruch, Oregon, travel south on Upper Applegate Road and go 18.8 miles to Carberry Creek Road (County Route 777). Turn right and follow mileposts on 777 to mile 6.9 at the junction with Steve Fork Road 1030. Turn left onto 1030 and continue 11.1 mi. to the Steve Fork Trailhead. Follow the Steve Fork Trail about 1 mile upstream to the signed junction with the Sucker Creek Gap Trail. Keep to the right for the beginning of the Sucker Creek Gap Trail.

FEATURES: This Rogue River National Forest trail ends at the Boundary/National Recreation Trail 1207 at Sucker Creek Gap. Directly across the Boundary Trail, what appears to be a continuation of Sucker Creek Gap Trail 906 is Sucker Cr. Trail 1237 dropping about 3 miles through the Siskiyou National Forest to Road 4616/098.

From Sucker Creek Gap, the Boundary Trail leads south about 5 mi. to Tannen Lakes, or north about 12 mi. to Sugarloaf Mtn.

HISTORY: "SUCKER CREEK GAP: The name 'Sucker Creek' resulted when large numbers of inexperienced men flocked to the placer deposits of that stream,a tributary of the Illinois River. Actually, Sucker Creek proved to pay quite well during the 1860's and 1870s." (USFS quote)

WHISKEY PEAK LOOKOUT TRAIL #910. (See map 25)

TRAIL BEGINS:	-Forest Road 1035/350.	ELEV. 6000'
TRAIL ENDS:	-Whiskey Peak Lookout.	ELEV. 6497'
DISTANCE:	-1/2 mile. Moderate, hiker only.	
SEASON:	-Usually snow-free July to October.	
BRING MAPS:	-USFS Applegate Ranger Dist. Rogue Riv. Ntl. For.	

ACCESS: From the town of Ruch, Oregon, travel south on Upper Applegate Road and go 18.8 miles to Carberry Creek Rd.(County Route 777). Turn right onto Route 777 and follow the mileposts 4.5 miles to Forest Road 1035. Turn left onto 1035 and travel 10.8 miles to the junction with Forest Road 1035/350. Turn right onto 350 and continue 2.3 miles to the trailhead near Whiskey Springs. The trail begins on a blocked Road 1035/356.

FEATURES: The trail to the lookout is maintained for hikers only. Views of the surrounding mountain tops are terrific! The lookout building is no longer being used.

HISTORY: "WHISKEY PEAK, CREEK: Named in the 19th Century when a group of inebriated hunters camped at the base of the steep-walled peak and one extremely drunk member of the party began running away, screaming that the mountain 'was falling over on them.'" (USFS quote)

BALDY PEAK TRAIL SYSTEM (See map on following page)

Mule Mtn./Mule Tie/Mule Creek/Charlie Buck-Baldy Peak Trails.

USE: -Hiker only at this time (1998) DIFFICULT

SEASON: -Year round except for occasional winter snows.

BRING MAPS: -USFS Applegate Ranger District-Rogue River N.F.

ACCESS TO LOWER END, MULE MTN./MULE CREEK TRAILS ELEV. 1760'

From the town of Ruch, go south on Upper Applegate Road to milepost 12. MULE MTN. TRAIL 919 climbs about 1/4 mi. to the junction with Tie Trail 919.01, that leads right 1.0 mile to the MULE CREEK TRAIL 920, or Trail 919 continues uphill left.

ACCESS TO LOWER END, CHARLIE BUCK/BALDY PEAK TRAIL 918.

From Ruch, follow Upper Applegate Road just beyond milepost 9, and turn left onto Forest Route 20. Go 1.25 mi. on 20 and turn right onto Road 941. After 1/4 mile turn left onto Road 940 and go 1.0 mile to a parking place near a rock quarry just before Road 940 makes a sharp uphill bend. ELEV. 2560. From here, Road 940 is undrivable! (Steep, narrow, rockfall, no turn-around. Hike 3/4 mi. to the ridge to where the road makes a sharp bend and 1/4 mi. further to the lower end of CHARLIE BUCK/BALDY PEAK TRAIL 918 on the right.

ACCESS TO UPPER END, MULE MTN, MULE CREEK, CHARLIE BUCK/BALDY PEAK TRAILS.

From the junction of Upper Applegate Road and Forest Road 20, go 3.6 miles and turn onto Forest Road 2010. Follow Road 2010 and go 4.8 miles to Road 2010-300. Park so as not to block the gate. The road is closed to vehicles. Follow Road 300 about 1.0 mile to a road triangle. From this triangle, Road 329 leads downhill left(west), appx. 1/4 mile to the UPPER TRAILHEAD of Mule Creek Trail 920. ELEV. 4000'.

From the above triangle, Road 300 continues north, about 200 feet to Road 330. Just before a gate on 330, Baldy Peak Trail 918 begins left as a Jeep trail, soon becoming a hiking trail. From here it is 2.0 mi. to the junction with CHARLIE BUCK/BALDY PEAK TR. #918. ELEV. 4240' (at the base of Baldy Peak). Look on the left (west) for Mule Mountain Trail sloping 4.0 miles down to Upper Applegate Road. From the above junction, Charlie Buck/Baldy Peak Trail leads 2.0 miles north to Road 940.

FEATURES: Trails can be combined for making LOOP or SHUTTLE trips. For example, a loop starting from Upper Applegate Road,up on MULE CREEK TRAIL 920 and down MULE MTN. TRAIL 919 would be almost 12.0 miles, rated strenuous for hikers. Shuttle trips starting from the upper elevations would be considerably easier.

From the upper elevations, there are wide-open views of the Mule Creek or Rock Gulch canyons, and of the surrounding area. The remoteness of the trails lead to a very memorable experience!

Mule Mountain, Mule Tie, Mule Creek and Charlie Buck/Baldy Peak Trails are maintained by "Lutheran Evergreens".

Middle Fork Trail 950, A beautiful trail but a little difficult in places in the upper portion of the trail.

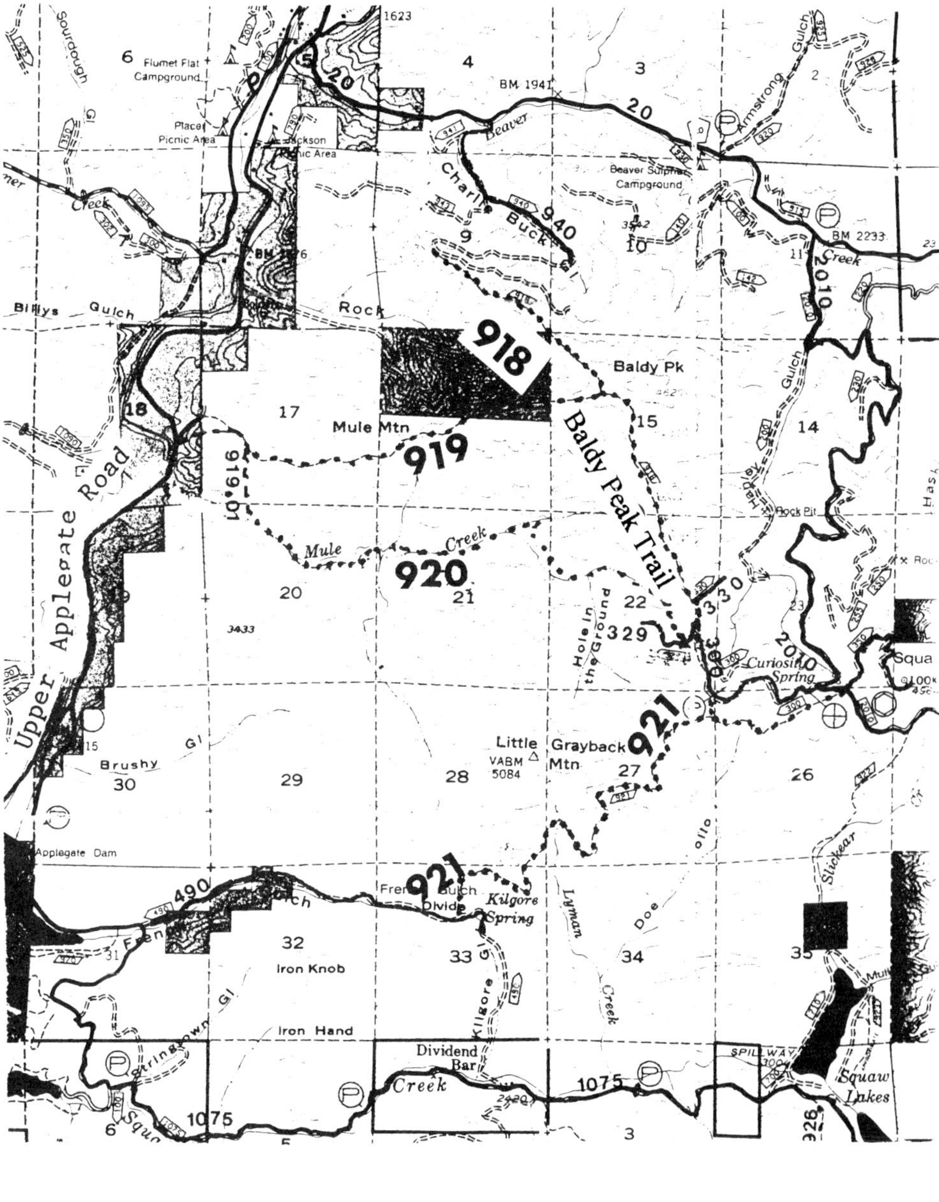
918
919
920
921
Baldy Peak Trail
Baldy Pk
Mule Mtn
Mule Creek
Little Grayback Mtn
VABM 5084
Upper Applegate Road
Flumet Flat Campground
Placer Picnic Area
Jackson Picnic Area
Beaver Sulphur Campground
Billys Gulch
Rock Pit
Curiosity Spring
Hole in the Ground
Applegate Dam
Brushy Gl
French Gulch
Divide
Kilgore Spring
Iron Knob
Iron Hand
Dividend Bar
Squaw Lakes
Spillway
Lyman Creek
Doe Creek
Armstrong Gulch
BM 1941
BM 2233
1623
20
940
2010
1075
490
330
329

LITTLE GRAYBACK TRAIL #921. (See map 26)

TRAIL BEGINS:	-French Gulch Road.	ELEV.	3200'
TRAIL ENDS:	-Forest Road 2010 near milepost 5.	ELEV.	4240'
DISTANCE:	-5.4 miles. Moderate for hikers and		
USE:	motor bikes. Difficult for horse/mountain bike.		
SEASON:	-Snow-free most of year, access roads may be hazardous during winter. Look for poison oak.		
BRING MAPS:	-USFS Applegate Ranger District -Rogue River N.F.		

LOWER ACCESS: From the town of Ruch, Oregon, follow mileposts on Upper Applegate Road to mile 14.9 and turn east across Applegate Dam onto Squaw Creek Road. Follow this road 1.5 miles then turn left onto French Gulch Road, past a row of mailboxes. Continue 2.1 miles to where the road reaches its crest at a logging road junction. The trailhead is on the left.

UPPER ACCESS: From the town of Ruch, travel 9.2 miles on Upper Applegate Road to the junction with Forest Rd. 20. (Beaver Creek Road). Follow Road 20 for 3.6 miles and turn right onto Forest Road 2010. Continue on Road 2010 for 5.1 miles and look on the right for Forest Road 2010-340.Take Road 340, 0.3 mi. west to a parking area on the left. The trailhead is just a short distance further on Road 340.

FEATURES: This trail climbs along the south slopes of Little Grayback Mountain, with open views of Squaw Lakes directly below, Elliott Ridge and of the Siskiyou Mtns. The one mile route to Squaw Peak Lookout begins near the upper trailhead.

LITTLE SQUAW TRAIL #923. (See map 26)

TRAIL BEGINS: -Squaw Lakes parking area. ELEV.3200'
TRAIL ENDS: -Mulligan Bay on Big Squaw Lake.
DISTANCE: -1.0 mile.
DIFFICULTY: -Easy. USE: Hiker/mountain bike.
SEASON: -All year.
BRING MAPS: -USFS Applegate Ranger Dist.Rogue River Ntl.Forest.

ACCESS: From the town of Ruch, Oregon, follow mileposts on Upper Applegate Road to mile 14.9 then turn left across the dam. Keep right at a junction 1.5 miles further.Squaw Creek Road becomes Forest Road 1075, and the Squaw Lakes parking area is just beyond milepost 8, uphill to the right.

From the parking area, the trail follows a maintenance road for 1/8 mile to Big Squaw Lake. Immediately after reaching the lake, continue east 100 yards further to a road junction. Turn right and follow this road for another 1/4 mi. to Little Squaw Lake.The trail crosses a foot bridge below the outlet of the lake,and then climbs a short distance before entering a mixed conifer and hardwood forest. Interpretative signs identify trees and vegetation along the trail.

The trail ends at Mulligan Bay on Big Squaw Lake. For those wishing to extend the hike, continue north on the lakeshore road that circles Big Squaw Lake. Visitors ending their hike at Mulligan Bay can return to the parking area by following the maintenance road west for 1/2 mile. CARRY WATER.

This outing provides the visitor with opportunities for picnicking, swimming, and fishing for rainbow and cutthroat trout.

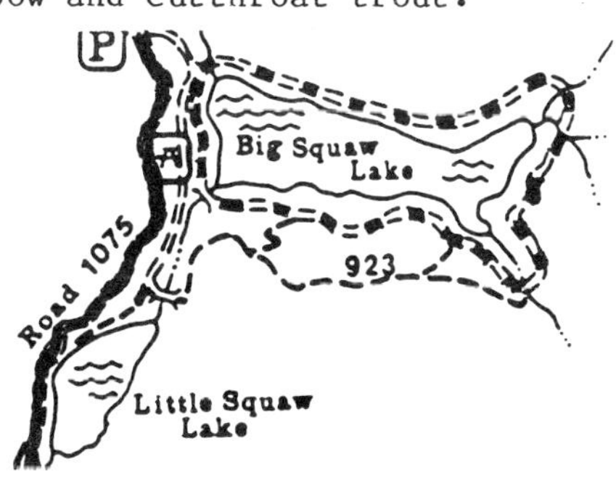

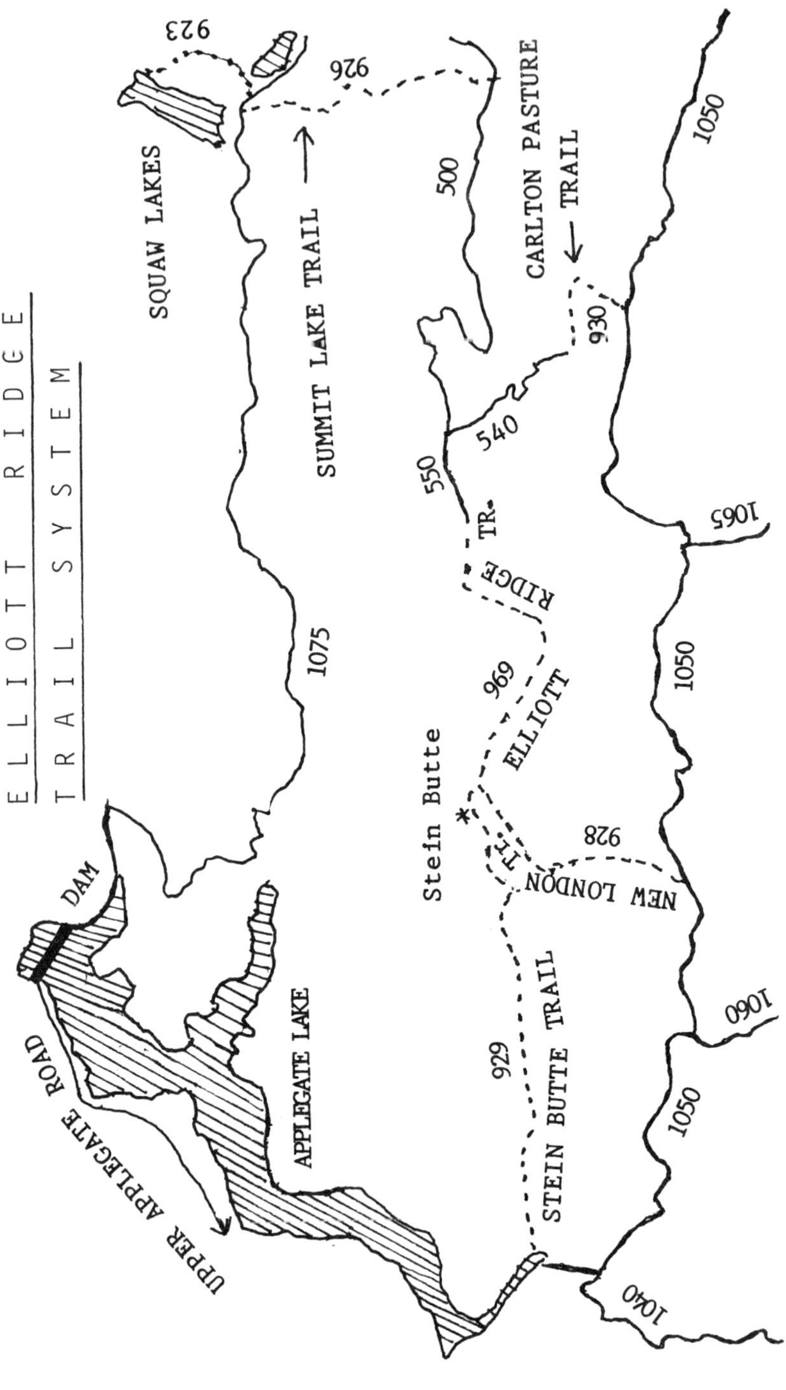
ELLIOTT RIDGE
TRAIL SYSTEM
SQUAW LAKES
923
926
SUMMIT LAKE TRAIL
500
CARLTON PASTURE
TRAIL
1050
930
540
550
TR.
RIDGE
ELLIOTT
969
1065
1075
1050
Stein Butte
928
NEW LONDON
TR.
DAM
APPLEGATE LAKE
STEIN BUTTE TRAIL
929
1060
1050
UPPER APPLEGATE ROAD
1040

SUMMIT LAKE TRAIL #926. (See map 26)

TRAIL BEGINS:	-Squaw Lakes parking area.	ELEV.	3040'
TRAIL ENDS:	-Elliott Creek Ridge.	ELEV.	4720'
DISTANCE:	-3.0 miles. Difficult.		
USE:	-1997 storm damage. Hiker only until repaired. Check with Star Ranger Station for updates.		
SEASON:	-All year except for occasional winter snows.		
BRING MAPS:	-USFS Applegate Ranger Dist.-Rogue River N.F.		

ACCESS: Follow directions to Little Squaw Trail. The Summit Lake Trail begins as an old logging track from the Squaw Lakes parking area, and leads uphill to the south.

FEATURES: Streams have washed out the logging track in three places. Hike approximately 1 mi. just beyond the third washout and look for blazes on another track leading uphill left. Follow this track 300 ft. to a meadow and keep left on the blazed trail to Summit Lake. (You can also reach the meadow by staying on the logging track 350' further to its end and turning left a few hundred feet.) The trail climbs steeply before reaching Road 1075-580. Do not cross the road-keep right and drop a short distance to Summit Lake.

Summit Lake is small and shallow and is surrounded by old growth ponderosa pines. It lies just below Elliott Creek Ridge. Paths lead up to the ridge for some good views of the surrounding area.

Summit Lake, Carlton Pasture, Elliott Ridge, New London and Stein Butte Trails comprise a trail system maintained by "Motorcycle Riders Association."

NEW LONDON TRAIL #928. (Map 26)
(Formerly the eastern portion of Stein Butte Trail #929)

TRAIL BEGINS: -Forest Road 1050. ELEV. 2160'
TRAIL ENDS: -Jnc. Stein Butte and Elliot Ridge Tr. ELEV. 4000'
DISTANCE: -2.5 miles, plus 5.0 miles on Stein Butte Trail if using a shuttle arrangement to Seattle Bar.
DIFFICULTY: -Difficult. Steep, sharp switchbacks.
SEASON: -All year except for occasional winter snows.
CONNECTING TR. Stein Butte Trail 929, Elliott Ridge Trail 969.
USE: -Hiker, mountain and motor bikes. Pack stock not recommended.
BRING MAPS: -USFS Applegate Ranger Dist.- Rogue River N.F.

ACCESS: From the town of Ruch, Oregon, follow mileposts on Upper Applegate Road 18.8 miles to Carberry Creek Road. Turn left (southeast) to the California-Oregon border near milepost 20 at the signed junction of Forest Roads 1040 and 1050. Turn left on 1050 and travel 2.7 mi.to the trailhead on the left. Parking is available directly across the road.

The 2.7 mile New London Trail meanders steeply, passing two mine adits and ends at a saddle just east of Stein Butte at the junction with the Stein Butte and Elliott Ridge Trails. Stein Butte Trail is on the left (west) leading 0.5 mi. to a ridge from where a side trail leads uphill left to Stein Butte. The Stein Butte Trail continues about 4.5 miles to its Seattle Bar Trailhead at Applegate Lake.

Elliott Ridge Tr. #969 leads right (east) from the above saddle, 1.7 mi. to Road 550. A road system from this point makes connections with Carlton Pasture Trail 930, and Summit Lake Trail 926. CARRY WATER ON ALL OF THE ABOVE TRAILS!

For a car shuttle using the above trails, cars could be placed at the appropriate lower trailheads.

New London, Stein Butte, Elliot Ridge, Summit Lake and Carlton Pasture Trails are maintained by Motorcycle Riders Association.

CARLTON PASTURE TRAIL #930. (See map 26)

TRAIL BEGINS: -Forest Road 1050. ELEV. 2640'
TRAIL ENDS: -Forest Road 1075/540. ELEV. 3680'
DISTANCE: -1.6 miles. DIFFICULT.
SEASON: -All year except for occasional winter snows.
USE: -Hiker, horse, mountain and motor bikes, horses not recommended.
BRING MAPS: -USFS Applegate Ranger Dist.- Rogue River N.F.

ACCESS: From the town of Ruch, Oregon, follow mileposts on Upper Applegate Road, 18.8 miles to Carberry Creek Road. Turn left (southeast) to the California-Oregon border near milepost 20 at the signed junction of Forest Roads 1040 and 1050. Turn left on 1050 and travel 6.6 mi.to CARLTON PASTURE TRAIL #930 trailhead on the left.

The 1.6 mile Carlton Pasture Trail climbs steeply, about 1/2 mile to the base of Carlton Pasture, and then heads west about 1.0 mi. to Forest Road 1075/540. To reach Elliott Ridge, follow Road 540 0.5 mile to Road 550. TURNING LEFT(West) onto Road 550 leads 0.5 mi. to ELLIOTT RIDGE TRAIL #969 that leads 1.7 mi.to the junction with STEIN BUTTE TRAIL #929 and NEW LONDON TRAIL #928.

From the above junction of Roads 540 and 550,TURNING RIGHT (east) onto Road 550 leads 0.5 mile to Road 500. Keep RIGHT onto Road 500 and go about 2.5 miles. Look on the left (downhill north)for Summit Lake and SUMMIT LAKE TRAIL #926.

For a car shuttle using the above trails, cars could be placed at the appropriate lower trailheads. This trail is maintained by the Motorcycle Riders Association.

MIDDLE FORK TRAIL #950. (See map 25)

TRAIL BEGINS: -Forest Road 1035, northern Calif. ELEV. 2640'
TRAIL ENDS: -Forest Road 1040/600. ELEV. 4200'
DISTANCE: -Lower section 3 miles, upper section 3.1 miles.
USE: -Hiker/horse. Temporarily closed to horses (1998).
SEASON: -May through October.
CONNECTING TR: -Frog Pond Trail 953.
BRING MAPS: -USFS Applegate Ranger Dist.-Rogue River Ntl. For.
-USFS "Red Buttes Wilderness" brochure.
-USFS Recreation Opportunity Guide-Middle Fork Tr.

ACCESS: From the town of Ruch, Oregon, follow mileposts on Upper Applegate Road to mile 18.8 at Carberry Creek Road. Turn left and continue 1.3 miles to the junction with Forest Road 1040 and 1050. Turn onto Road 1040 and drive the following distances:

LOWER TRAILHEAD-5 miles to junction with Rd. 1035. Turn right onto Road 1035 and go .2 mile to the trailhead on the left.

MIDDLE TRAILHEAD: Continue 7.0 mi. on Road 1040 to where Middle Fork Trail crosses the road and continues upstream from the Frog Pond Trailhead.

UPPER TRAILHEAD: Continue 2.0 miles on Road 1040 to the junction with Road 1040/600. Turn left onto Road 600 and go 1/8 mile to a new trailhead on the left.

FEATURES: The lower end of the trail begins as a rough road that very soon breaks into a trail on the right. It follows the Middle Fork of the Applegate River and passes two old mining cabin sites along the way (ca.1930). The trail continues its climb and crosses Road 1040 at the Frog Pond Trailhead. It then continues 3.1 mi. to the Upper Trailhead. There is an abundance of autumn color from the vine maples, alder, yew, dogwood, huckleberry and other surrounding plants.

FROG POND TRAIL #953. (See map 25)

TRAIL BEGINS: -LOWER END: Forest Road 1040. ELEV. 3440'
TRAIL ENDS: -UPPER END: Forest Road 1040. ELEV. 3880'
DISTANCE: -5.4 miles, steep grades. HIGHPOINT ELEV. 5200'
DIFFICULTY: -Moderate for hikers/difficult for horses and they are not recommended.
SEASON: -Early July through October.
CONNECTING TR: -Middle Fork Trail 950. NO MOTORIZED VEHICLES.
BRING MAPS: -USFS Applegate Ranger Dist.-Rogue River N.F.
-USFS "Red Buttes Wilderness" brochure.

ACCESS: From the town of Ruch, Oregon, follow mileposts on Upper Applegate Road 18.8 miles to Carberry Creek Road. Turn left and continue 1.3 miles to the junction with Forest Roads 1050 and 1040. Keep right onto 1040 and go 9.7 miles to the lower trailhead or 2 miles more to the upper trailhead.

FEATURES: From the lower end, the trail begins along a faint track soon becoming a good trail. Near the top end of the loop the trail may become obscure. Follow the blazes, stakes, and green "X" trail signs. At one point the trail passes a small pond into a larger meadow and becomes difficult to follow. Follow cairns in the center of the meadow and head for the uprooted tree on the far side. The trail becomes easy to follow then climbs steadily to the north with views of the Red Buttes. After reaching a crest, the trail descends sharply to the southwest shore of Frog Pond and then passes an old cabin that uses a cluster of cedar trees as its mainstay. The cabin was built by John Knox McCloy in about 1900. The trail drops sharply about 1 mile to the upper trailhead on Road 1040.

FIR GLADE TRAIL #955. (A ROUTE TO AZALEA LAKE see map 25)

TRAIL BEGINS: -Forest Road 1040/800. ELEV. 5200'
TRAIL ENDS: -Azalea Lake. ELEV. 5400'
DISTANCE: -5.8 miles. HIGH POINT ELEV. 6000'
SEASON: -Usually open late June through October.
USE: -Hiker/horse MODERATE GRADE, NO ORV'S.
BRING MAPS: -USFS Applegate Ranger Dist.-Rogue River N.F.
-USFS "Red Buttes Wilderness" brochure.
CONNECTING TR.-Steve Fork Trail 905, Phantom Meadows Trail 955A, Butte Fork Trail 957.

ACCESS: There are two routes to Forest Road 1040/800,both subject to winter road washouts--check with USFS Star Ranger Sta. for best route. 18.8 MILES SOUTH OF RUCH ON UPPER APPLEGATE ROAD:
ROUTE 1: Turn LEFT and go 1.3 mi. to the road 1050/1040 junction. Turn RIGHT onto 1040 and go about 17 mi. to Road 800 on the left.
ROUTE 2: Turn RIGHT onto Carberry Road(777) and go 6.9 mi to Road 1030. Take 1030 4.8 miles to Road 400 (Low Gap Road). Follow Rd. 400 4.2 mi. just beyond the ridge crest. At the junction of Roads 700 and 1040, keep RIGHT on 1040 for 0.1 mi. to Road 800. Low Gap Road had heavy 1997 storm damage (Check for repair status).

Turn onto Road 800 and go 0.4 mi. to Hinkle Lake junction. Turn left and go 0.1 mi. to Fir Glade Trailhead. (Very rough Road).

FEATURES: This trail affords open views of the Middle Fork drainage, Buck Peak, Figurehead Mountain and Klamath Mountains. Not far from the trailhead, the route follows an old road for a short distance. Look left to where the trail continues to Fir Glade, a large open meadow with a collapsed shelter. On the near edge of the meadow, look left for the continuation of the trail. 1 mile further, pass the junction with the Steve Fork and Phantom Meadows Trails then continue to the crest of the divide between Rogue River and Klamath Ntl. Forests. The trail switchbacks to a saddle N.W. of Figurehead Mountain before dropping down to Azalea Lake. At Azalea Lake,hikers camp is north of the lake and stock camp east of the lake. "No camping in the day-use area between the perimeter trail and the lake. LIMIT PER GROUP 8 persons,12 stock. Bring pellets/grain for stock" (USFS)

BUTTE FORK TRAIL #957. (See map 25)

TRAIL BEGINS: -From Horse Camp Trail 958,or from SHOO FLY TRAILHEAD on Forest Road 1040.

TRAIL ENDS: -Azalea Lake.

DISTANCE: -10 miles to Azalea Lake via the Horse Camp Trail, or 8 miles from the Shoo Fly Trailhead.

SEASON: -June through October. USE: hiker/horse only.

CONNECTING TR. -Horse Camp Trail #958, Shoo Fly Trail #954, Fort Goff Trail #956, Fir Glade Trail #955.

BRING MAPS: -USFS "Red Buttes Wilderness" brochure.
-USFS Applegate Ranger Dist. -Rogue River N.F.

ACCESS: From the town of Ruch, Oregon, follow mileposts on Upper Applegate Road, 18.8 miles to Carberry Creek Road. Turn left and go 1.3 mile to the signed junction of Forest Roads 1040 and 1050. Turn right onto Road 1040 and go 3.6 miles to the Horse Camp Trailhead on the left (At the former Cook and Green Campground).Take the Horse Camp Trail about 3/4 mile to where the Butte Fork Trail leads RIGHT.

SHOO FLY TRAILHEAD is 4 mi. further on Road 1040 near milepost 9. The trail drops 0.7 mile to the Butte Fork Trail. Turn right and continue about 7.5 miles upstream to Azalea Lake.

FEATURES: From its junction with Horse Camp Trail,the Butte Fork Trail passes below the Butte Fork Slide before dropping to Echo Canyon and the Butte Fork of the Applegate River. In another 0.5 miles,you reach a bridge taking you to the north bank of the river with a good view of Hello Canyon. Follow the trail about 0.5 mile to the lower end of the Shoo Fly Trail.

Butte Fork Trail continues upstream,passing an old Forest Service toolhouse and a marked grave of persons killed in a 1945 airplane crash, before reaching Cedar Basin and the junction of Fort Goff Trail 956. Azalea Lake is one mile west of Cedar Basin.

HORSE CAMP TRAIL #958. (See map 26)

TRAIL BEGINS: -Forest Road 1040. ELEV. 2400'
TRAIL ENDS: -Pacific Crest National Scenic Trail. ELEV. 5900'
DISTANCE: -3.9 miles, very steep grades. CARRY WATER.
SEASON: -June through Oct. USE: As of 1988: hikers. Not recommended for pack stock, mountain/motor bikes.
CONNECTING TR: -Butte Fork Trail 957.
-Pacific Crest National Scenic Trail.
BRING MAPS: -USFS Applegate Ranger Dist. -Rogue River N.F.
-USFS "Red Buttes Wilderness" brochure.
-USFS Recreation Opportunity Guide-Horse Camp Tr.

ACCESS: From the town of Ruch, Oregon, follow mileposts on Upper Applegate Road, 18.8 miles to Carberry Creek Road. Turn left and go 1.3 miles to the junction of Roads 1050 and 1040. Turn right onto Road 1040 and go 3.6 miles to the trailhead on the left. (At the former Cook and Green Campground).

FEATURES: Horse Camp Trail is popular with backpackers as an access to the Pacific Crest National Scenic Trail. About 3500 ft. of elevation is gained in only four miles, rating the trail one of the steepest in the Siskiyou Mountains.

In about 0.5 mi. KEEP LEFT at the new Butte Fork Trail junction. It is 1.0 mile further to Horse Camp and a nearby spring. WATER TREATMENT IS RECOMMENDED. The trail continues another 1.5 miles to a high mountain meadow before reaching the Echo Lake junction. The trail to the right leads to Echo Lake nestled in a small cirque basin below Red Buttes. To reach the Pacific Crest National Scenic Trail, keep left at the above junction and go 0.5 miles.

A 15 mile loop is possible by using the Horse Camp, Pacific Crest and Cook and Green Trails. MOTORIZED VEHICLES ARE NOT ALLOWED ON THE PACIFIC CREST TRAIL OR IN THE RED BUTTES WILDERNESS.

HISTORY: "Horse Camp: Named by John Knox McCloy in the early 20th century." (USFS quote)

COOK AND GREEN TRAIL #959. (See map 26)

TRAIL BEGINS: -(Lower Trailhead) Forest Road 1040. ELEV. 2280'
TRAIL ENDS: -(Upper Trailhead) Cook and Green Pass ELEV. 4765' Forest Road 1055.(Road directions in Chapter 14).
DISTANCE: -About 8.2 miles.
DIFFICULTY: -Moderate for hikers, horses, mountain bikes and motor bikes.
SEASON: -Usually snow-free June through October.
CONNECTING TR: -Pacific Crest National Scenic Trail.
BRING MAPS: -USFS Applegate Ranger Dist.-Rogue River Ntl. For.
-USFS Recreation Opportunity Guide-this trail.
-USFS Pacific Crest Trail-Oreg. Southern Portion.

ACCESS: (LOWER TRAILHEAD). From Ruch, Oregon, turn left onto Upper Applegate Road and continue 18.8 miles to the junction with Carberry Creek Road. Turn left and go 1.3 miles to the junction of Forest Roads 1050 and 1040. Turn right onto Road 1040 and go 2.8 mi. to the trailhead on the left.

FEATURES: The trail passes through a sizable stand of the rare Brewer spruce trees recognizable by its four to eight foot long, string-like branchlets hanging down from its limbs. Noble and white fir are also seen at higher elevations. No-See-Em Camp is reached just before crossing Cook and Green Cr. The trail then climbs along the west side of Bear Gulch and passes a small spring just before reaching Cook and Green Pass. See Chapter 14 for road directions to Cook and Green Pass. MOTORIZED VEHICLES NOT ALLOWED ON THE PCNST OR IN RED BUTTES WILDERNESS. WATER TREATMENT IS RECOMMENDED.

HISTORY: "COOK AND GREEN CREEK, PASS, CAMPGROUND: Robert Cook and the two Green brothers were partners in several mining ventures in this vicinity during the 1870s and 1880s; the name undoubtedly resulted from their activities."
"NO-SEE-EM CAMP: Probably named by early day Forest Service employees, for the clouds of small gnats (no-see-ums) which harass campers during the spring and summer months." (USFS quotes)

TIN CUP TRAIL #961. (See map 26)

TRAIL BEGINS: -End of Forest Road 1060/600. ELEV. 5240'
TRAIL ENDS: -Siskiyou crest. ELEV. 6000'
DISTANCE: -1.6 miles, moderate grades. USE: hiker/horse.
SEASON: -Usually snow-free July through October.
CONNECTING TR. -Pacific Crest National Scenic Trail.
BRING MAPS: -USFS Applegate Ranger Dist.- Rogue River N.F.

ACCESS: From the town of Ruch, Oregon, follow mileposts on Upper Applegate Road 18.8 miles to Carberry Creek Road. Turn left (southeast) to the California-Oregon border near milepost 20 at the signed junction of Forest Roads 1040 and 1050. Turn left on 1050 and travel 1.6 miles to the junction with Forest Road 1060. Turn right onto 1060 and continue 3.5 mi. to a hairpin turn leading back to the north. (The old Blue Ledge Copper Mine is located on the right, southwest of this turn.) Continue northeast on 1060, gaining Nabob Ridge in about 2 miles at the junction with Forest Road 1060/600. Turn right onto Road 600 for about 1.5 miles to its end. (In 1997 Road 600 was damaged ~~1/4~~ 1.5 mile before reaching the trailhead).

FEATURES: This short trail connects with the Pacific Crest National Scenic Trail near Lowdens' Cabin and Slaughterhouse Flat. MOTORIZED VEHICLES ARE NOT ALLOWED ON THE PCNST OR IN RED BUTTES WILDERNESS.

HISTORY: "JOHN LOWDEN settled at the mouth of Seiad Creek in 1860 and operated a ferry across the Klamath River for several years. He and his two sons mined, raised wheat and began a small dairy. Their beef cattle ranged on the high meadows of the Siskiyou crest during the summers."

"SLAUGHTERHOUSE FLAT may have been the site of an early hog butchering operation providing meat for the sudden influx of miners during the 1850s." (USFS quotes)

CHAPTER 6 - SKY LAKES WILDERNESS

Sky Lakes Wilderness is a land of lakes, rocky ridges and timbered slopes, and was designated by Congress in 1984. Its 113,590 acres straddles southern Oregon's Cascade Range from Crater Lake National Park southward to Highway 140. It is approx. six miles wide and twenty seven miles long, with elevations ranging from 3800 feet in the canyon of the Middle Fork of the Rogue River to a lofty 9495 feet at the top of Mt. McLoughlin.

More than 200 pools of water, from small ponds to lakes of 30-40 acres, dot the landscape. Fourmile Lake, near the southern end of the area, exceeds 900 acres. The lake basins can sometimes be crowded with other campers, but the wilderness has thousands of acres of forest and scenic ridges where the visitor can find solitude.

<u>SPECIAL RULES</u> are enforced to protect the Wilderness resource:

1) Campsites must be at least 100 ft. from lakeshores and 50 ft. from streams.

2) Graze and tether horses and pack animals at least 200 feet from lakes or ponds and 50 feet from streams. Avoid tying animals directly to trees and do not picket. Use a "high-line" stretched between two trees.

3) Stay out of specially marked areas being revegetated.

4) Visitors should travel in groups no larger than 8 people and twelve animals throughout Sky Lakes Wilderness.

5) Bicycles, motorbikes, hang gliders, carts, wagons and other forms of mechanized transport are not allowed (disabled persons in wheelchairs permitted).

6. Bring adequate food (pellets or grain, not hay) for your animals because feed is scarce in the Wilderness, use nosebag.

(continued on next page)

SPECIAL RULES CONTINUED:

7. Refrain from operating loud radios or other audio devices. Discharging of firearms within or near occupied areas or across lakes is prohibited.

8. Grazing is not allowed before August 1, unless otherwise posted at trailhead bulletin boards.

THE WILDERNESS CONTAINS TWO LAKE BASINS WHERE FURTHER RESTRICTIONS APPLY (SEVEN LAKES BASIN and BLUE CANYON BASIN).

A. In sensitive areas of these two basins, groups with pack/saddle animals must camp only within designated "horse camp" sites. These sites are marked with signs; sensitive areas and horse camp locations are shown on maps posted at trailheads.

B. In the two basins, grazing is permitted only in designated meadows and only after August 1 (unless otherwise posted at trailhead bulletin boards).

Be sure to check the trailhead bulletin board for current rules and other information pertaining to the Sky Lakes Wilderness. The complete management regulations enforced in the area may be reviewed in the Forest Supervisor or District Ranger offices.

A SKY LAKES WILDERNESS MAP, and other very detailed information, can be obtained from:

Forest Supervisor, Rogue River National Forest, 333 W. 8th St., Medford, OR 97501.
-District Ranger, P.O. Box 227, Butte Falls, OR 97522.

Forest Supervisor, Winema National Forest, 2819 Dahlia St., Klamath Falls, OR 97601.
-Klamath District Ranger, 1936 California Ave., Klamath Falls, OR 97601.

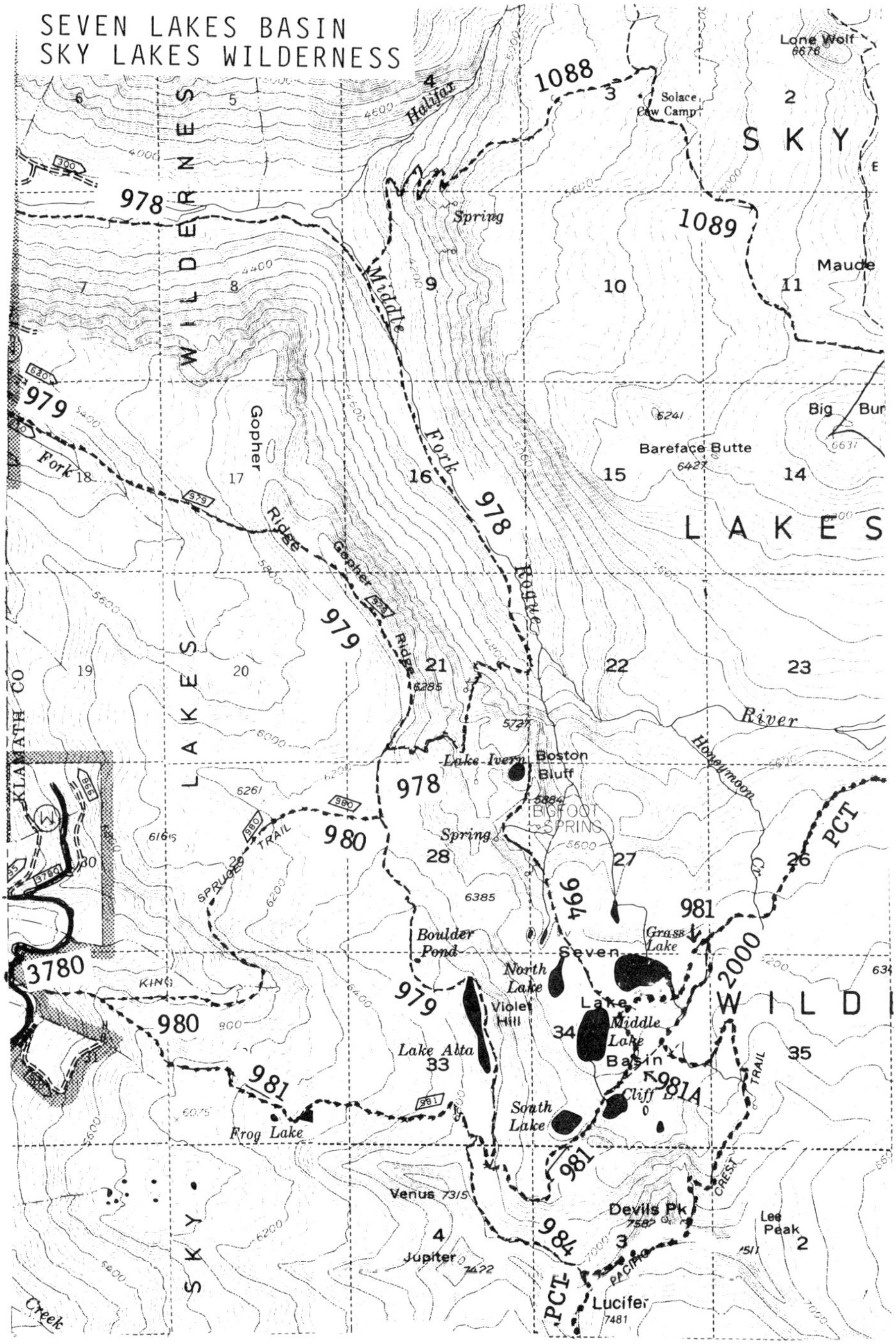
SEVEN LAKES BASIN
SKY LAKES WILDERNESS
1088
1089
978
979
980
981
981A
984
994
2000
3780
PCT
Halifax
Solace Cow Camp
Lone Wolf
6676
Spring
Maude
Middle Fork Rogue
River
Gopher Ridge
Big Bur
Bareface Butte
6427
6241
6637
Honeymoon Cr
Lake Ivern
Boston Bluff
5884
BIGFOOT SPRING
6285
5727
6261
6385
SPRUCE TRAIL
KING
Boulder Pond
North Lake
Grass Lake
Seven Lake Basin
Middle Lake
Violet Hill
Lake Alta
South Lake
Cliff L
Frog Lake
Venus 7315
Jupiter 7472
Devils Pk 7582
Lee Peak
Lucifer 7481
PACIFIC CREST TRAIL
KLAMATH CO
Fork
Creek
SKY LAKES WILDERNESS

MIDDLE FORK TRAIL #978. (See map 11)

TRAIL BEGINS: -Middle Fork Trailhead Road 3790. ELEV. 3500'
TRAIL ENDS: -Alta Lake Trail junction. ELEV. 6200'
DISTANCE: -8.5 miles, moderate/difficult. Hiker/horse.
SEASON: -Lower segment of trail usually open by May 15.
-Upper segment of trail, July-October.
CONNECTING TR. -Halifax Tr. 1088 *
-Alta Lake Trail 979.
BRING MAPS: -Butte Falls Ranger Dist.-Rogue River Ntl.Forest.
USFS Sky Lakes Area-Rogue River/Winema Ntl. For.
USFS Rec. Opportunity Guide, Middle Fork Trail.

ACCESS: From the town of Butte Falls, Oreg., travel east out of town 1.0 mile to County Route 992,leading north to the town of Prospect. Turn onto this road and follow it 8.7 miles to Forest Route 34. Turn east and continue 8.2 miles to Forest Route 37. Turn left on 37 and continue 5.2 miles to Forest Road 3790. Travel 3 miles east on 3790 to the trailhead.

FEATURES: For the first six miles, the trail follows along the south bank of the river. There are a number of camp spots, though not obvious from the trail. (The junction with Halifax Tr.*is reached after the first 3.5 miles).The Middle Fork Trail then climbs steeply out of the canyon to the junction with Alta Lake Trail on Gopher Ridge.

The USFS advises that there is no horse feed in the canyon, and that water is available not far from the trail along most of its length. Visitors should recognize that water in wilderness and backcountry areas may not be safe to drink. Water is not tested. (Excerpts USFS Recreation Opportunity Guide)

See beginning of chapter 6 for historical notes and regulations.

* HALIFAX TRAIL CLOSED IN 1997 DUE TO SLIDES AND WASHOUT. CHECK WITH BUTTE FALLS RANGER STATION FOR STATUS.

ALTA LAKE TRAIL #979. (See map 11)

TRAIL BEGINS:	-Forest Road 3785.	ELEV. 4800'
TRAIL ENDS:	-Seven Lakes Trail junction.	ELEV. 6800'
DISTANCE:	-6.2 miles, moderate to difficult.	
SEASON:	-Usually snow-free July to October. Preferred use: hikers. No horse feed at Alta Lake.	
CONNECTING TR.	-Middle Fork Trail 978, King Spruce Trail 980 and Seven Lakes Trail 981.	
BRING MAPS:	-Butte Falls Ranger Dist.-Rogue River Ntl. Forest. -USFS Rec. Opportunity Guide-Alta Lake Trail. -USFS Sky Lakes Area-Rogue River/Winema Ntl. For.	

ACCESS: From the town of Butte Falls, Oreg., travel east one mile to County Route 992 leading north to the town of Prospect. Turn onto this road and follow it 8.7 miles to Forest Route 34. Turn right onto 34 and go 8.2 miles to the junction with Forest Route 37. Keep left onto 37 and travel 2.2 miles to the junction with Forest Road 3785. Turn onto Road 3785 and go 3.5 miles to the Alta Lake Trailhead. Parking is limited to roadside turnouts with space for horse trailer turn-around.

FEATURES: This trail gets little use. It begins at Wallowa Creek and climbs to the open parklands on the south slope of Gopher Ridge. The trail junctions with the Middle Fork and King Spruce Trails, then ends at Seven Lakes Trail 981. Camp sites are on high ground both east and west of Alta Lake. A 9.1 mile loop uses the upper section of the Alta Lake Trail, the Seven Lakes Trail 981 and King Spruce Trail 980. Water is available at Alta Lake and seasonally at Boulder Pond, but should be treated. Alta Lake has no horsefeed. See beginning of Chapter 6 for Sky Lakes Wilderness regulations and historical notes.

HISTORY: "ALTA LAKE: One of the lakes in the Seven Lakes Basin, probably named by early Forest Svc. personnel because of its location on the slopes of a bluff, several hundred feet higher than the other six lakes." (USFS quote)

KING SPRUCE TRAIL #980. (See map 11)

TRAIL BEGINS: -Near Seven Lakes Trailhead, Road 3780. ELEV. 5600'
TRAIL ENDS: -Junction with Alta Lake Trail. ELEV. 6350'
DISTANCE: -2.8 miles, moderate, preferred use: Hikers.
SEASON: -Usually snow-free July to October.
CONNECTING TR.-Alta Lake Trail 979, Seven Lakes Trail 981.
BRING MAPS: -Butte Falls Ranger Dist.-Rogue River Ntl. Forest.
-USFS Sky Lakes Area-Rogue River/Winema Ntl. For.

ACCESS: From the town of Butte Falls, travel east one mile to County Route 992, leading north to the town of Prospect. Turn onto this route and follow it 8.7 miles to Forest Route 34. Turn onto 34 and go 8.2 miles to Forest Route 37. Keep left onto 37, and travel 0.4 miles to Forest Road 3780. Turn onto 3780 and go 3.6 miles to the Seven Lakes Trailhead. There is ample parking/turnaround space at the trailhead. Water not available. The lower end of the KING SPRUCE TRAIL is reached by hiking along the Seven Lakes Trail, 0.5 mile from its trailhead.

FEATURES: The 2.8 mi. King Spruce Tr. passes the site of the old King Spruce Camp before climbing to the junction with the Alta Lake Trail 979. TURNING LEFT at this junction leads to the Middle Fork Trail in less than 1 mile, or 3.6 miles to the Alta Lake lower trailhead.

TURNING RIGHT from King Spruce Trail leads 2.5 miles, past Alta Lake, to the Seven Lakes Trail. See beginning of Chapter 6 for Sky Lakes Wilderness regulations and history.

It is a good idea to keep
Raingear in your pack

SEVEN LAKES TRAIL #981. (See map 11 and 12)

TRAIL BEGINS: -Forest Road 3780. ELEV. 5000'
TRAIL ENDS: -Pacific Crest National Scenic Trail, ELEV. 6200'
DISTANCE: -6.1 miles, moderate to difficult. Hiker/horse.
SEASON: -Usually snow-free July to October.
CONNECTING TR. -King Spruce Trail 980, Alta Lake Trail 979, Devils Peak Trail 984, Lake Ivern Trail 994, and Pacific Crest Trail.
BRING MAPS: -USFS Butte Falls Ranger Dist., Rogue River N.F.
-USFS Rec. Opportunity Guide, Seven Lakes Trail.
-USFS Sky Lakes Area-Rogue River/Winema Ntl. For.

ACCESS: From the town of Butte Falls, travel east 1 mile to County Route 992,leading north to the town of Prospect.Turn onto this route and travel 8.7 mi. to Forest Route 34. Turn east on 34 and travel 8.2 miles to the junction with Forest Route 37 and keep left for 0.4 mi. to Forest Road 3780. Follow 3780, 3.6 miles to the trailhead. Parking and turnaround space is ample. Water is not available.

FEATURES: Seven Lakes Trail passes the lower King Spruce Trailhead in the first 0.5 mile before climbing 1700 feet to a saddle at a junction with Alta Lake and Devils Pk. Trails. Seven Lakes Trail then drops into Seven Lakes Basin and the junction with Lake Ivern Trail 994, before ending on the Pacific Crest Trail.

For a cross-wilderness experience, follow the PCT 2.5 miles northeast to the junction with Sevenmile Trail 3703 that travels northeast to its trailhead in Winema National Forest.

A 9.1 mile loop uses Trail 981, the upper end of Alta Lake Trail 979 and King Spruce Trail 980. The Seven Lakes Trail may be dusty due to overuse. Cliff Lake may be overcrowded. CARRY WATER, as lake water in the area is not recommended for drinking without treatment. Mosquitos are bad from June to mid-August.

Please see beginning of Chapter 6 for historical information and for a mention of wilderness regulations.

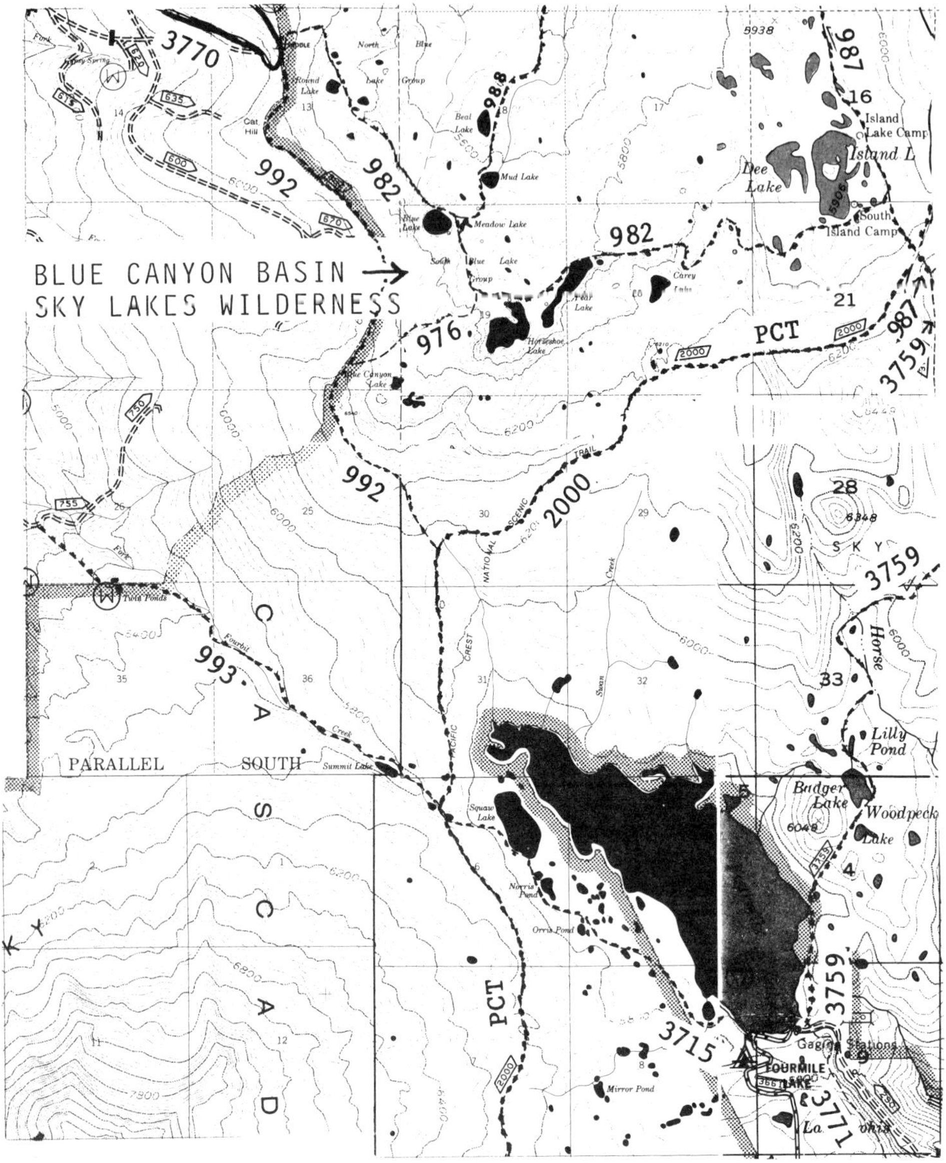
BLUE CANYON BASIN
SKY LAKES WILDERNESS
3770
992
982
988
987
976
PCT
2000
3759
993
3715
3771
Island Lake Camp
Island L
Dee Lake
South Island Camp
Mud Lake
Meadow Lake
Horseshoe Lake
Blue Canyon Lake
Twin Ponds
Summit Lake
Squaw Lake
Norris Pond
Orris Pond
Mirror Pond
Lilly Pond
Budger Lake
Woodpeck
Lake
FOURMILE LAKE
Gaging Stations
PARALLEL
SOUTH
C A S C A D
NATIONAL SCENIC TRAIL
PACIFIC CREST

BLUE CANYON TRAIL #982 (See maps 11 and 16)

TRAIL BEGINS: -Road 3770 at Saddle Camp. ELEV. 6200'
TRAIL ENDS: -Junction with Red Lake Trail 987. ELEV. 6000'
DISTANCE: -5.1 miles, easy to moderate. USE: hiker/horse.
SEASON: -Usually snow-free June to October, trailhead often not accessible by car until the end of June or the first of July. Mosquitos are numerous until about August 15.
CONNECTING TR. -Cat Hill Way Tr.992, Meadow Lake Tr. 976, South Fork Tr. 988, Red Lake Tr. 987.
BRING MAPS: -USFS Butte Falls Ranger Dist., Rogue River N.F.
-USFS Sky Lakes Area, Rogue Riv.-Winema Ntl. For.
-USFS Rec. Opportunity Guide-Blue Canyon Trail.

ACCESS: From White City, OR., follow mileposts on State Hwy. 140, 28.6 miles to the junction with County Route 821.Continue north on 821,8.8 mi. just beyond milepost 26 to a junction where Route 37 leads right(east). Follow mileposts on 37, 10.9 miles to the junction with Road 3770 on the right. Follow 3770, 6 miles to the trailhead. Parking and turn-around space is adequate.

FEATURES: Trail 982 passes Blue, Meadow, Horseshoe, Pear and Island Lakes. The trail may be dusty from overuse, and the surrounding lakes may be overcrowded. There is no horsefeed in the Blue Canyon Area. A 5.6 mile day loop hike is possible by using the Cat Hill Way Trail 992 (trailhead just a few hundred feet down from the Blue Canyon Trailhead), Meadow Lake Trail 976 and the Blue Canyon Trail. A longer 12.5 mile loop uses the Cat Hill Way, the Pacific Crest and Blue Canyon Trail.

Please see beginning of chapter 6 for Sky Lakes Wilderness regulations and history notes.

SOUTH FORK TRAIL #988 (See maps 11 and 16)

TRAIL BEGINS: -Forest Road 37/720. ELEV. 4000'
TRAIL ENDS: -Junction with Blue Canyon Trail. ELEV. 5700'
DISTANCE: -5.1 miles, moderate to difficult.
SEASON: -Usually snow-free June to October. Mosquitos bad until mid-August. USE: Recommended, hiker only.
CONNECTING TR: -Blue Canyon Trail 982.
BRING MAPS: -Rogue River Ntl. Forest-Butte Falls Ranger Dist.
-USFS Sky Lakes Area-Rogue River/Winema Ntl. For.
-USFS Rec. Opportunity Guide-South Fork Trail.

ACCESS: From White City OR., follow mileposts on State Hwy. 140, 28.6 miles to the junction with County Route 821.Turn north on 821 and go 8.8 miles(just beyond Milepost 26) to where Forest Route 37 leads right (east). Follow mileposts on 37, 13.3 miles to the junction with Forest Road 37/720 on the right. Turn and continue on 720, 1 mile to the end of the road at the South Fork Trailhead.

ALTERNATE ALL PAVEMENT ROUTE: From Butte Falls, travel east one mi.to County Route 992, that leads north to the town of Prospect. Turn onto this route and go 8.7 miles to the junction with Forest Route 34. Turn right onto 34 and go 8.2 miles to the junction with Forest Route 37. Turn right onto 37 and go 5.7 miles to the junction with Road 720. Turn left and follow 720 one mile to the trailhead at the end of the road.

FEATURES: This trail is recommended for hiker use only. It passes Beal, Mud and Meadow Lakes before terminating at Blue Lake and Blue Canyon Trail 982. If using a car shuttle, the hike could be made easier by hiking from the Blue Canyon Trailhead to Blue Lake, and taking the South Fork Trail down to Forest Road 37/720. Water is plentiful along the trail, but like all wilderness water, should be treated before drinking. (See the beginning of Chapter 6 for historical notes and a mention of Wilderness regulations).

CAT HILL WAY TRAIL #992. (See maps 11 and 16)

TRAIL BEGINS: -Road 3770 at Saddle Camp. ELEV. 6200'
TRAIL ENDS: -Junction with Pacific Crest Trail. ELEV. 6160'
DISTANCE: -3.4 miles, moderate. Preferred use: hikers.
SEASON: -Usually snow-free June to October, trailhead often not accessible by car until the end of June or first of July. Mosquitos are numerous until mid August.
CONNECTING TR. -Blue Canyon 982, Meadow Lake 976 and Pacific Crest Trails.
BRING MAPS: -USFS Butte Falls Ranger Dist., Rogue River N.F.
-USFS Sky Lakes Area-Rogue River/Winema Ntl. For.

ACCESS: From White City, OR., follow mileposts on State Hwy. 140, 28.6 miles to the junction with County Route 821. Continue north on 821, 8.8 miles just beyond milepost 26, to where Forest Route 37 leads right (east). Follow mileposts on 37, 10.9 miles to the junction with Road 3770 on the right. Follow 3770, 6 miles to the trailhead. Parking and turn-around space is adequate.

FEATURES: To reach the Cat Hill Way Trail, hike a few hundred feet down from the Blue Canyon Trailhead. Look for a trailhead sign on the right.

A 5.6 mile day loop hike is possible by using the Cat Hill Way Trail 992, Meadow Lake Trail 976 and Blue Canyon Trail 982. A longer 12.5 mile loop uses the Cat Hill way, Pacific Crest and Blue Canyon Trails.

The Cat Hill Way Trail is maintained by the Rogue Chapter of the Sierra Club. Please see beginning of Chapter 6 for Sky Lakes Wilderness regulations and historical notes.

TOM AND JERRY TRAIL #1084. (See map 6)

TRAIL BEGINS: -Forest Road 3795/600. ELEV. 5000'
TRAIL ENDS: -McKie Shelter. ELEV. 5500'
DISTANCE: -5 miles, moderate, hiker/horse, June to October.
CONNECTING TR: -Mudjekeewis Trail 1085 and McKie Camp Tr. 1089.
BRING MAPS: -USFS Butte Falls Ranger Dist., Rogue River N.F.
-USFS Sky Lakes Area-Rogue River/Winema Ntl. For.
-USFS Rec. Opportunity Guide, Tom and Jerry Trail.

ACCESS: From the town of Prospect, Oregon, travel east on County Route 992,leading toward Butte Falls for 2.5 miles to Forest Route 37. Turn onto 37 and continue east, 2.8 miles to Road 3795. Turn left onto 3795 and continue 5.7 miles to the junction with Forest Road 3795/600. Turn right onto 600 and go 0.6 mile to the trailhead. Parking and turn-around space is adequate.

FEATURES: After 1.5 miles, you reach the junction with the 5.1 mile Mudjekeewis Trail 1085 (that skirts the south edge of Kerby Peak with views of the Middle Fork Canyon before re-joining the Tom and Jerry Trail at Mckie Shelter). KEEP LEFT AT THE 1.5 MILE JUNCTION to reach McKie Shelter via the Tom and Jerry Trail. Water is usually available on the first portion of the trail and at McKie Camp. Horse feed is plentiful in the McKie vicinity. Returning (westbound) on the Tom and Jerry Trail, a saddle is reached in about 1.5 miles. Just west of the saddle look for the trail as it leads southwest. BEWARE OF A TREE BLAZE ON AN OLD ABANDONED TRAIL THAT LEADS NORTHWEST. The Tom and Jerry Trail is maintained by the Oregon Hunters' Assn., and Mudjekeewis Trail by the Jackson County Horsemans' Assn.

If making a 11.5 mile loop with the Tom and Jerry and the Mudjekeewis Trails, stay along the west edge of the meadow at McKie Camp. See beginning of Chapter 6 for Sky Lakes Wilderness information and regulations.

HISTORY: "McKIE SHELTER: (now collapsed), is an old trail camp location. The shelter was built between 1934 and 1936 and was named after a sheepherder, Tom McKie." (USFS quote)

RED BLANKET TRAIL #1090. (See map 6 and 7)

TRAIL BEGINS: -End of Road 6205. ELEV. 3900'
TRAIL ENDS: -Stuart Falls Trail 1078. ELEV. 5400'
DISTANCE: -3.9 miles, moderate grades. USE: hiker/horse.
SEASON: -Usually snow-free June to October. Closed to all use from the end of elk hunting season until April 1 for protection of winter range.
CONNECTING TR: -Lucky Camp Tr. 1083, and Stuart Falls Tr. 1078.
BRING MAPS: -USFS Butte Falls Ranger Dist., Rogue River N.F.
-USFS Sky Lakes Area-Rogue River/Winema Ntl. For.

ACCESS: From the town of Prospect, Oregon, drive east on County Route 992, leading toward Butte Falls, 1.1 mile to the junction with Red Blanket Road. Follow Red Blanket Road 0.3 mile and turn left onto Forest Road 6205. Continue on 6205, about 12 miles to the trailhead at the end of the road.

FEATURES: The Red Blanket Trail begins near the southwest corner of Crater Lake National Park. After 1/4 mile, look for the large concrete corner post on the left. The trail follows along Red Blanket Creek and reaches the Lucky Camp Trail 1083 in approx. three miles. Keeping to the left at this junction brings you to Stuart Falls Trail 1078 in about one mile. To reach Stuart Falls, keep left for about 1/2 mile. This is a popular access route to Sky Lakes Wilderness and Crater Lake National Park. See beginning of Chapter 6 for Sky Lakes Wilderness information and regulations.

HISTORY: "RED BLANKET CREEK, MOUNTAIN: Said to have been named in about 1865 after a white man purchased a large parcel of land from a group of Indians for one red blanket." (USFS quote)

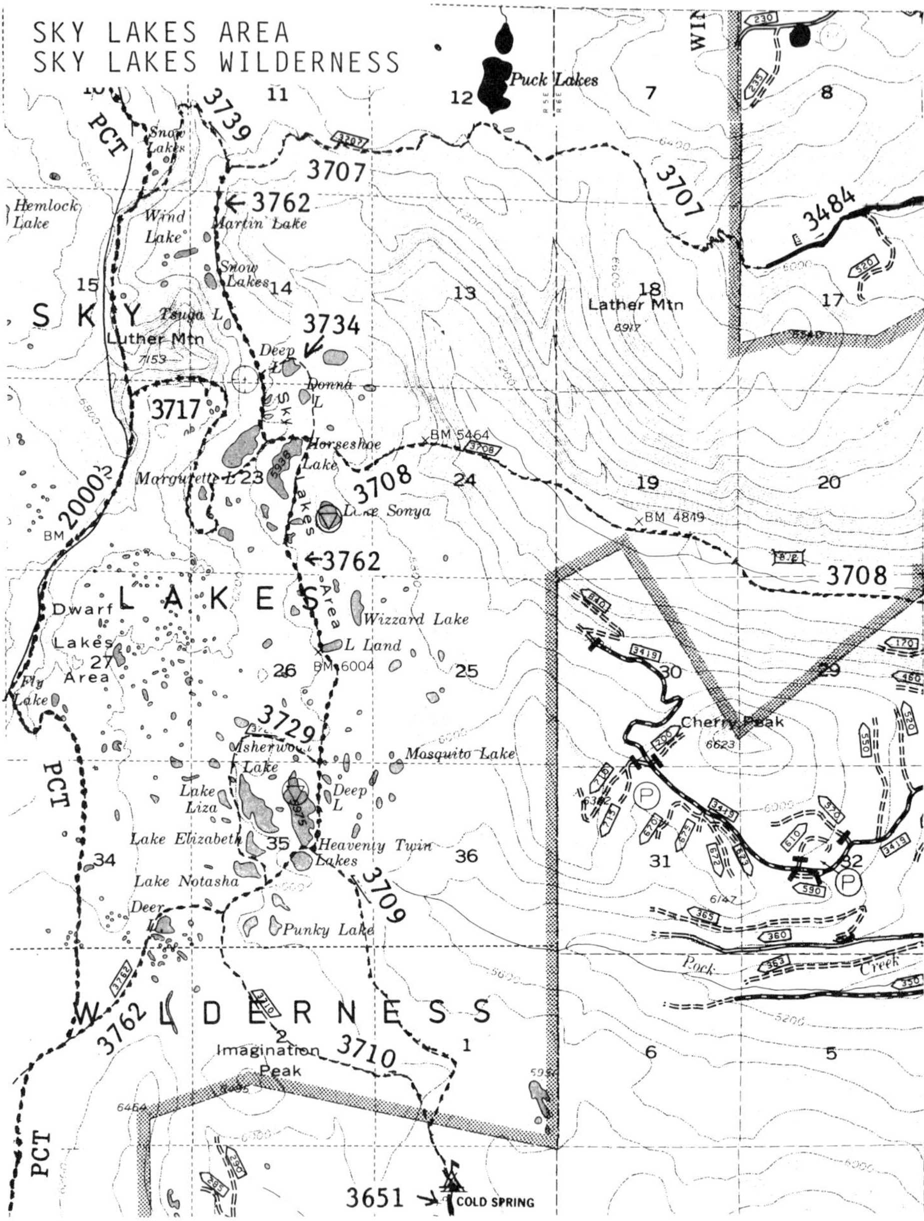
SKY LAKES AREA
SKY LAKES WILDERNESS
Puck Lakes
PCT
Snow Lakes
3739
3707
Hemlock Lake
Wind Lake
3762
Martin Lake
Snow Lakes
3484
Lather Mtn
SKY
Tsuga L
Luther Mtn
3734
Deep L
Donna L
3717
Horseshoe Lake
BM 5464
2000
Marguerette L
3708
Lake Sonya
BM 4849
LAKES
Dwarf Lakes Area
Wizzard Lake
L Land
BM 6004
Fly Lake
3729
Cherry Peak
Isherwood Lake
Mosquito Lake
Lake Liza
Deep L
Lake Elizabeth
Heavenly Twin Lakes
Lake Notasha
3709
Deer L
Punky Lake
Rock Creek
WILDERNESS
Imagination Peak
3710
3651
COLD SPRING

SKY LAKES TRAIL #3762 and connecting trails. (See map 12)

TRAIL BEGINS: -PCNST South of Deer Lake. ELEV. 5900'
TRAIL ENDS: -Snow Lakes Trail #3739, Nannie Creek Tr. #3707.
DISTANCE: -6.0 miles, moderate grades. USE: hiker/horse.
SEASON: -June through October.
BRING MAPS: -USFS Sky Lakes Wilderness.
-USFS Pacific Crest National Scenic Trail-Oregon Central Portion.
-USFS Recreation Opportunity Guide (this trail).
-USFS Winema National Forest.

ACCESS: The Sky Lakes Trail,once called the Skyline Trail, parallels the Pacific Crest through the Sky Lakes Basin. This intra-wilderness trail departs from the Pacific Crest Trail south of Deer Lake, and passes the trailhead access trails of Cold Springs, South Rock Creek, Cherry Creek and Nannie Creek. This route ends at the junction with Snow Lakes Tr. on the north, which is not maintained for stock users.

TRAIL LOG-MILEAGE READINGS ARE APPROXIMATE.
Mile 0.6 Deer Lake.
Mile 0.9 Junction (Right) COLD SPRINGS TRAIL #3710.
Mile 1.3 Junction (Left) South end of ISHERWOOD LOOP TR. #3729.
Mile 1.5 Junction (Right) SOUTH ROCK CREEK TRAIL #3709, just past Heavenly Twin Lakes.
Mile 2.0 Junction (Left) North end of ISHERWOOD LOOP TR. #3729.
Mile 4.0 Junction (Right) CHERRY CREEK TRAIL #3708.
Mile 4.1 Junction (Right) (North end of Trapper Lake) South end DONNA LAKE LOOP TR. #3734-NOT MAINTAINED FOR STOCK USE.
Mile 4.4 Junction (Left) Between Lakes Margurette and Trapper, DIVIDE TRAIL #3717, 2.9 miles,elevation gain 600',maintained for stock users,connects to Pacific Crest Trail.
Mile 4.7 Junction (Right) North end-DONNA LAKE LOOP TRAIL #3734.
Mile 5.6 Martin Lake.
Mile 6.0 Junction (Right) NANNIE CREEK TRAIL #3707.
SNOW LAKES TRAIL #3739 begins from this junction,a 2.3 mile steep climb to re-join the Pacific Crest Trail.Not maintained for stock users. Elevation gain 800'.

Please see beginning of Chapter 6 for Sky Lakes Wilderness information and regulations.

SEVENMILE TRAIL #3703. (See map 12)

TRAIL BEGINS: -Sevenmile Trailhead Forest Road 3334, ELEV. 5600'
TRAIL ENDS: -Pacific Crest Trail. ELEV. 5825'
DISTANCE: -1.9 miles, easy grades. USE: hiker/horse.
SEASON: -June through October.
CONNECTING TR. -Pacific Crest National Scenic Trail (PCNST).
BRING MAPS: -USFS Sky Lakes Area-Rogue River/Winema Ntl. For.
-USFS Winema National Forest.
-USFS Pacific Crest Trail-Oregon Southern Portion.

ACCESS: This description begins from State Hwy. 140 just east of milepost 43 (43.6 miles east of White City). Turn north onto Westside Road (County Route 531), and go 16.9 miles to the junction with Forest Route 33. Follow Route 33, 2.8 miles to a 3-way junction,then go northwest on Road 3334, 5.7 miles to the trailhead at the end of the road.

FEATURES: This 2 mile trail provides a quick and easy access to the Pacific Crest National Scenic Trail. From the PCNST, options exist for a side-trip to Ranger Springs, an entry into Seven Lakes Basin near Devils Peak and Cliff Lake, or numerous other possibilities.

Ranger Springs is one of the headwater springs that feed the Middle Fork of the Rogue River. To get there, take Sevenmile Trail 3703 to the junction with the Pacific Crest Trail. Turn right and go 1/4 mile north to a junction on the left leading another mile to the springs.

See beginning of Chapter 6 for Sky Lakes Wilderness information and regulations.

NANNIE CREEK TRAIL #3707. (See map 12)

TRAIL BEGINS: -End of Forest Road 3484. ELEV. 6000'
TRAIL ENDS: -Jnc. Snow Lakes & Sky Lakes Trails. ELEV. 6000'
DISTANCE: -4.3 miles, strenuous. HIGH POINT 6520'
USE: -Hikers/horses.
SEASON: -June through October, mosquitos till mid-August.
BRING MAPS: -USFS Winema National Forest.
-USFS Sky Lakes Area-Winema/Rogue River Ntl. For.

ACCESS: This description begins from State Hwy. 140 just east of milepost 43 (43.6 mi. from White City). Turn north onto Westside Road (County Route 531), and go 12.1 mi. to the junction with Forest Road 3484 on the left. Travel north and west on 3484, about 5.5 miles to the trailhead at the end of the road.

FEATURES: From the trailhead, the trail climbs up a steep slope and follows the rocky contours,through the heavily forested slopes of Lather Mtn.(Elev. 6917') to the southwest. After coursing across a relatively level basin, the trail passes the southern shore of Puck Lakes and up through towering mixed conifer groves. The trail reaches the junction of the Snow Lakes and Sky Lakes Trails about 0.3 mile south of the Snow Lakes group.

See the page describing SKY LAKES TRAIL 3762, and the map showing how it connects with other lakes in Sky Lakes Basin.

Sky Lakes Wilderness information and regulations are noted at the beginning of Chapter 6.

SNOW LAKES TRAIL #3739. (See map 12)

TRAIL BEGINS: -Junction of Sky Lakes Trail #3762. and Nannie Creek Trail #3707. ELEV. 5800'
TRAIL ENDS: -Pacific Crest National Scenic Trail ELEV. 6600'
DISTANCE: -2.3 miles, moderate. USE: hiker/horse.
SEASON: -Summer season: July-Oct.
BRING MAPS: -USFS Sky Lakes Wilderness.
-USFS Pacific Crest National Scenic Trail-Oregon Central Portion.
-USFS Recreation Opportunity Guide.
-USFS Winema National Forest.

ACCESS: The Snow Lakes Trail is an intra-wilderness trail connecting Sky Lakes Trail and Pacific Crest Tr. It has a rather steep section that is not maintained for stock use. This trail departs from the northern end of Sky Lakes Trail at the junction with Nannie Creek Trail #3707.

FEATURES: The Snow Lakes Trail begins at elevation 5800', as it departs from Sky Lakes Trail.The route initially climbs gradually along the northern slopes of Sky Lakes Basin, crossing flower-splashed meadows. The trail then climbs steeply up the rock outcrops and windswept ridges offering breathtaking vistas to the south and east. Gaining nearly 1000 feet in elevation in just under 1 mile, the trail joins the Pacific Crest Trail on the backbone of the Cascade Mountain Range. The rugged scenery and magnificent views along this trail are a vivid reminder of our responsibility to practice minimum impact visitation so the primitive wilderness environment may remain. (USFS INFO)

See the page describing SKY LAKES TRAIL 3762, and the map showing how it connects to other lakes in Sky Lakes Basin. Sky Lakes Wilderness information and regulations are listed in Chapter 6.

CHERRY CREEK NATIONAL RECREATION TRAIL #3708. (See map 12)

TRAIL BEGINS: -Forest Road 3450. ELEV. 4672'
TRAIL ENDS: -Sky Lakes Trail 3762. ELEV. 6000'
DISTANCE: -5.3 miles, strenuous. USE: hiker/horse.
SEASON: -Usually snow-free June to October. Mosquitos bad until mid-August.
BRING MAPS: -USFS Winema National Forest.
-Sky Lakes Area-Winema/Rogue River Ntl. Forests.

ACCESS: FROM WHITE CITY, Oregon, follow mileposts east on State Hwy. 140, 43.6 miles to the junction of Westside Road (County Route 531). FROM ASHLAND, take Dead Indian Memorial Road (Jackson County 722, Klamath County 533), 36 miles to the junction with State Highway 140. Turn right (east) on 140 and go 6 miles to Westside Road.

Follow Westside Road 11 miles to the junction with Road 3450 (on the left). Turn west onto Road 3450 and go 1.6 mile to the trailhead at the end of the road. Trailhead parking and turn-around space is limited.

FEATURES: Although strenuous, this trail is a good access route to the Sky Lakes Wilderness. The Cherry Creek drainage, a U-shaped canyon formed by glaciation, is being proposed as a Research Natural Area. The USFS encourages "horseback riders to dismount and walk their horses through the (creek) crossings and wet boggy areas."

See the page describing SKY LAKES TRAIL 3762, and the map showing how it connects to other lakes in Sky Lakes Basin.

Cherry Creek Trail became a part of the National Recreation Trail System in 1979. Sky Lakes Wilderness information and regulations are noted at the beginning of Chapter 6.

DIVIDE TRAIL 3717. (See map 12)

TRAIL BEGINS: -Sky Lakes Trail #3762. ELEV. 6000'
TRAIL ENDS: -Pacific Crest National Scenic Trail. ELEV. 7000'
DISTANCE: -2.9 miles, moderate grades. USE: hiker/horse.
SEASON: -June through October.
BRING MAPS: -USFS Sky Lakes Wilderness.
-USFS Pacific Crest National Scenic Trail-Oregon Central Portion.
-USFS Recreation Opportunity Guide (this trail).
-USFS Winema National Forest.

ACCESS: The Divide Trail is an intra wilderness trail connecting Sky Lakes Trail and the Pacific Crest Tr. Although the trail is steep, it is maintained for stock use. It departs from Sky Lakes Trail between Margurette Lake and Trapper Lake, and climbs to the west to join the Pacific Crest Trail.

FEATURES: The Divide Trail begins at an elevation of 6000' as it departs from the Sky Lakes Trail. The route climbs gradually along the southwestern shores of Lake Margurette crossing flower-splashed meadows,then climbs steeply up the rock outcrops and wind swept ridges of Luther Mountain.The trail gains 1000 feet in elevation in just under 3 miles. The rugged scenery and magnificent vistas along this trail are a vivid reminder of our responsibility to practice minimum impact visitation so the primitive wilderness environment may remain. (USFS info)

See the page describing SKY LAKES TRAIL 3762, and the map showing how it connects to other lakes in Sky Lakes Basin.

Please see beginning of Chapter 6 for Sky Lakes Wilderness information and regulations.

SOUTH ROCK CREEK TRAIL #3709. (See map 12)

TRAIL BEGINS:	-Cold Springs Trail, Forest Road 3651, ELEV. 5800'
TRAIL ENDS:	-Sky Lakes Trail 3762. ELEV. 6000' (At Heavenly Twin Lakes).
DISTANCE:	-1.6 mile.
USE:	-Hiker/horse.
SEASON:	-Usually snow-free June to October.
CONNECTING TR:	-Cold Springs Trail 3710, Sky Lakes Trail 3762.
BRING MAPS:	-USFS Winema National Forest. -USFS Rec. Opportunity Guides, Winema Ntl. For. -Sky Lakes Area-Rogue River/Winema Ntl. Forests.

ACCESS: FROM WHITE CITY, Oregon, follow mileposts east on State Hwy. 140, 40.9 miles to the junction of Lost Creek Road 3651. If driving FROM ASHLAND, take Dead Indian Memorial Road (Jackson County 722, Klamath County 533) to State Highway 140,and turn right 3.1 miles to Road 3651.

Turn onto Road 3651 and go 10.5 miles to the COLD SPRINGS TRAILHEAD at the end of the road.

After about 0.7 mi. along the Cold Springs Trail, the SOUTH ROCK CREEK Trail begins on the right and continues about 1.6 mile to the Sky Lakes Trail near Heavenly Twin Lakes. From here, a loop trip back to Cold Springs Campground is possible by taking a left turn (southwest) on the Sky Lakes Trail and going 1.0 mile to the junction with Cold Springs Trail 3710 on the left. Follow Cold Springs Trail,2.7 miles southeast to the campground on Road 3651.

See the page describing SKY LAKES TRAIL 3762, and the map showing how it connects to other trails in Sky Lakes Basin.

Mosquitos are bad, especially at Cold Springs Campground, usually until mid-August. Sky Lakes Wilderness information and regulations are noted at the beginning of Chapter 6.

COLD SPRINGS TRAIL #3710. (See map 12)

TRAIL BEGINS: -Cold Springs Camp, Forest Road 3651. ELEV. 5800'
TRAIL ENDS: -Sky Lakes Trail 3762. ELEV. 6000'
(Near Lake Notasha).
DISTANCE: -2.7 mile.
USE: -Hiker/horse.
SEASON: -Usually snow-free June to October.
Mosquitos bad till about mid-August.
CONNECTING TR. -South Rock Creek Trail 3709 and Sky Lakes Trail 3762.
BRING MAPS: -USFS Winema National Forest.
-USFS Rec. Opportunity Guides, Winema Ntl. For.
-Sky Lakes Area-Rogue River/Winema Ntl. Forests.

ACCESS: FROM WHITE CITY, Oregon, follow mileposts east on State Hwy. 140, 40.9 miles to the junction of Lost Creek Road 3651. If driving FROM ASHLAND, take Dead Indian Memorial Road (Jackson County 722, Klamath County 533) to State Highway 140 and turn right for 3.1 miles to Road 3651.

Turn onto Road 3651 and go 10.5 miles to COLD SPRINGS TRAILHEAD at the end of the road.

After about 0.7 mile on the Cold Springs Trail, keep left at the junction with the South Rock Creek Trail and continue on the Cold Springs Trail to the Sky Lakes Trail near Lake Notasha.

FEATURES: This is a short and easy access to Dwarf Lakes-Sky Lakes Basin. A loop trip back to Cold Spr. Campground is possible by turning right (northeast) onto the Sky Lakes Trail and go one mile to the junction with South Rock Creek Trail 3709 on the right just beyond Heavenly Twin Lakes. Follow 3709 southeast 1.6 miles to its junction with Cold Springs Trail, turn left and go 0.7 miles back to Cold Springs Camp.

See the page describing SKY LAKES TRAIL 3762, and the map showing how it connects to other lakes in Sky Lakes Basin.

Sky Lakes Wilderness information and regulations are noted at the beginning of Chapter 6.

TWIN PONDS TRAIL #3715, Winema National Forest. (See map 16)

TRAIL BEGINS: -Fourmile Lake Campground. ELEV. 5700'
TRAIL ENDS: -Pacific Crest National Scenic Trail. ELEV. 5900'
DISTANCE: -2.5 miles.
SEASON: -June to October. USE: hiker/horse.
CONNECTING TR. -Pacific Crest Trail, Twin Ponds Trail #993.
BRING MAPS: -Sky Lakes Area-Rogue River/Winema Ntl. Forests.
-USFS Recreation Opportunity Guides.

ACCESS: FOURMILE LAKE. From White City, follow mileposts on Hwy. 140, 35.7 miles to the junction of Road 3661. Go 5.6 miles north on 3661 to a road junction at Fourmile Lake. Turn left and go 0.1 mile to a spur leading left to a PARKING FACILITY FOR ALL TRAILS. 400ft. south of a trailhead sign, KEEP RIGHT at a junction where Twin Ponds Tr.leads toward the PCT.

FEATURES: In the vicinity of Fourmile Lake, Trail #3715 is often swampy or partly submerged. After passing Squaw Lake, it joins the Pacific Crest Trail about 2.5 miles northwest of the trailhead.

TWIN PONDS TRAIL #993,managed by the Rogue River National Forest, continues northwestward for 3.5 miles down Fourbit Creek. Summit Lake is reached within the first 0.5 mi., Twin Ponds 2.0 mile beyond, and 1.0 mile further to the lower trailhead on Road 3760. These waters sometimes dry-up in late summer.

Trail 993 has a very rocky surface in places but is much easier to follow than in previous years. In a couple of places, it is still suggested to look carefully for rock cairns and tree blazes.

ACCESS TO LOWER TRAILHEAD, TRAIL #993. From White City OR, follow mileposts on Hwy. 140, 28.6 mi. to County Route 821. Turn north onto 821 and go 8.8 mi. to where Forest Route 37 turns east. Follow Route 37, 1.5 mi. to Road 3760 on the right. Go 4.4 miles on 3760 to the trailhead at the end of the road.

Trails #3715 and 993 follow the route of the 1864 Fort Klamath-Jacksonville Military Wagon Road. Sky Lakes Wilderness information and regulations are listed at the beginning of Chapter 6.

MT. McLOUGHLIN

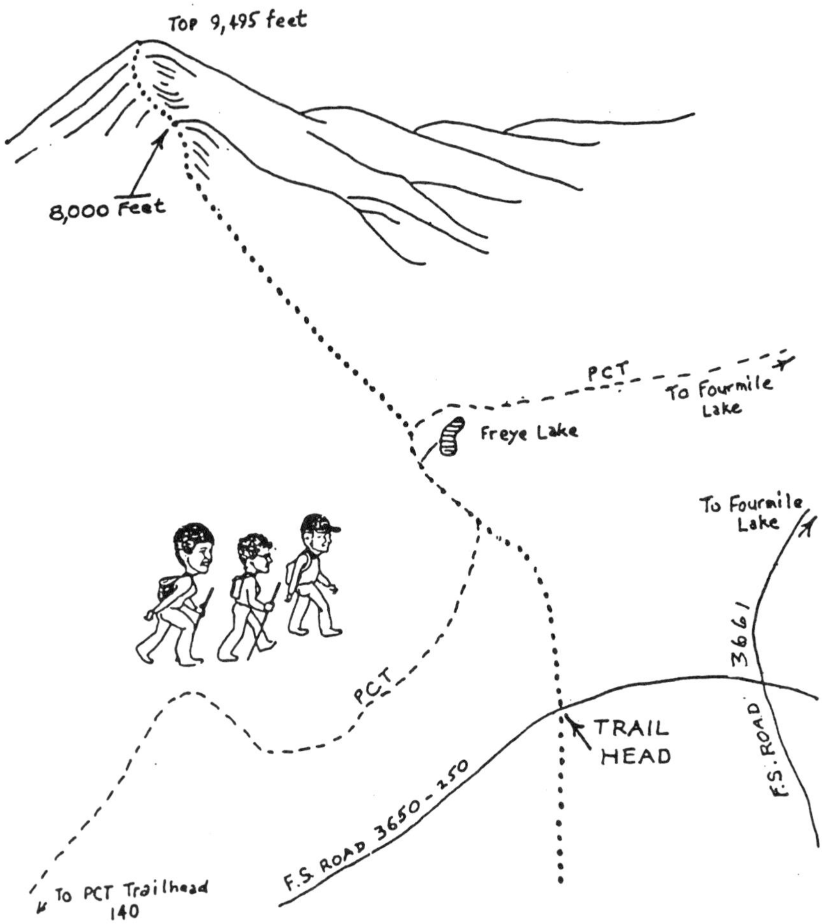

Mt. McLOUGHLIN TRAIL #3716. (See Map 16)

TRAIL BEGINS:	-Trailhead, Forest Road 3650.	ELEV. 5580'
TRAIL ENDS:	-Mt. McLoughlin summit.	ELEV. 9495'
DISTANCE:	-About 4.9 miles, strenuous-time up 4 to 5 hours.	
SEASON:	-July thru September.	
CONNECTING TR.	-Pacific Crest National Scenic Trail.	
BRING MAPS:	-USFS Sky Lakes Area-Rogue River/Winema Ntl. For.	
	-USFS Winema National Forest.	
	-USFS "Mt. McLoughlin" information leaflets.	
	-USGS Mount McLoughlin, 7.5 minute series.	

ACCESS: From White City, Oregon, follow mileposts east on State Hwy. 140, 35.7 miles to the junction of Forest Road 3661. Turn left and follow mileposts on 3661, 2.9 miles to the junction with Road 3650. Turn left on 3650 and continue 0.3 mi. to the trailhead and parking area.

ROUTE: The Mt. McLoughlin Trail meets the Pacific Crest (PCNST) Trail in about 1 mile. Turn right (N.W.) and follow the PCNST, 1/2 mile to where the Mt. McLoughlin Trail continues its northwesterly ascent to the summit. The trail is not maintained beyond the tree line. ON THE WAY UP, NOTICE THAT THE ROUTE PARALLELS A RIDGE THAT SLOPES IN AN EAST TO WEST DIRECTION.

ON THE RETURN TRIP.....KEEP THE SAME RELATIONSHIP WITH THE RIDGE! INFORMAL PATHS CAN BE MISLEADING! NOTE THAT THE RIDGE RUNS MORE EAST THAN IT DOES SOUTH. THERE IS NO TRAIL OUT FROM THE SOUTH SLOPES OF THE MOUNTAIN OTHER THAN THE PACIFIC CREST TRAIL! WATCH ALSO FOR THE JUNCTIONS WITH THE PACIFIC CREST TRAIL. The McLoughlin Trail follows the Pacific Crest Trail southeast for 1/2 mile and turns southeast to the Road 3650 Trailhead.

From the summit; Mt. Shasta, the Klamath Basin,Rogue River Valley, Crater Lake Rim and points into Central Oregon come into view. A fire lookout building was once located at the summit.

PRECAUTIONS: (Quotes from USFS -HIKING THE McLOUGHLIN TRAIL) "Remember.....Every year someone gets lost hiking Mt. McLoughlin. This could be prevented by following three basic rules: 1). Never travel alone. 2). Stay with your group. 3). Stay on the trail. Allow plenty of time for your climb (average 8 hours round trip). Travel only during the daylight hours and don't attempt to travel during unsettled weather or when storms are forecast. Wilderness areas challenge your skills in traversing using map and compass."

"BE AWARE OF THE SYMPTOMS OF HYPOTHERMIA. Hypothermia is a rapid and progressive mental and physical collapse, resulting from lowering the inner temperature of the body. Left untreated, hypothermia can result in death. Briefly, the symptoms to watch for are: uncontrollable shivering; vague, slow speech; memory lapses; immobile or fumbling hands; frequent stumbling; drowsiness and apparent exhaustion. The best treatment is to eliminate exposure. Get the victim out of the wind and rain. Strip off all wet clothing and put him in a sleeping bag with another person........also stripped. Keep the victim awake and give warm drinks. If possible, build a warming fire."

BRING DRINKING WATER: THERE IS NO WATER ALONG THE SUMMIT TRAIL.
FOOD: "High energy foods such as nuts, raisins, hard candy, fruit, fruit juices and grain products are excellent choices."
CLOTHING AND EQUIPMENT: "Vibram-soled hiking boots, extra wool socks, light/warm clothing (preferably wool) that can be layered, raingear, gloves, and hat. EQUIPMENT: MAP AND COMPASS, FIRST AID KIT with matches, moleskin or tape for blisters, goggles or sunglasses, suntan cream and a flashlight for emergencies.

NOTE: The Mt. McLoughlin trail can also be accessed by hiking the Pacific Crest Tr. about 4 mi. north from its Hwy. 140 Trailhead, located between mileposts 32 and 33 on State Highway 140. Sky Lakes Wilderness information and regulations are noted at the beginning of Chapter 6.

BADGER LAKE TRAIL #3759 (See Maps 16,17)

TRAIL BEGINS: -Fourmile Lake Campground. ELEV. 5750'
TRAIL ENDS: -Jnc. Red Lake Trail and unmaintained Lost Creek Trail. ELEV. 5950'
DISTANCE: -Woodpecker Lake 1.3 mile, Badger Lake 1.6 mile, Long Lake 3.6 Mile. Easy grades. Hiker/horse.
SEASON: -July to October, mosquitos until mid-August.
CONNECTING TR. -Rye Spur 3771, Red Lake 987, unmaintained Lost Creek 3712.
BRING MAPS: -USFS Sky Lakes Area-Rogue River/Winema Ntl. For.
-USFS Winema National Forest.

ACCESS: From White City, follow mileposts on State Highway 140, 35.7 miles to the junction with Forest Road 3661. Turn north onto 3661 and go 5.6 miles to the junction at Fourmile Lake.

A PARKING AREA FOR ALL TRAILS can be reached by turning left for 0.1 mile, then left again to the parking area. A sign indicates the Twin Ponds, Pacific Crest, and Badger Lake Trails. 400' south of this sign is a junction leading left to Rye Spur Trail. When reaching the Rye Spur Trail, turn left (north) and cross the Cascade Canal to the BADGER LAKE TRAILHEAD.

FEATURES: This is an easy access route into Sky Lakes Wilderness leading north to Woodpecker,Badger,Lilly Pond, and Long Lakes before ending at the junction with Red Lake Trail 987 and unmaintained Lost Creek Trail 3712.

Traveling southward on the Pacific Crest Trail to the Twin Ponds Trail and back to Four Mile Lake Campground makes for an adventurous day trip, total loop distance about 13 miles.

Sky Lakes Wilderness information and regulations are noted at the beginning of Chapter 6.

CHAPTER 7 - MOUNTAIN LAKES WILDERNESS

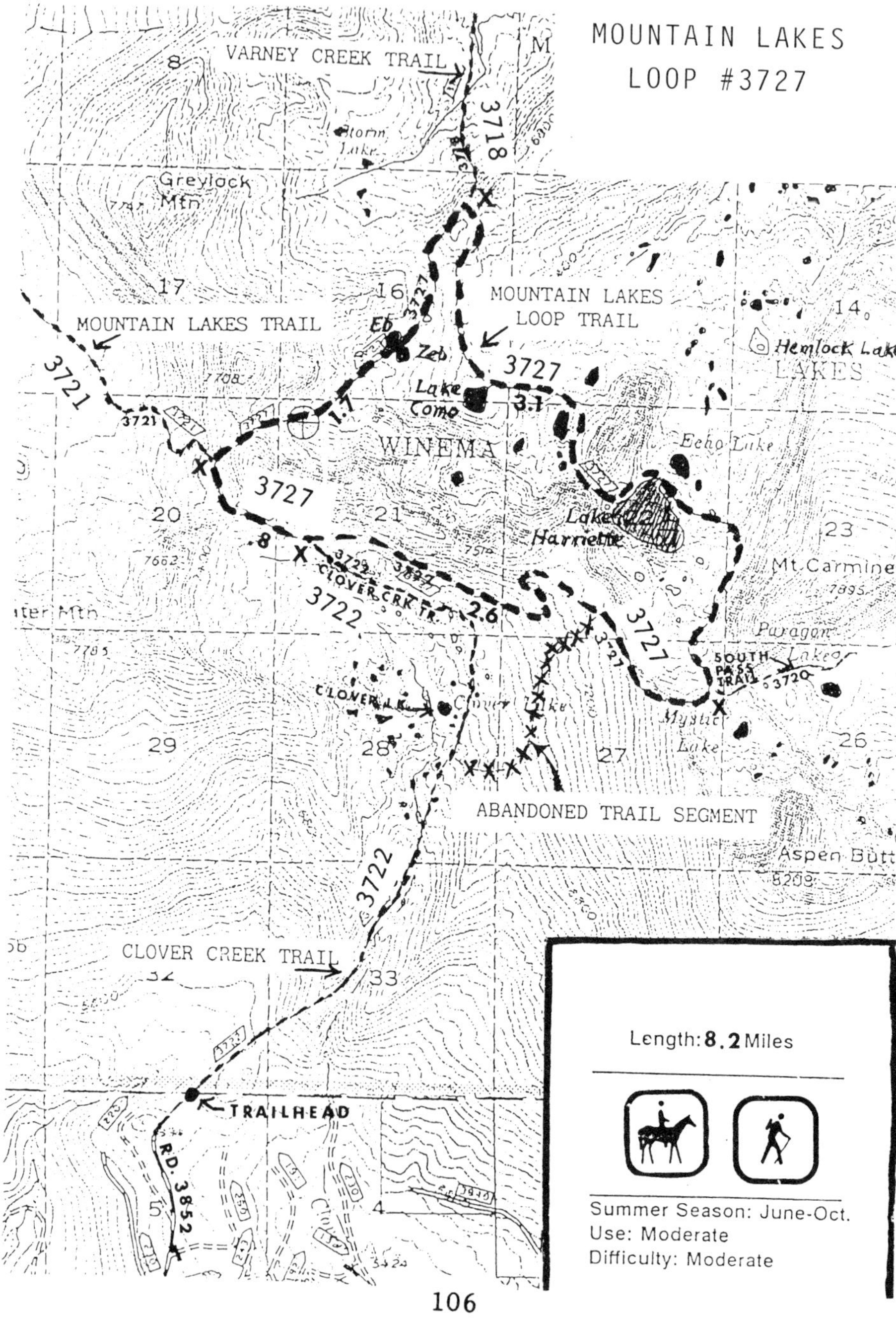

Length: **8.2** Miles

Summer Season: June-Oct.
Use: Moderate
Difficulty: Moderate

MOUNTAIN LAKES WILDERNESS AREA. (See map 17)

HISTORY: "In 1930 Mountain Lakes was established as one of the first three primitive areas in the Pacific Northwest Region. In 1940 the original 13,444 acres was increased to 23,071 acres and the name was changed to the Mountain Lakes Wild Area. The Mountain Lakes became a part of the National Wilderness System in 1964." (Quote: USFS Winema National Forest)

FEATURES: Most of the area is above 6000 ft. elevation. The "hub" of the maintained trail system is the Mountain Lakes Loop Trail that circles the old volcanic caldera rim in the heart of the wilderness. It is accessed by the Varney Creek Trail 3718 from the north, Mountain Lakes Trail 3721 from the west and Clover Creek Trail 3722 from the south. Eb and Zeb Lakes, Lake Como, Lake Harriette and Clover Lake are just a few of the highlights on the loop trail. Aspen Butte (elevation 8208') is the highest point in the wilderness.

REGULATIONS. "To protect the wilderness resource, the following regulations are enforced:

1. Hiking and camping group size is limited to 10 people and/or stock in any combination.
2. Hikers must camp at least 100 feet from lakeshores, streams and springs.
3. Pack and saddle stock should stay at least 200 feet away from all water sources,except when traveling on established trails.
4. Campers with pack and saddle stock must camp at least 200 feet from lakeshores, streams and springs.
5. Bicycles, motorbikes, and other mechanized equipment are not allowed within the wilderness area. Please contact the Klamath Ranger District Office for information on areas designated for these and other recreation opportunities."

(Quote: Winema National Forest-Klamath Ranger District)

VARNEY CREEK TRAIL #3718. (See map 17)

TRAIL BEGINS: -End of Forest Road 3664. ELEV. 5600'
TRAIL ENDS: -Mountain Lakes Loop Trail 3727. ELEV. 6630'
DISTANCE: -4.4 miles, moderate. USE: hikers/horses.
SEASON: -Usually snow-free June through October, carry insect repellant during early summer months.
BRING MAPS: -USFS Recreation Opportunity Guide, Varney Cr. Tr.
-USFS Mountain Lakes Wilderness.
-USFS Winema National Forest.

ACCESS: The Varney Creek Trailhead is located at the end of Forest Road 3664, and can be reached from two points on STATE HIGHWAY 140:

NEAR MILEPOST 43 (mile 43.3). Turn south on Forest Road 3610 and continue 1.7 miles to the junction with Forest Road 3667. Turn left and continue 3.0 miles to Forest Road 3664. Turn right and continue 2 miles to the trailhead at the end of the road.

NEAR MILEPOST 48. Turn south onto Forest Road 3667 and continue 1.8 miles to Forest Road 3664. Turn left and continue 2 miles to the trailhead at the end of the road.

FEATURES: Trail 3718 maintains a steady uphill grade as it follows Varney Cr. into the wilderness area. The "hub" of the maintained trail system is the Mountain Lakes Loop Trail 3727, forming a 8.2 mile loop around the old caldera rim in the heart of the wilderness. This loop trail can also be accessed by Mountain Lakes Trail 3721 from the west and Clover Cr. Trail 3722 from the south. THE SOUTH END OF THE LOOP TRAIL HAS BEEN REROUTED THROUGH MAP SECTIONS 21 and 22 AT THE 7000' LEVEL AND NO LONGER DROPS DOWN TO CLOVER LAKE. THE CLOVER CREEK TRAIL HAS BEEN EXTENDED NORTHWEST OF CLOVER LAKE TO JOIN THE LOOP TRAIL REROUTE. THE SECTION OF THE OLD LOOP TRAIL LEADING EAST FROM CLOVER LAKE TO THE LOOP TRAIL HAS BEEN ABANDONED. See beginning of Chapter 7 for information and wilderness regulations.

MOUNTAIN LAKES TRAIL #3721. (See map 17)

TRAIL BEGINS: -Forest Road 3660. ELEV. 5200'
TRAIL ENDS: -Mountain Lakes Loop Trail 3727, ELEV. 7400'
DISTANCE: -5.1 miles. USE: hiker/horse. Moderate. HIKERS can also access the trail from Rainbow Bay Picnic Area, across from the restrooms.
SEASON: -Usually snow-free June through October.
BRING MAPS: -USFS Winema National Forest Recreation Map/Guide.
-USFS Mountain Lakes Wilderness map.

ACCESS: Follow mileposts (numbering from WHITE CITY) on State Hwy. 140 to mile 37.7 at the junction with Dead Indian Memorial Road (Klamath County Rte. 533). If using the UPPER ACCESS where parking is limited and there is no turn-around facility, turn right onto Dead Indian Memorial Road and go 0.1 mi. to Road 3610. Turn left onto Road 3610, and go 0.8 mile to Road 3660. The trailhead is 0.8 mile up Road 3660.

Using the LOWER, Lake of the Woods facility where horses are not allowed: across from the restrooms at the Rainbow Bay Picnic Area follow the Family Loop(Mtn.Lake) Trail a short distance, crossing the Sunset Trail and Road 3704. A junction is soon reached at the beginning of the Family Trail Loops, and where MOUNTAIN LAKES TR. turns right to cross Dead Indian Memorial Rd. and on to the upper Mountain Lakes Trail access on Road 3660.

FEATURES: The trail climbs up Seldom Creek through tranquil meadows and along volcanic outcrops. The scenery gradually changes to higher elevation mountain hemlock/subalpine fir communities before ending at Mountain Lakes Loop Trail #3727.

Mountain Lakes Loop Trail makes an 8.2 mile loop around the old caldera rim in the heart of the wilderness.The loop trail is also accessed by Varney Creek Trail 3718 from the north and Clover Cr. Trail 3722 from the south. THE SOUTH END OF THE LOOP TRAIL HAS BEEN REROUTED THROUGH MAP SECTIONS 21 and 22 AT THE 7000' LEVEL, AND NO LONGER DROPS TO CLOVER CREEK TRAIL SOUTH OF CLOVER LAKE. THE CLOVER CREEK TRAIL HAS BEEN EXTENDED NORTHWEST OF CLOVER LAKE TO JOIN THE LOOP TRAIL REROUTE. See beginning of Chapter 7 for Mountain Lakes historical notes and regulations.

CLOVER CREEK TRAIL #3722. (See map 17)

TRAIL BEGINS:	-End of Forest Road 3852.	ELEV. 5600'
TRAIL ENDS:	-Mountain Lakes Loop Trail 3727.	ELEV. 7000'
DISTANCE:	-About 3.4 miles. Moderate grades.	
SEASON:	-Usually snow-free June-Oct. Hiker/horse.	
BRING MAPS:	-USFS Mountain Lakes Wilderness.	
	-USFS Winema National Forest.	
	-USFS Recreation Opportunity Guide, Clover Creek Trail 3722.	

ACCESS: From Interstate Hwy. 5, Ashland-Klamath Falls Exit 14, travel 0.6 mi. east on State Highway 66 to the junction with Dead Indian Memorial Road(Jackson County Route 722, Klamath County 533). Turn left and follow this road 28.3 miles to the junction with Clover Creek Road (Klamath County Route 603). Travel southeast on Clover Creek Road, 5.8 miles to the junction with Forest Road 3852 on the left. Turn onto Road 3852 and go 3.3 miles to the trailhead at the end of the road.

FEATURES: It is 2.3 miles up the trail to an older,abandoned section of the Mountain Lakes Loop Trail heading east. The Clover Creek Trail has been extended from this point, passing Clover Lake and junctions WITH A RELOCATED SECTION OF THE MOUNTAIN LAKES LOOP TRAIL 1.1 MILE FURTHER THROUGH MAP SECTIONS 20 and 21, elevation 7000'.

Mountain Lakes Loop Trail 3727 is an 8.2 mile loop around an old caldera rim in the heart of the wilderness and can also be accessed via Mountain Lakes Trail 3721 from the west, and Varney Creek Trail 3718 from the north.

See beginning of Chapter 7 for Mountain Lakes historical notes and regulations.

MOUNTAIN LAKES LOOP TRAIL #3727. (See map 17)

DISTANCE: -8.2 miles,moderate grade. USE: hiker/horse.
SEASON: -June to October.
CONNECTING TR. -Mountain Lakes #3721; Varney Creek #3718, Clover Creek #3722.
BRING MAPS: -USFS Recreation Opportunity Guide-Trail #3727.
-USFS Mountain Lakes Wilderness.
-USFS Winema National Forest.

ACCESS: This trail can be accessed by entering the wilderness from any of the 3 Mountain Lakes Trailheads; Varney Creek, Clover Creek, and Mountain Lakes(See text).

FEATURES: "Following this trail clockwise FROM THE JUNCTION OF THE LOOP TRAIL WITH MOUNTAIN LAKES TRAIL, the Loop Trail climbs gently through a pass north of Whiteface Peak and descends into the caldera between crystal blue Lake Eb & Lake Zeb. Past the junction with Varney Creek Trail, the Loop Trail passes along gentle slopes north of Lake Como and many small wilderness lakes. The trail then climbs a short steep pass to skirt the windblown waters of Lake Harriette, the largest lake in the Mountain Lakes Wilderness. From Harriette, the trail meanders up the lower slopes of Mt.Carmine before steeply climbing the southern caldera rim. Views of the wilderness lakes and peaks, as well as vast southern vistas, are spectacular from this vantage point. The section of trail from here to the Clover Creek Trail has been relocated and is easily found. The new route switchbacks down a rugged rock scree, then follows this land feature to the west, where the trail completes the circuit at the Mountain Lakes Trail junction. The wet meadows, stream banks, and lakeshores which the traveller discovers in this high elevation setting are both beautiful and extremely fragile microenvironments which require the practice of minimum trace visitation in order to survive"
(USFS Quote)

See beginning of Chapter 7 for Mountain Lakes historical notes and regulations.

CHAPTER 8 - FISH LAKE - LAKE OF THE WOODS

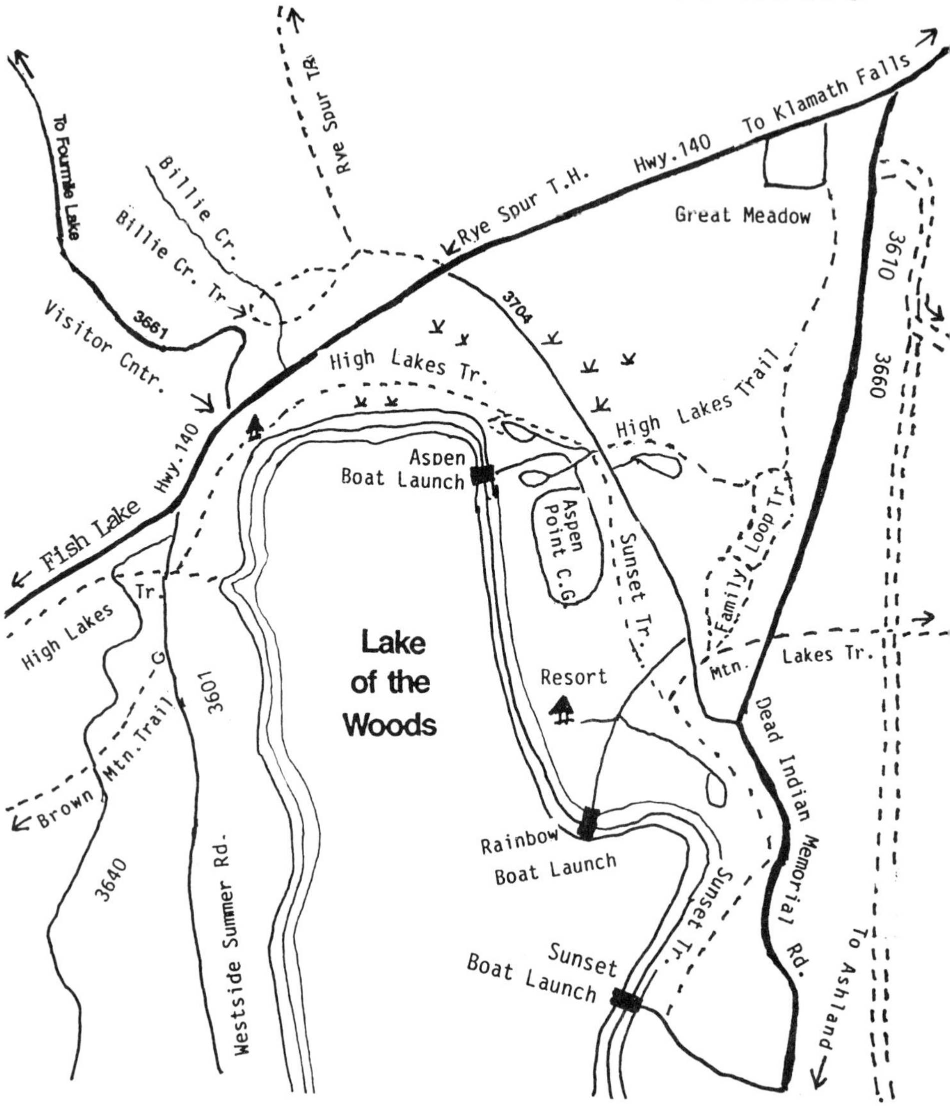

SEE MAPS 16 AND 17 (IN BACK PAGES OF BOOK)

HIGH LAKES TRAIL #6200. (See map page 112)

TRAIL BEGINS: -WEST TRAILHEAD-Fish Lake,Hwy.140 near Milepost 30.
-EAST TRAILHEAD-Great Meadow- 140 near Milepost 37.
DISTANCE: -9.3 mile, easy. USE: hiker/jogger/mtn. bikes, motorized wheelchairs:NO OTHER MOTORIZED VEHICLES.
SEASON: -May through October. Winter skiing, snowmobiles.
CONNECTING TR. -Family Loop,Sunset,Pacific Crest,Fish Lake Trails.
BRING MAPS: -Info from Rogue River-Winema Ntl. Forest Offices.

ACCESS POINTS ALONG HIGHWAY 140,MILEPOSTS NUMBER FROM WHITE CITY.
-Mile 30.4: FISH LAKE TRAILHEAD, Boat ramp parking area.
-MILE 35.4 ROAD 3601 JUNCTION. Turn right and go 0.1 mile to Road 3640. Follow Road 3640, 0.3 mile to a HIGH LAKES TRAILHEAD.
-Mile 36.4: ROAD 3704 JUNCTION. Turn right onto Road 3704 and go 0.6 mile to the entrance of Aspen Point Campground. Drive to the end of the first campground loop on the right, HIGH LAKES TRAILHEAD is located near the restrooms.
-Mile 36.4: ROAD 3704 JUNCTION leading 1.0 mile to the Resort turnoff. Turn right and go 0.1 mile to the RAINBOW BAY PICNIC AREA. Across from the restrooms, the Family Loop Trail uses the Mtn. Lakes Trail to a junction where the Family Loops keep LEFT to join a portion of HIGH LAKES TRAIL in less than 1.0 mile.
-Mile 37.5: GREAT MEADOW TRAILHEAD. The trail begins just beyond the restrooms and crosses a spillway before skirting the far end of the meadow, on its way to the west terminus at Fish Lake.

FROM ASHLAND, Follow Dead Indian Memorial Road, (Jackson County Route 722,Klamath County 533),36 miles to State Highway 140. Turn left onto Hwy. 140, GREAT MEADOW is immediately to the left. Hwy. 140 leads west to Fish Lake and other access points of the trail.

FEATURES: The High Lakes Trail travels through 2.5 miles of lava flows and groves of aspen and fir. You can also experience views of Mt. McLoughlin and Pelican Butte. Interpretive signs indicate geological, wildlife and botanical features. A map at the beginning of Chapter 8 shows loops and connection opportunities with other trails. The trail crosses the Pacific Crest Trail (closed to mechanized vehicles),to co-locate with Fish Lake Tr. #1013 for one mile before the Fish Lake Trail departs left to Fish Lake,and High Lakes Trail keeps right to end north of Fish Lake Resort.

SUNSET TRAIL #6202. (See map beginning of Chapter 8)

TRAIL BEGINS: -Sunset Campground, Lake of the Woods, milepost 34, Dead Indian Memorial Road (Klamath County Rte.533).
TRAIL ENDS: -Aspen Point Campground, Lake of the Woods.
DISTANCE: -About 2 miles. USE: bikers/hikers.
SEASON: -Usually snow-free June through October.
CONNECTING TR. -Family Loop, Mtn. Lakes and Highlakes Trails.
BRING MAPS: -Info from Rogue River-Winema Ntl. Forest Offices.

FROM ASHLAND, Follow Dead Indian Memorial Road (Jackson County Route 722, Klamath County 533), 34 miles to SUNSET CAMPGROUND. Turn left to the boat launch parking area.
RAINBOW BAY PICNIC AREA. Continue 1.0 mile on Dead Indian Memorial Road to Road 3704. Turn onto 3704 and go 0.3 mi. to the Resort turnoff. Take the turnoff 0.1 mi. to RAINBOW BAY PICNIC AREA and turn left past the restrooms to Sunset Tr.(end of road).
ASPEN POINT CAMPGROUND turnoff is located 0.4 miles further along Road 3704.

FROM WHITE CITY, Follow State Highway 140, 36.4 miles to Road 3704 on the right. Take Road 3704, 0.6 miles to ASPEN POINT CAMPGROUND turnoff and 0.4 miles further to the Resort turnoff leading to RAINBOW BAY PICNIC AREA. To reach SUNSET CAMPGROUND, continue 0.3 mile further on Road 3704 to Dead Indian Memorial Road and turn right to milepost 34.Turn right to boat dock area.

FEATURES: Sunset Trail begins from the SUNSET BOAT LAUNCH parking lot and continues 1.0 mile northwest along the Lake of the Woods shoreline to the parking spaces at RAINBOW BAY PICNIC AREA. Go straight across the parking spaces, and look immediately left for the trail leading about 0.5 mile to the junction with Family Loop Trail, and about 0.5 miles further to ASPEN POINT CAMPGROUND where Sunset Trail terminates at the HIGHLAKES TRAIL.

NOTE: Family Loop Trail uses the Mtn. Lakes Trail to a junction where the family loops begin left to join a portion of Highlakes Trail in less than one mile.

A map at the beginning of Chapter 8 shows the many loop and connection opportunities with other trails.

RYE SPUR TRAIL #3771. (See maps 16 and 17)

TRAIL BEGINS:	-Fourmile Lake Campground.	ELEV. 5750'
TRAIL ENDS:	-State Hwy. 140, near milepost 36.	ELEV. 5000'
DISTANCE:	-6.1 miles, SEASON: July-October.	
USE:	-Hikers, horses. Motor bikes allowed, but beginning riders may find lower 1.5 mi. too steep.	
BRING MAPS:	-USFS Winema Ntl. Forest/Rec. Opportunity Guide.	

ACCESS: From White City,OR,follow mileposts on State Highway 140, 35.7 mile to the jnc. with Road 3661. UPPER TRAILHEAD: Turn left (north) onto 3661 and go 5.6 miles to the signed PARKING AREA FOR ALL TRAILS, at Fourmile Lake Campground. South of a trail sign, a trail leads east, crossing Road 3661, to the jnc. with Rye Spur Trail, just below the dam at the southeast end of the lake. Turn right (south) to continue toward the lower trailhead.

LOWER TRAILHEAD: From the above junction of Highway 140 and Road 3661, continue east on Hwy.140, 0.4 mile,just beyond milepost 36, and turn left (north) onto a road track paralleling Hwy.140. Make an immediate right turn leading toward RYE SPUR TRAILHEAD.The one mile BILLIE CREEK NATURE TRAIL, for hikers and horses only,is located 1000ft. up the trail and loops through stands of ponderosa pine, white fir and other coniferous trees. It crosses Billie Cr. in two locations. Decayed logs from past logging activities provide food and cover for wildlife. After passing Billie Creek Tr., Rye Spur Trail continues about 6 mi. to Fourmile Lake Campground.

HIKERS would benefit mostly by hiking 3.4 mi.from the upper trailhead to the viewpoint and return. From the viewpoint, there are views of Pelican Butte,Mountain Lakes Wilderness and of the fault systems below, leading north into Sky Lakes Wilderness and south into California.You could also return to the campground by hiking beyond the viewpoint to the Cascade Canal and turning left(northeast) along the canal road. Total loop distance is 9.0 miles.

South of the Cascade Canal, Rye Spur Trail continues,crossing Rd. 3633, and 0.9 more miles to the junction with BILLIE CREEK NATURE TRAIL, for hikers and horses only. Keep left and go about 1000ft. to Rye Spur lower trailhead. Rye Spur Trail,a portion of the former Oregon Skyline Trail, is maintained by "Desert Trail Riders" of Klamath Falls.

F I S H   L A K E   A R E A   T R A I L S

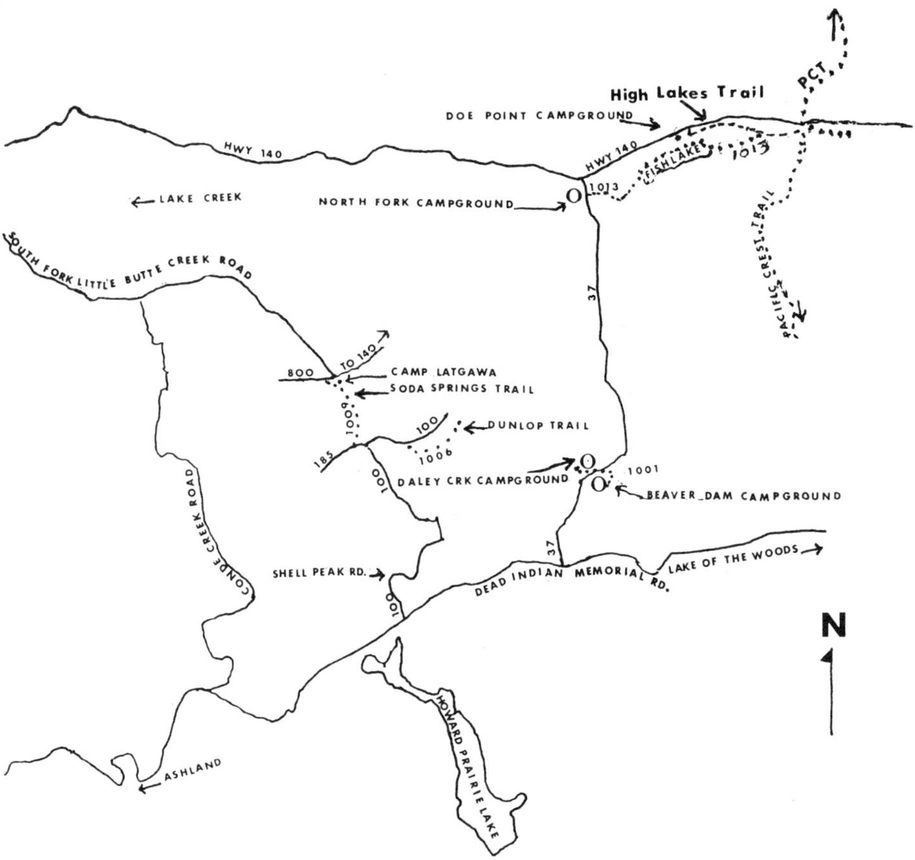

FISH LAKE TRAIL #1013. (See map 16)

TRAIL BEGINS: -North Fork Campground,Forest Route 37-ELEV. 4560'
TRAIL ENDS: -Pacific Crest National Scenic Trail. ELEV. 4950'
DISTANCE: -5 miles (one way), EASY, MAY-OCTOBER.
USE: -Hikers/mountain bikes. Bikes not allowed on PCT!
CONNECTING TR. -Pacific Crest and High Lakes Trails.
BRING MAPS: -USFS Ashland Ranger Dist.-Rogue River Ntl. Forest.
-USFS Pacific Crest Trail-Oregon Southern Portion.
-USFS Recreation Opportunity Guide-(this trail).

ACCESS: From Interstate Hwy. 5, Ashland-Klamath Falls Exit 14, travel 0.6 mile east on State Hwy. 66 to the junction with Dead Indian Memorial Road (County Route 722). Turn left onto this road and go 22 miles to the junction with Forest Route 37 (Big Elk Road). Turn left onto Route 37 and go 7 miles to NORTH FORK CAMPGROUND. The western end of the FISH LAKE TRAIL is across Route 37 from the campground.
TO BEGIN AT DOE POINT OR FISH LAKE CAMPGROUNDS, continue 1.0 mile north on Route 37 to Highway 140. Turn right and go 2.0 miles to the Fish Lake turnoff. Turn right and follow signs.Parking is at either of the day use picnic areas.
TO BEGIN AT THE PCNST SUMMIT TRAILHEAD: continue 2 miles east on Highway 140 just beyond milepost 32, to the trailhead entrance on the left. Hike the PCNST south (crossing Hwy. 140) and go 0.5 mi to the junction with Fish Lake and High Lakes Trails that are co-located for one mile west before Fish Lake Tr. keeps left to Fish Lake and beyond to terminate at Forest Route 37.

FEATURES: From the trailhead at North Fork Campground, the trail follows the North Fork of Little Butte Creek and after 0.5 mi., a side trail leads right to Fish Lake Dam. The main trail turns left and follows the north shore of Fish Lake. The picnic areas at DOE POINT and FISH LAKE campgrounds are good midpoints to begin a hike either direction on the trail. Continuing through these campgrounds, the trail leads past Fish Lake Resort, skirts the end of the lake and heads east through a forest with large openings of basalt lava. Fish Lake Trail reaches the High Lakes Trail and the two trails co-locate for one mile east, to where Fish Lake Trail terminates. PACK/SADDLE STOCK NOT PERMITTED IN DEVELOPED RECREATION SITES AT FISH LAKE. SEE THE LATEST USFS RECREATION GUIDES FOR DETAILS OF A NEARBY TETHERING AREA.

PACIFIC CREST NATIONAL SCENIC TRAIL-HWY. 140 TO FOREST ROAD 700. (See maps 16 and 23)

TRAIL BEGINS: -PCNST parking area off Hwy. 140 ELEV. 5100'
TRAIL ENDS: -Forest Road 700. ELEV. 5200'
DISTANCE: -10.6 miles (one way) MODERATE.
SEASON: -June through October.
CONNECTING TR:-Fish Lake, High Lakes, Brown Mountain Trails.
BRING MAPS: -USFS Pacific Crest Trail-Oregon Southern Portion.
-USFS Ashland Ranger Dist.-Rogue River Ntl. Forest.
-USFS Recreation Opportunity Guide.

FEATURES: Beginning from the Pacific Crest Trailhead on Hwy. 140,a 0.2 mile access trail leads to the PCNST. At this junction, turn left (SOUTH) and follow the trail along the Cascade Canal for 0.5 mile to Hwy. 140. The trail crosses the Hwy. and continues 0.5 miles to the junction with High Lakes Trail and Fish Lake Trail 1013 that are co-located for one mile, before Fish Lake Trail keeps left (south) on its way to Fish Lake Resort, and High Lakes Trail keeps RIGHT (north) to end north of the resort.

Continuing south, the trail begins a 5.0 mile traverse over Brown Mountain lava flows (on a cinder trail surface), gaining 800 ft. in elevation. Once leaving the lava flows, the trail enters a dense conifer forest. Solomon's seal, prince's pine, and huckleberries blanket the forest floor. A small campsite is reached just prior to the junction with the Brown Mountain Trail. (8.6 mile point). From this junction, the trail continues south another 2 miles to Forest Road 700. This is the ending point for this hike. (See below for PCT shelter and water pump location).

Along this section of trail, there are good views of Brown Mtn., Robinson Butte and Mt. McLoughlin. (Excerpts USFS Recreation Opportunity Guide).

Some folks may wish to extend the trip to PCNST trailhead on Dead Indian Memorial Road, 1.9 trail miles further south. Just 800 ft. south of Road 700, a short side-trail leaves the PCNST to the SOUTH BROWN MOUNTAIN SHELTER. A WATER PUMP HAS BEEN INSTALLED AT THIS LOCATION.

-continued

PCNST Hwy. 140 to Road 700--continued:

HWY.140 ACCESS From Ashland Interstate 5 Exit 14, drive east on Highway 66, 0.6 mile to Dead Indian Memorial Road (Jackson County Route 722, Klamath County 533). Turn onto this road and go 22 miles to the junction with Forest Route 37. Turn left onto Route 37 and proceed 8 miles to the junction with Highway 140. Turn right onto 140 and go 4.2 miles to Forest Rd. 3650. Turn left onto Rd. 3650 and an immediate left onto Road 010 leading to the Pacific Crest Summit Trailhead. A short 0.2 mi. access trail leads to the Pacific Crest Trail.

RD. 700 ACCESS From Ashland Interstate 5 Exit 14, drive east on Highway 66, 0.6 mile to Dead Indian Memorial Road (Jackson County Route 722, Klamath County 533). Turn onto this road and go 26.5 miles to Forest Road 3720. Turn left onto 3720 and go 2 miles to Road 700. Turn right onto 700 and continue 0.4 miles to where the PCNST crosses the road. Parking is available between the Road 500 spur and the trail.

DEAD INDIAN MEMORIAL ROAD ACCESS: From Ashland Interstate 5 Exit 14,drive east on Highway 66, 0.6 mile to Dead Indian Memorial Rd. (Jackson County Route 722, Klamath County 533). Travel left onto this road, 27.2 miles to the Pacific Crest Trail parking area, at Pederson Snow Park.

SHUTTLE ARRANGEMENTS:

Driving distance between Pederson Park-PCT Trailhead and the PCT Summit Trailhead on Hwy. 140 is 15.1 miles, (north on Dead Indian Memorial Rd. to Hwy. 140 and turning west 5.1 mi. to the PCT Summit Trailhead).

Driving distance from the Road 700 PCT crossing-to the PCT Summit Trailhead on Hwy. 140 is 12.8 miles,by returning 0.4 miles to Rd. 3720. Turn right and go 2 miles to Road 3705. Turn right again and go 4 miles to Route 37. Turn right onto 37 and go 2.2 miles to Hwy. 140. Turn right and go 4.2 miles to Road 3650 (PCT Trailhead) on the left.

BROWN MTN. TRAIL #1005-ROGUE RIV. NTL. FOREST SECTION. (Map 16)

TRAIL BEGINS: -Forest Road 3705. ELEV. 4850'
TRAIL ENDS: -Forest Road 3640. ELEV. 5650'
DISTANCE: -5.3 miles (one way), moderate.
SEASON: -Mid May to October.
USE: -Hikers, horses, mountain bikes when trail surfaces are dry.
CONNECTING TR. -Pacific Crest National Scenic Trail #2000.
-Brown Mtn. Trail 3724 (Winema Ntl. Forest).
BRING MAPS: -USFS Ashland Ranger Dist.-Rogue River Ntl. Forest.
-USFS Pacific Crest Trail-Oregon Southern Portion.
-USFS Rec. Opportunity Guide-Brown Mountain Trail.

ACCESS: FOREST ROAD 3705 TRAILHEAD. From Interstate Hwy. 5 Ashland-Klamath Falls Exit 14,go 0.6 mile east on State Hwy. 66 to the junction with Dead Indian Memorial Road (County Route 722). Turn left onto this road and travel 22 miles to the junction with Forest Route 37 (Big Elk Road). Turn left onto Route 37 and go 6.0 miles to Forest Road 3705. Turn right on 3705 and continue 3.0 miles to the trailhead.

FOREST ROAD 3640 TRAILHEAD. From the above Road 3705 Trailhead, continue southeast on Road 3705 for 1.0 mile to the junction with Forest Road 3720. Turn left onto Road 3720 and continue for 1.5 miles to the junction with Road 700. Turn left onto Road 700 and travel 3 miles to Road 3640. Turn left onto Road 3640 and proceed 1.5 miles to the trailhead.

FEATURES: From the Rd. 3705 Trailhead, the Brown Mtn. Trail crosses Road 500 in 1.5 miles. At 2.5 miles you cross Road 560 and at 2.9 miles you cross the Pacific Crest National Scenic Trail. At 5.2 miles the trail forks; TAKE THE TRAIL TO THE RIGHT 0.1 MI. TO THE RD. 3640 TRAILHEAD. The trail to the left is Brown Mtn. Trail 3724 (Winema Ntl. Forest section) that continues 2.5 miles to Lake of the Woods.

BROWN MTN. TRAIL #3724 WINEMA NTL. FOREST SECTION. (Maps 16 & 17)
(See preceding page for continuation in Rogue River Ntl. Forest).

TRAIL BEGINS:	-Forest Road 3640 Trailhead.	ELEV. 5640'
TRAIL ENDS:	-Forest Road 3601 Trailhead.	ELEV. 4960'
DISTANCE:	-2.5 miles.	
SEASON:	-June-October.	
USE:	-Hiker/horse.	
CONNECTING TR.	-Brown Mtn. Trail 3705- Rogue River Ntl. Forest.	
BRINC MAPS:	-USFS Winema National Forest.	

ACCESS: Take State Highway 140 to summer home Road 3601, located at the west end of Lake Of The Woods near milepost 35. Turn south on Road 3601 and go 0.1 mile to the junction with Forest Road 3640 and:

Keep left on Road 3601 and go 0.4 mi. to the LOWER TRAILHEAD near Camp McLoughlin, OR.....

Turn right onto Rd. 3640 and go 3 miles to the UPPER TRAILHEAD on the right side of the road.

DUNLOP TRAIL #1006. Moderate, May-Oct., hiker only beyond meadow.
SODA SPRINGS TRAIL #1009. Moderate, yearlong from Soda Springs.
BRING MAPS: -USFS Recreation Opportunity Guides.
-Rogue River Ntl. Forest- Ashland Ranger District.
(See maps 15-16 back of this book).

ACCESS to UPPER TRAILHEADS-SHELL PEAK ROAD-FOREST ROAD 2500-100.
From Interstate Hwy. 5 Ashland-Klamath Falls Exit 14, go 0.6 mile east on State Hwy. 66 to the junction with Dead Indian Memorial Road (County Route 722) and travel 18.5 miles to Shell Peak Road on the left. Follow Shell Peak Road 5.6 miles to the junction of Road 2500-185 and turn left 250 ft. to SODA SPRINGS TRAILHEAD.

SODA SPRINGS TRAIL #1009 begins at ELEVATION 4060' dropping steeply 2.5 miles to the lower trailhead on Forest Road 3730-800 ELEVATION 2740'. The trail begins through heavy timber and soon comes to a site of a clearcut that affords a wide view of the surrounding area before re-entering the forest. A grove of oak and maple is reached at the lower elevations, soon to be followed by a rocky ledge with more good views. Descending further, you come to the junction with the trail leading right to Latgawa Church Camp. But turn left to the soda springs, cross a foot bridge, and continue to the lower trailhead on Road 3730-800. See next page for access.

The DUNLOP TRAILHEAD is reached by going 0.9 mile further on ROAD 2500-100 at a road gate just before MILEPOST 7, ELEVATION 3700'. Trail distance is 1.5 miles one way, that takes you past beautiful meadows, an interesting old homestead site, and some of the grandest ponderosa pines that you will ever see. The trail ends in the canyon of the South Fork of Little Butte Creek where fishing for small cutthroat trout is usually very good. ELEVATION 2400'.

Sierra Club volunteers and Forest Service trail crews rebuilt the Dunlop Trail in 1990. Soda Springs Trail was rebuilt in 1992 by Forest Service crews and the Northwest Youth Corps.

"The Dunlop Ranch was said to have been settled by a bootlegger referred to as 'ol' man Dunlop-in the 1920's. During the 1930's a family named Nickerson 'got by' raising goats, whose hides were used for car upholstery and convertible tops. The site has been abandoned since the late 1930's."

-Continued

ACCESS TO SODA SPRINGS LOWER TRAILHEAD. (See maps 14 and 15)

Normally the lower trailhead could be reached from the community of Lake Creek by following SOUTH FORK LITTLE BUTTE CREEK ROAD 13 miles to the junction with Road 3730-800. Crossing the bridge on Road 800 led 0.5 mile to the trailhead.

The above bridge was washed out in the 1997 flood with no immediate date of replacement. Contact USFS Ashland Ranger District to see if reroute plans develop.

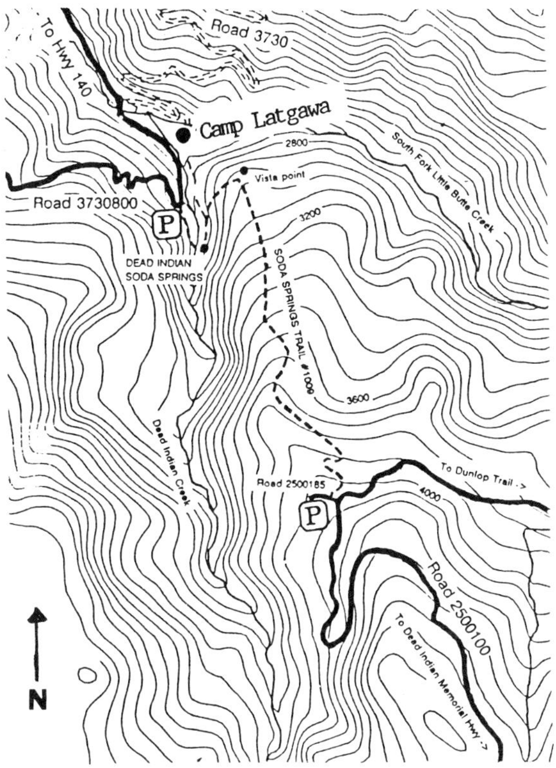

BEAVER DAM TRAIL #1001, hiker only.
2.1 mi.,easy, May-Oct. Elev. 4500'.

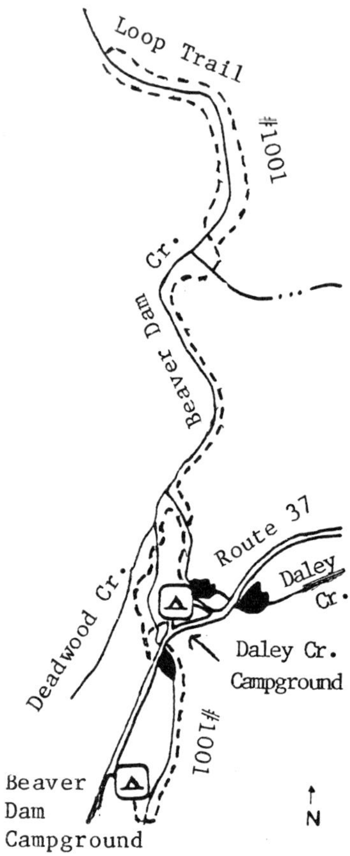

Beaver Dam Trail is between two different types of habitat; streamside and forest. The setting is the confluence of three small creeks which drain the southern Dead Indian Plateau. Beaver Dam Creek, Daley Creek and Deadwood Creek flow through an area of grassy banks, willows, false hellbore and beaver ponds. The trail connects Beaver Dam and Daley Creek Campgrounds, forming a partial loop.

TREES: Douglas fir, white pine. Pacific yew is poisonous, eating foliage or seeds contained in bright red berries can result in death.

WILDFLOWERS: bleeding heart,calypso orchid and trillium.

BIRDS: CAVITY NESTERS:pileated woodpecker, red-breasted nuthatch. ALSO, watch and listen for the belted kingfisher who makes his livlihood capturing small fish.

BEAVERS may be spotted in early morning or evening. Gnawed branches and several active dams are visible from the trail.

ACCESS: From Ashland Interstate 5, Exit 14, drive east on Hwy.66, 0.6 mi. to Dead Indian Memorial Road (County 722). Turn left onto this road and go 22 mi. to the junction of Forest Route 37. Turn left onto Route 37 and go 1.5 miles to Beaver Dam and Daley Creek Campgrounds. You can begin in either campground. (Excerpts: Rogue River National Forest, Ashland Ranger District, Recreation Opportunity Guide)

CHAPTER 9 - BUTTE FALLS AREA

WHISKEY SPRINGS INTERPRETIVE TRAIL. (See map 16)

TRAIL BEGINS/ENDS: WHISKEY SPRINGS CAMPGROUND PICNIC AREA.
DISTANCE: -1.0 mile. ELEV. 3200'
DIFFICULTY: -Easy, wheelchair accessible.
SEASON: -June thru October. USE: hikers only.
BRING MAPS: -Butte Falls Ranger Dist.-Rogue River Ntl. Forest.

ACCESS: From Butte Falls: Go 10 miles east on the Butte Falls-Fish Lake Hwy.(County Route 821)to Whiskey Springs Campground.

From Ashland: Go 0.6 mile east on Hwy. 66, turn left onto Dead Indian Memorial Road (County Route 722), and continue 22 miles to the junction with Forest Route 37. Follow Route 37, 8 mi. to Hwy. 140. Turn right and go 1/4 mi. to County Route 821 that continues north 9.3 miles to Whiskey Springs Campground.

FROM WHITE CITY: Follow mileposts on Highway 140, 28.6 miles and turn north onto County Route 821. Follow 821, 9.3 mi. to Whiskey Springs Campground.

FEATURES: The one mile loop trail starts at the picnic area and leads through a forested area before arriving at a viewing platform that overlooks a marshland created by beavers. Wood Ducks, frogs,and other wildlife habitats may be seen along the way. Interpretive signs are frequently located throughout the area.

ALSO: NEARBY SKY LAKES WILDERNESS AREA TRAILS: (See Chapter 6)

-continued

SOUTH FORK ROGUE RIVER TRAILS

SOUTH FORK TRAILS

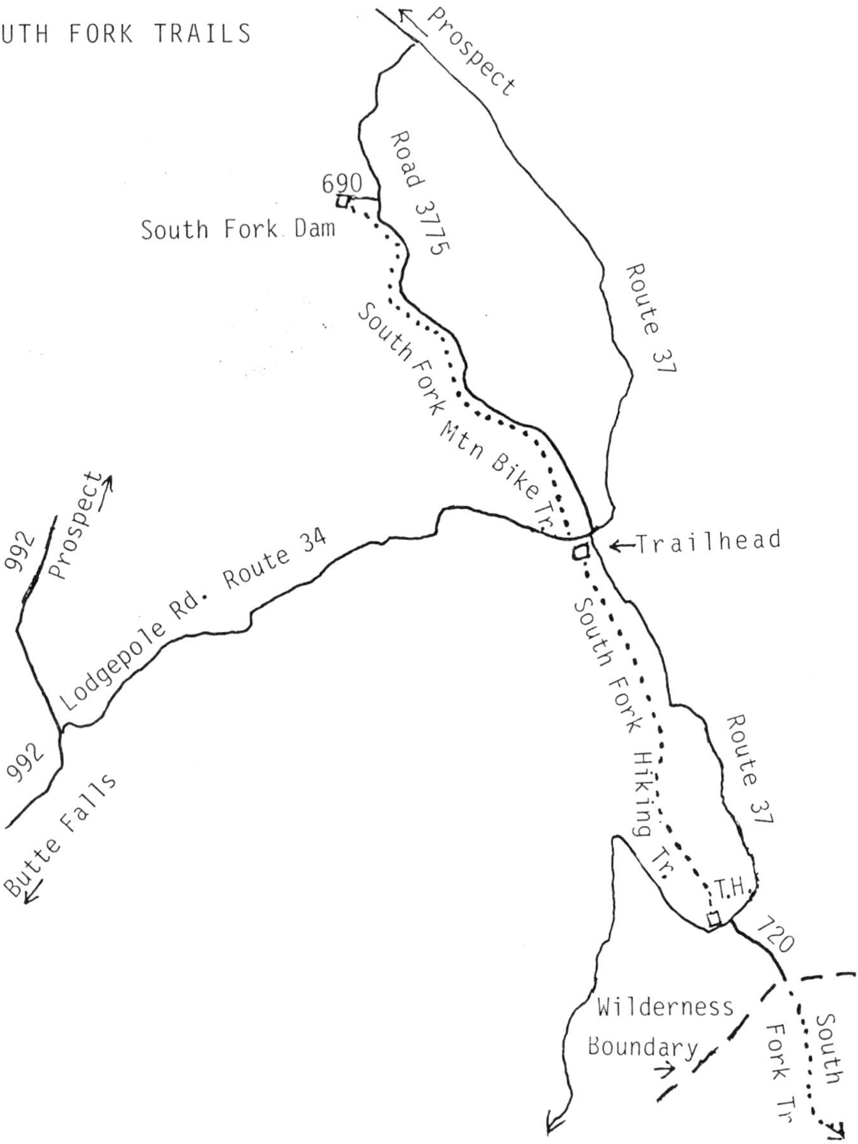

LOWER SOUTH FORK ROGUE RIVER TRAIL #986. (See map 11)

TRAIL BEGINS: -Upper Trailhead-(Hiker) Route 37. ELEV. 4400'
MID-POINT: -Middle Trailhead-Forest Route 34. ELEV. 4000'
TRAIL ENDS: -Lower Trailhead- (Mtn. bike) Rd. 3775/690 near South Fork Dam. ELEV. 3400'
DISTANCE: -HIKER SECTION, 5.3 mi., MTN.BIKE SECTION 6.8 mi.
SEASON: -Spring, summer, fall. Mosquitos can be very bad in late spring and early summer. They should be virtually absent by the first of July.
BRING MAPS: -Butte Falls Ranger Dist.-Rogue River Ntl. Forest.

ACCESS: From Butte Falls, Oregon, travel east one mile to the County road leading north to the town of Prospect. Turn onto this road and go 8.7 mi. to the junction of Forest Route 34. Turn right onto 34 and go 8.1 miles. The MID-POINT TRAILHEAD is on the right just before reaching the junction with Forest Route 37 and Rd.3775. South of this trailhead is the South Fork Hiking Trail and north is the South Fork Mtn. Bike Trail.You may hike on the bike tr.but please keep bikes off hiking section.

UPPER (HIKER) TRAILHEAD: Continue on Route 34 to the junction of Route 37. Turn right (south) onto 37 and go 5.6 mi. to the trailhead on the right. This HIKER ONLY trail proceeds 5.3 miles along the river,downstream to the parking area on Forest Route 34.

LOWER (MTN. BIKE-HIKER) TRAIL SECTION continues directly across Route 34 and leads 6.8 miles downstream to the lower trailhead on Forest Road 3775/690. If making a car shuttle, Forest Road 3775 parallels just east of this section of trail. Drive 5.2 miles northwest on Road 3775 to Forest Road 3775/690 on the left (Just beyond milepost 5). Follow Road 690 0.5 mile to the trailhead at the end of the road. (Road 690 may be unmarked and impassible for larger vehicles due to overgrowth of roadside brush.)

FEATURES: Parking and turn-around is adequate at the trailheads. The trails follow the river along its entire length.

CHAPTER 10 - PROSPECT AREA

MILL CREEK FALLS. (See map 5)

TRAILS BEGIN: -Mill Creek viewpoint parking area, 1 mile south of Prospect; and from the State Park at the south town limits of Prospect.
DIFFICULTY: -Easy. USE: hikers only.
SEASON: -All year except for occasional winter snows.

ACCESS: From Medford, take Crater Lake Highway (Hwy. 62) to the community of Cascade Gorge (milepost 38). Mill Creek Drive junctions on the right (east). Follow mileposts on Mill Creek Drive, 5.4 miles to the Mill Creek viewpoint parking area on the right. A large sign-map is erected here; giving directions to the Avenue of the Giant Boulders, and viewpoints of Barr Creek Falls and Mill Creek Falls. The trail to these points begins from the south end of the parking area. While hiking these trails note the signs that are posted to alert visitors:

"DANGER: POWER DAM SPILLWAY UPSTREAM. WATCH OUT FOR ANY FAST RISE OF WATER AT ANY TIME AND WITHOUT WARNING. BE SURE THAT YOU CAN REACH SHORE SAFELY."

AN OREGON STATE PARK, WITH RESTROOMS, is located one mile further north on Mill Creek Drive, just at the south town limits of Prospect. THE TRAIL TO PEARSONY FALLS begins here. Metal posts indicate the names of the various trees. After about one mile, the trail descends to the Rogue River bed, sometimes dry due to water diversion from a power company dam upstream. DANGER SIGNS WARN THAT WATER COULD SUDDENLY BE RELEASED FROM THE DAM, and should be taken seriously.

These trails were designed for public use by BOISE CASCADE TIMBER AND WOOD PRODUCTS GROUP.

MAMMOTH PINES NATURE TRAIL. (See map 5)

TRAIL BEGINS/ENDS: -State Highway 62 between mileposts 50 and 51.
DISTANCE: -1/4 mile loop, easy.
SEASON: -June through October.
BRING MAP: -USFS Prospect Ranger Dist.-Rogue River N.F.
-USFS brochure-Mammoth Pines Nature Trail.

ACCESS: From the town of Prospect, take State Highway 62 to milepost 50. Road 6200/060 is 0.6 mile further. Turn left onto Road 060 that leads to a parking area.

FEATURES: An information board is located at this parking area. Brochures may be available from a receptacle at this point. The short loop trail travels through a mixed conifer forest. Each "station" is numbered and is keyed to the brochure as follows:

1. Snowbrush
2. Western Hemlock
3. California Hazel
4. Mammoth Sugar Pine
5. Douglas Fir
6. Grand Fir
7. Ponderosa Pine
8. Oregon Grape
9. Mixed Coniferous Forest
10. Serviceberry
11. Thimbleberry
12. Mountain Ash
13. The Continuing Story of Succession
14. Bracken Fern
15. Pacific Yew
16. The End and the Beginning
17. Sugar Pine
18. Pacific Dogwood
19. Golden Chinquapin
20. Scouler's Willow

HISTORY: In October 1979, Douglas fir trees infected by laminated root rot were felled by a windstorm. This disease weakens the root system, and eventually kills the tree. In May 1981, the trees were removed for visitor safety. Laminated root rot is spread from tree to tree through the root system, and future generations of trees can become re-infected. The area has been replanted with ponderosa pines, and other species resistant to laminated root rot.

Upper Rogue Trails

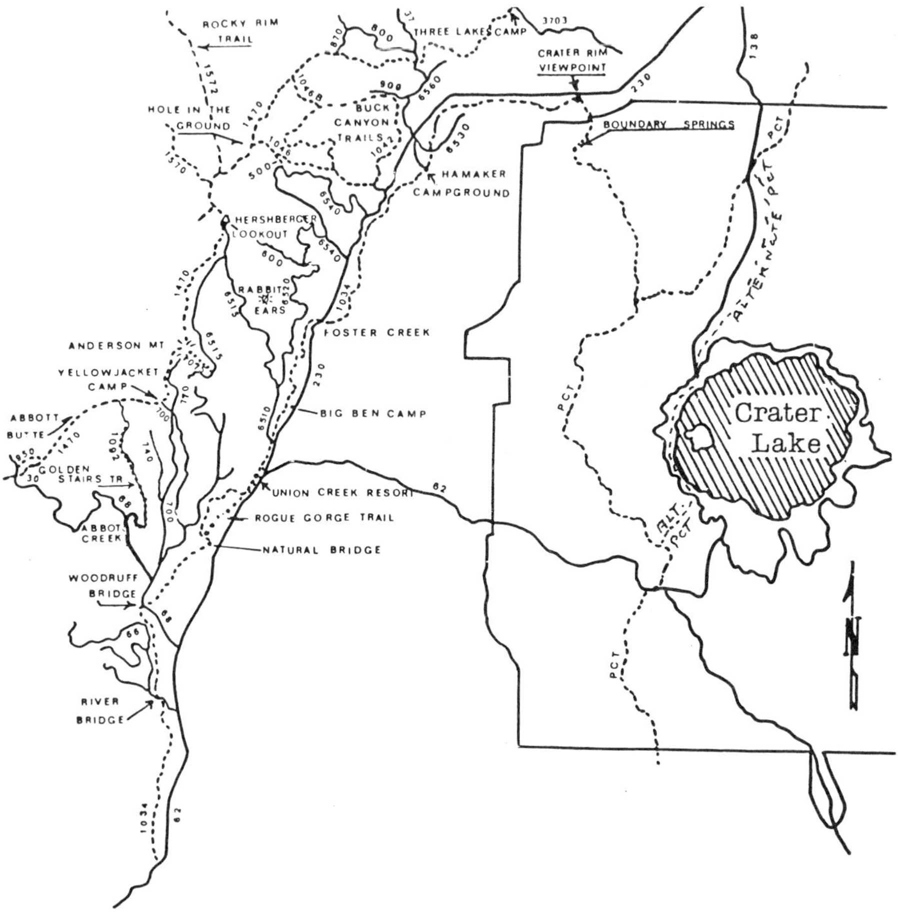

UPPER ROGUE RIVER TRAIL #1034-CRATER RIM VIEWPOINT TO HAMAKER MEADOWS. Segment 1 (See map 2)

DISTANCE: -9.3 miles, easy to moderate. USE: hikers only.
SEASON: -June to October. Wildflowers until mid-August.
CONNECTING TR.-Boundary Springs Trail 1057.
BRING MAPS: -Prospect Ranger District-Rogue River Ntl. Forest.
-USFS Rec. Opportunity Guide-Upper Rogue River Tr.

ACCESS TO CRATER RIM VIEWPOINT, ELEV. 5174'.
Just north of the Union Creek Resort, at the junction with State Hwys. 62 and 230, follow mileposts northeast on 230, 18.6 miles to the viewpoint parking area and trailhead. Hike 0.6 mile to the junction with Boundary Springs Trail 1057, that begins a 7.2 mile hike to the Pacific Crest Trail. KEEP RIGHT at this junction onto Trail 1034, which reaches Hamaker Campground in 9.3 miles.

FEATURES: Starting from Crater Rim Viewpoint, the trail travels downstream. After 1/2 mile, it drops to the river's edge, crosses a small creek before climbing to 200 foot cliffs of compacted pumice. The next two miles offer impressive sights, Ruth Falls can be heard below but is hard to see. Rough Rider Falls is 2 miles further. Another waterfall is located 1.5 miles downstream. The trail leaves the river and winds 2.5 miles through the woods, crosses Forest Road 6530 and then returns to the river's edge at Hamaker Campground on Forest Road 900. THIS IS 1 OF 7 SEGMENTS OF THE 48 MILE UPPER ROGUE RIVER TRAIL.

ACCESS TO HAMAKER CAMPGROUND, see next page.

HISTORY: "The Upper Rogue River Trail is a National Recreational Trail. Some segments of the trail were built by the Civilian Conservation Corps as access routes for recreation and fire supression purposes. The construction of the rest of the trail began in 1975 as a Volunteer Bicentennial commemorative project, and was completed in late 1977. Long range plans envision the Upper Rogue Trail extending from the Pacific Crest Trail to the Pacific Coast." (USFS quote)

UPPER ROGUE RIVER TRAIL #1034....HAMAKER CAMPGROUND TO NEW TRAILHEAD FOREST ROAD 6530/070. Segment 2 (See map 2)

DISTANCE: -About 7.5 miles, easy to moderate.

SEASON: -June through October. USE: hiker/horse. Motor vehicles not allowed.

BRING MAPS: -Prospect Ranger District-Rogue River Ntl. Forest.
-USFS Rec. Opportunity Guide-Upper Rogue River Tr.

ACCESS: HAMAKER CAMPGROUND, ELEV. 4000'.

From the junction of State Hwys. 62 and 230, follow mileposts northeast on 230, 12.1 miles to the junction with Forest Road 6530. Turn right onto Road 6530 and go 0.6 mi. to the junction with Forest Road 6530/900. Turn right onto 900, and go 0.8 mi. to Hamaker Campground at the end of the road. Trail 1034 heading north is along the left side of the road just before you reach the Rogue River bridge.

FEATURES: From Hamaker Campground, Trail 1034 begins right (south) just after crossing the bridge. It first leads away from the river and rejoins it two miles later near the confluence of Muir Creek and the Rogue River. The trail follows through grassy meadows, crosses Hurryon Creek, then rejoins Rogue River near Highway Falls. Beyond Highway Falls, the trail climbs to the top of a pumice cliff with views of the Rogue River below. After descending to the river bank and then crossing National Cr. on a footlog, the trail meets Forest Road 6530. Hike across the bridge and make a left turn to continue south along the west bank of the river. About 1/4 mile further, look for an access trail leading to a NEW (1989) trailhead/parking area on Road 6530/070, replacing the Foster Creek Trailhead on Hwy. 62 that was difficult to reach.

THIS IS ONE OF 7 SEGMENTS OF THE 48 MILE UPPER ROGUE RIVER TRAIL.

ACCESS TO FOREST ROAD 6530/070 TRAILHEAD, see next page.

UPPER ROGUE RIVER TRAIL #1034-ROAD 6530/070 TRAILHEAD TO BIG BEND
Segment 3 (See maps 2,5,and 6)

DISTANCE: -About 9.5 miles, easy to moderate.
SEASON: -June through October. USE: hiker/horse. Motorized vehicles not allowed.
BRING MAPS: -Prospect Ranger District-Rogue River Ntl. Forest.
-USFS Rec. Opportunity Guide-Upper Rogue River Tr.

ACCESS: FOREST ROAD 6530/070 TRAILHEAD.
North of the Union Creek Resort, at the junction of State Hwys. 62 and 230, follow mileposts on 230 to milepost 6 at the County line.Turn right onto Forest Road 6530 and go 0.7 mi. to the junction with Road 070 on the right. Turn right and go 0.1 mile to the trailhead and parking area. This new trailhead was built in 1989 by Gregory Forest Products and USFS to replace the old, difficult to reach, Foster Creek Trailhead.

FEATURES: An access trail leads to the Upper Rogue River Trail. Turn right to continue south and after a short distance the trail climbs away from the river, crosses Hwy. 230 two miles south, and continues 0.5 mile to the former Foster Creek Trailhead.

Hiking south from Foster Creek,it is necessary to wade the creek. In about 1 mile downstream, the trail leaves the Rogue River and climbs a pumice cliff. It then continues through a series of wet marshy areas. 5 miles downstream, on the south side of a foot-bridge, Trail 1034 passes the abandoned 0.5 mile trail that went to the Brown's Cabin Trailhead. Continuing south along the river, the trail climbs and traverses a pumice bluff. It then follows the river's edge as it winds around Big Bend and terminates on Forest Road 6510, 3/4 mile north of its junction with Hwy. 230.

THIS IS ONE OF 7 SEGMENTS OF THE 48 MILE UPPER ROGUE RIVER TRAIL.

ACCESS TO BIG BEND, see next page.

UPPER ROGUE RIVER TRAIL #1034-BIG BEND TO NATURAL BRIDGE CAMPGROUND AND VIEWPOINT. Segment 4 (See map 5)

DISTANCE: -7 miles, moderate grades, must ford Flat Creek.
SEASON: -June through October.
USE: -Hiker only.
CONNECTING TR. -Rogue Gorge Trail 1034A.
BRING MAPS: -Prospect Ranger District-Rogue River Ntl. Forest.
-USFS Rec. Opportunity Guide-Upper Rogue River Tr.

ACCESS: BIG BEND TRAILHEAD, ELEV. 3500'.
North of the Union Creek Resort, at the junction with State Hwys. 62 and 230, continue 0.9 mi. northeast on 230 to the junction with Forest Road 6510. Turn left across Rogue River bridge, and continue 3/4 mile to the crossing of the Upper Rogue River Trail. Hiking north leads 7 miles to Foster Creek. Hiking south leads 6 miles toward Natural Bridge Campground.

FEATURES: From Big Bend Trailhead, the trail climbs a rocky embankment, and traverses a steep slope overlooking the Rogue River. Fish Mountain to the north, becomes visible through a brief opening in the trees. Further south, after frequent switchbacks, a steep forested slope overlooks Farewell Bend Campground across the river. The trail then momentarily descends to river level to view the water raging through the long, narrow chute of a collapsed lava tube. South of Union Creek Campground, the trail returns to a calm river and crosses Flat Creek, 4 miles further south. The river regains its turbulent nature and Trail 1034 then reaches the first of 2 footbridges crossing to the east bank of the river, at the junction with Rogue Gorge Trail 1034A, 1/4 mile north of Natural Bridge Campground. Traveling one mile further along the west bank, leads one mile to the Natural Bridge Viewpoint facility and footbridge. This area is 0.5 mile west of Hwy. 62 accessible by Forest Road #300.

THIS IS ONE OF 7 SEGMENTS OF THE 47 MILE UPPER ROGUE RIVER TRAIL.

ACCESS TO NATURAL BRIDGE CAMP/VIEWPOINT FACILITY (See next page)

UPPER ROGUE RIVER TRAIL #1034-NATURAL BRIDGE CAMPGROUND/VIEWPOINT TO WOODRUFF BRIDGE. Segment 5 (See map 5)

DISTANCE: -3.5 miles, easy. USE: hikers only.
SEASON: -June through October.
CONNECTING TR. -None.
BRING MAPS: -Prospect Ranger District-Rogue River Ntl. Forest.
-USFS Rec. Opportunity Guide-Upper Rogue River Tr.

ACCESS: NATURAL BRIDGE CAMPGROUND, ELEV. 3200'.
From the town of Prospect, follow mileposts north on State Highway 62 to mile 54.8 at the junction with Forest Road 300. Turn left and go 1/2 mile to Natural Bridge Viewpoint parking lot. Follow a paved path to a footbridge. Do not cross the footbridge if you are going toward Woodruff Bridge. Crossing the bridge leads to the Natural Bridge Viewpoint facility interpretative stations, and then on further north to other segments of the Upper Rogue River Trail.

FEATURES: From the above footbridge, continue downstream on the east bank of the river, over a rough tread of mossy lava rock which becomes slippery in wet weather. The trail later climbs to view the river as it makes a sharp bend and rages through a narrow chute of a collapsed lava tube. This rapids is known as Knob Falls.

Several old skid roads are encountered, as trail 1034 approaches Woodruff Bridge developed picnic area. The U.S. Forest Service advises, "The pools and river can be dangerous due to cold water and a forceful current." THIS IS ONE OF 7 SEGMENTS OF THE 48 MI. UPPER ROGUE RIVER TRAIL.

ACCESS TO WOODRUFF BRIDGE, see next page.

UPPER ROGUE RIVER TRAIL #1034-WOODRUFF BRIDGE TO RIVER BRIDGE CAMPGROUND. Segment 6 (See map 5)

DISTANCE: -4.6 miles, easy, some moderate pitches. The tread is rocky on the southern end.
SEASON: -June through October. USE: hikers only.
CONNECTING TR. -None.
BRING MAPS: -Prospect Ranger District-Rogue River Ntl. Forest.
-USFS Rec. Opportunity Guide-Upper Rogue River Tr.

ACCESS: WOODRUFF BRIDGE, ELEV. 3000'.
From the town of Prospect, follow mileposts north on State Highway 62 to mi. 51.3 at the junction with Forest Route 68. Turn left onto 68 and travel northwest 1.8 miles to Woodruff Bridge. Trailhead signs are on the east bank of the river indicating NORTH, 3.5 miles to Natural Bridge Campground; and SOUTH, 4.6 miles to River Bridge Campground.

FEATURES: From Woodruff Bridge Picnic Area, the trail heads downstream along the east bank of the river, and after about 1.5 miles, approaches the dark-colored cliffs of Takelma Gorge. The river drops through a series of rapids and turns sharply to enter the gorge itself. The narrow channel continues for nearly 1.25 miles. The tread on this section of the trail is quite rocky and the grades become steeper.

Below Takelma Gorge, the trail goes past the Upper Rogue Baptist Church Camp, and then continues 1.4 miles to River Bridge Campground on Road 6210. (Excerpts USFS Recreation Opportunity Guide)

THIS IS ONE OF 7 SEGMENTS OF THE 48 MILE UPPER ROGUE RIVER TRAIL.

ACCESS TO RIVER BRIDGE CAMPGROUND, see next page.

UPPER ROGUE RIVER TRAIL #1034-RIVER BRIDGE CAMPGROUND TO PROSPECT
Segment 7 (See map 5)

DISTANCE: -6.5 miles, easy. USE: hikers only.
SEASON: -June through October.
CONNECTING TR: -None.
BRING MAPS: -Prospect Ranger District-Rogue River Ntl. Forest.
-USFS Rec. Opportunity Guide-Upper Rogue River Tr.

ACCESS: RIVER BRIDGE CAMPGROUND, ELEV. 2800'.
From the town of Prospect, follow mileposts north on State Highway 62 to mile 49.2 at the junction with Forest Road 6210. Turn left and continue 1 mile to the trail crossing at the near (east) end of the bridge. Trail signs are on the east bank of the river and indicate 4.6 miles north to Woodruff Bridge, and 6.5 miles south to Prospect.

PROSPECT TRAILHEAD, southern terminus of the trail, ELEV. 2598'.
On State Hwy. 62, travel to the northern edge of Prospect,0.1 mi. north of milepost 45. Turn left (west) onto the narrow dirt access road leading 1/2 mile to a picnic area and a power company reservoir. Follow the road leading north along the east bank of the river to the Upper Rogue River Trailhead. River Bridge Campground is 6.5 miles north.

FEATURES: From River Bridge Campground, the trail continues south along the east bank of the river, crosses a sandy beach, then enters a forest of tall sugar pines. Views of the river occur where the trail nears the edge of 20 foot bluffs bordering the river channel. The last four miles of trail leaves the river, and the backwaters of the reservoir later become visible as the trail returns to the river bank. The trail joins and follows an old road to the reservoir and a picnic area near Prospect. A 1/2 mile access road connects to Hwy. 62 from the dam.

THIS IS ONE OF 7 SEGMENTS OF THE 48 MILE UPPER ROGUE RIVER TRAIL.

ROGUE GORGE TRAIL #1034A (See map 5)

TRAIL BEGINS: -Rogue Gorge Viewpoint, Highway 62. ELEV. 3363'
-Also accessed from Farewell Bend Campground.
TRAIL ENDS: -Near Natural Bridge Campground. ELEV. 3200'
DISTANCE: -3.5 miles, easy grade. USE: hiker only.
SEASON: -June through October-wildflowers through August.
CONNECTING TR. -Union Creek Trail 1035.
-Upper Rogue River Trail 1034.
BRING MAPS: -Prospect Ranger Dist.-Rogue River Ntl. Forest.

ACCESS: ROGUE GORGE VIEWPOINT, ELEV. 3363'. From Union Creek Resort, travel northeast on Highway 62, 0.3 mile to the Rogue Gorge viewpoint on the left. This viewpoint is also reached from Farewell Bend Campground. Trail 1034A runs south to Natural Bridge Campground on the east bank of the Rogue River.

NATURAL BRIDGE CAMPGROUND, ELEV. 3200'. From the town of Prospect, follow mileposts north on State Hwy. 62 to mile 54.8 at the junction with Forest Road 300. Turn left onto 300 and go 0.5 mi. to the campground. Trail 1034A runs north along the east bank of the Rogue River.

FEATURES: From the Rogue Gorge Viewpoint, the trail reaches Union Creek Campground in 0.5 mile. 1.5 miles further, a footbridge crosses to the west bank to join the Upper Rogue River Trail 1034. Continuing south on the east bank of the river leads 1/4 mile to Natural Bridge Campground.

The views of the Rogue River as it winds its way through the narrow channel of basalt lava, are very impressive. Autumnal color may be enjoyed from mid-September through mid-October.

UNION CREEK TRAIL #1035. (See maps 5 and 6)

TRAIL BEGINS: -Union Creek Campground. ELEV. 3240'
TRAIL ENDS: -Forest Road 6200/610. ELEV. 3730'
Some maps and signs may show this as Road 700.
-4.4 miles, easy. USE: hiker/fishermen/camping.
SEASON: -June through October.
CONNECTING TR. -Rogue Gorge Trail 1034A.
BRING MAPS: -Prospect Ranger District-Rogue River Ntl. Forest.
-USFS Rec. Opportunity Guide -Union Creek Trail.

ACCESS: FROM UNION CREEK CAMPGROUND: At the confluence of Union Creek and the Rogue River, cross a footbridge over Union Creek and follow the trail east to a point just south of the Union Creek Resort on State Hwy. 62.

The trail crosses Hwy. 62, just south of the resort and then continues east along the north bank of the creek with a good view of Union Falls in about 3 miles. The upper trailhead is 1 mile further.

By road, the UPPER TRAILHEAD is reached by travelling 1.3 miles northeast of Union Creek Resort to the junction of State Highways 230 and 62. Continue northeast on 62, 2 miles to the junction of Forest Road 6200/600. (Some maps/signs may show the upper trailhead on Forest Road 700.) Turn right onto Road 600 and continue 0.2 mi. to the junction with Forest Road 6200/610. Turn left onto 610 and go 0.1 mi. to the trailhead on the right.

HISTORY: "UNION CREEK, PEAK: Named in 1862 (the Civil War had begun the year before) by 'patriotic' prospectors Chauncy Nye and Hiram G. Abbott. (Pro-confederate feelings, however, ran high among a large segment of the Jackson County population.)" (USFS quote)

SPHAGNUM BOG TRAIL #1038. (See map 2)

TRAIL BEGINS: -Forest Road 6535 near milepost 5. ELEV. 5360'
TRAIL ENDS: -West Boundary Crater Lake Ntl. Park. ELEV. 5572'
DISTANCE: -1.1 mile. Easy grades. USE: hiker/horse.
SEASON: -Usually snow-free July through September.
CONNECTING TR: -Crater Springs Trail, Crater Lake Ntl. Park.
BRING MAPS: -USFS Prospect Ranger Dist. Rogue River Ntl.Forest.
-CRATER LAKE map/brochure-National Park Service.
-USGS Crater Lake West, 7.5' series, 1985.

ACCESS: Just north of Union Creek Resort from the junction with State Highways 62 and 230, follow Hwy. 230 to milepost 6 at the junction with Forest Road 6530. Turn RIGHT onto Road 6530 and go 1.3 miles to the second junction with loop Road 6535. Follow Road 6535, 5.5 miles (just beyond milepost 5) to the trailhead on the left. This trailhead was constructed in 1995 to provide adequate parking and turn-around space for stock trailers and other vehicles.

The trail begins its climb to a road gate at the upper end of Rd. 6535/660. The trail continues beyond the gate,1/2 mi. to the West Boundary of Crater Lake Park, at the junction with Crater Springs Trail. A sign reads; Sphagnum Bog 1.7 mi., PCT 4.7 mi., Boundary Springs 7.9 mi.

Crater Springs Trail continues 1.2 mi. to the junction with Oasis Butte Trail on the left, that leads 6.7 miles to Boundary Springs. Keep right at the above junction and follow Crater Springs Trail, 0.5 mile south to Crater Springs, where a short spur leads south to unmarked routes to SPHAGNUM BOG. Crater Springs Trail continues east from this spur to Pacific Crest Trail.

FEATURES: It is possible to continue south along unmarked routes to Sphagnum Bog, thru wet meadows filled with bog dwelling plants. Care should be taken not to trample the fragile plant life or to accidently step into deep, cold water pools. Water is available at Crater Springs. Camping is not allowed within a 0.5 mile radius of Sphagnum Bog. SEE BEGINNING OF CHAPTER 11 FOR CRATER LAKE PARK BACKCOUNTRY USE REGULATIONS.

MINNEHAHA TRAIL #1039. (See map 2)

TRAIL BEGINS: -Forest Road 6530/800. ELEV. 3825'
TRAIL ENDS: -Soda Springs. ELEV. 4400'
DISTANCE: -3.1 miles,easy. USE hiker,horse,mtn.& motorbikes.
SEASON: -Usually snow-free June through October.
BRING MAPS: -Prospect Ranger Dist. -Rogue River Ntl. Forest.

ACCESS: From the Union Creek Resort, travel northeast on Crater Lake Hwy. 62, 1.3 miles to the junction with State Hwy. 230. Follow mileposts on 230, 12.1 miles to the junction with Forest Road 6530. Turn right onto 6530 and go 1.0 mile to Road 800. Turn right onto Road 800 and go 0.1 mi. to the Minnehaha Trailhead on the left, near the old Minnehaha Camp.

FEATURES: The route begins as an old road that diminishes to a trail, then follows Minnehaha Creek to Soda Springs. Along the way, the trail passes at the edge of a large, grassy meadow from where there are good views of Minnehaha Creek with its beautiful waterfalls.

HISTORY: "MINNEHAHA CREEK, CAMP: The date of this name is unknown; probably post-1900. The term is an Indian name from the eastern United States, made famous in Longfellow's poem 'Song of Hiawatha'." (USFS quote)

SHERWOOD CREEK TRAIL #1041. (See map 2)

TRAIL BEGINS:	-State Hwy. 230 near milepost 15.	ELEV. 4634'
TRAIL ENDS:	-Three Lakes Camp, Road 3703.	ELEV. 6000'
DISTANCE:	-4.5 miles, MORE DIFFICULT, stream crossings.	
SEASON:	-June thru Oct. Snow often till Aug. on Road 3703.	
USE:	Hiker/horse.	
CONNECTING TR.	-Beaver Meadows Trail (Abandoned)	
BRING MAPS:	-USFS Rec. Opportunity Guide-Sherwood Creek Trail. -Prospect Ranger District-Rogue River Ntl. Forest.	

ACCESS: LOWER END OF TRAIL: Just north of the Union Creek Resort, at the junction of State Highways 62 and 230, go northeast on Hwy. 230, 0.2 mile beyond milepost 15. Turn left to a parking area and trailhead.

UPPER END OF TRAIL: Continue east on Hwy. 230 following mileposts to mile 20.6 at the junction with Three Lakes Road 3703. Turn left onto 3703 and go about 5.7 miles to the junction with Forest Road 3703/400 at the far (west) end of Three Lakes Camp. Turn left onto 3703/400 for 0.2 mile to the parking area at the west end of the lake. Follow blazes along an old road,0.8 mile to the beginning of the trail.

FEATURES: FROM THE LOWER TRAILHEAD: The trail rises through a series of small meadows and high elevation forests. Stream crossings can be difficult even in late summer. In a few places the trail may be hard to follow when it passes thru meadows and stream crossings, as cattle trails can look like the main trail. Watch carefully for blazes and trail signs and note your route for the return trip. TRAIL LOG IS AS FOLLOWS:

.25 mile: Junction with ABANDONED Beaver Meadows loop trail,keep left.

1.25 mile: Junction with upper end of the Beaver Meadows Trail. Keep left.

1.5 mile SHERWOOD MEADOW: CAUTION:About half way along the west edge of the meadow, look for trail signs on trees.What looks like the continuation of the trail is an informal trail to a forest road. FROM SIGNS,THE TRAIL LEADS AT RIGHT ANGLES ACROSS THE MEADOW. LOOK FOR A ROCK DUCK AT THE FAR END OF THE MEADOW.The trail continues about 3 miles to Three Lakes Camp.

MUIR CREEK TRAIL #1042. (See map 2)

TRAIL BEGINS:	-State Hwy. 230 near milepost 10.	ELEV. 3825'
TRAIL ENDS:	-Buck Canyon Trail 1046.	ELEV. 4100'
DISTANCE:	-3.9 miles, easy. USE: hiker/horse.	
SEASON:	-June through October.	
CONNECTING TR.	-Buck Canyon Trail 1046.	
BRING MAPS:	-Prospect Ranger Dist. -Rogue River Ntl. Forest. -USFS Rec. Opportunity Guide-Muir Creek Trail.	

ACCESS: Just north of the Union Creek Resort, at the intersection of State Highways 62 and 230, follow mileposts on 230, 10.4 miles just before crossing the bridge at Muir Creek. Muir Creek Trailhead is on the left (west) side of the road at the site of a horse unloading ramp and hitching rail.

FEATURES: Muir Creek Trail winds along the west bank of the creek, passing Muir Creek Falls in about 2.5 miles, and ends at Buck Canyon Trail 1046. Turning RIGHT onto Trail 1046 leads 0.5 mile to Forest Road 6560. This is a popular trail for fishermen.

I Think We Should Have Checked The Map Sooner.

BUCK CANYON TRAILS

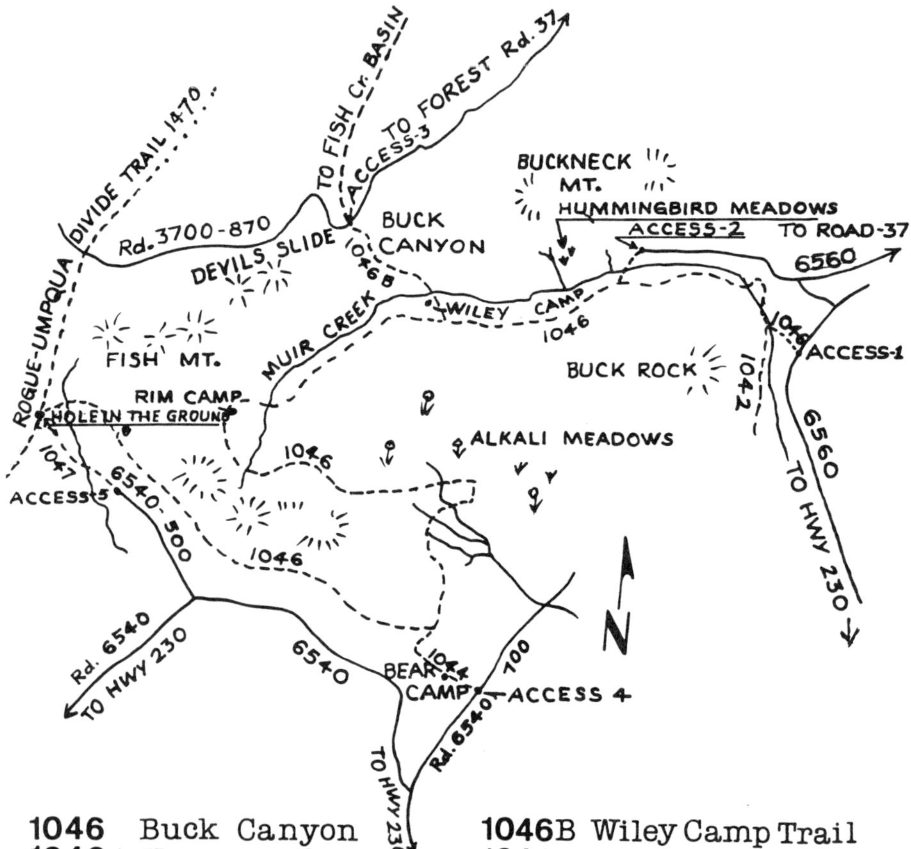

1046 Buck Canyon
1046A Hummingbird Meadows trail.
1047 Hole In The Ground Trail.
1046B Wiley Camp Trail
1044 Meadow Creek Tr.

BUCK CANYON TRAIL #1046 (See map 2)

TRAIL BEGINS: -Forest Road 6560. ELEV. 4160'
TRAIL ENDS: -Hole In The Ground Camp. ELEV. 5300'
DISTANCE: -10.7 mi. plus 3 miles of access trails. High-point ELEV. about 6000 feet. USE: hiker/horse.
-Usually snow-free June through October.
CONNECTING TR. -Muir Creek Trail 1042.
-Hummingbird Meadows Trail 1046A. (Access #2)
-Wiley Camp Trail 1046B. (Access #3)
-Meadow Creek Trail 1044. (Access #4)
-Hole In The Ground Trail 1047. (Access #5)
BRING MAPS: -Prospect Ranger Dist. -Rogue River Ntl. Forest.
-USFS Rec. Opportunity Guide-Buck Canyon Trail.

ACCESS #1 BUCK CANYON TRAILHEAD, ELEV. 4160'. MORE DIFFICULT.
From the junction of Highways 62 and 230 just north of Union Cr. Resort,follow mileposts northeast on Highway 230 to mile 12.1, at the junction with Road 6560 on the left. Follow Road 6560,one mi. and turn left onto Road 6560-190. Follow this road 0.5 mi. to the trailhead. Distance: 0.25 mi. to Muir Creek Trail and 10.5 mi. to Hole-In-The-Ground.

ACCESS #2 HUMMINGBIRD MEADOWS TRAIL 1046A, ELEV. 4000'. EASIEST.
Continue 0.8 mi. north on Road 6560 to the junction with Forest Road 6560/400 on the left. Follow Road 400 1.2 mi. to the trail-head at the end of the road. A sign indicates: "Hershberger Mtn. 13 miles". This 1/2 mile access trail passes through Hummingbird Meadows and then fords Muir Creek. There is no bridge, the crossing may be difficult early in the season. The junction with the Buck Canyon Trail is just beyond. ELEV. about 4400'.

Good hikers always leave a trail cleaner than they find it.

BUCK CANYON TRAIL #1046, page 2. (See map 2)

ACCESS #3 WILEY CAMP TRAIL 1046B, ELEV. 5200'. Near milepost 12 on State Hwy. 230 at the junction with Forest Road 6560, turn and travel northwest on Road 6560, 4 miles to the Rogue-Umpqua Divide where the road number changes to Forest Route 37. Continue on 37 for 1/2 mile to Forest Road 3700/800. Turn left and follow Road 800, 2.3 mi. to the junction with Forest Road 3700/870. Turn left and follow 870, 2.5 mi. to the trailhead on the left side of the road. The 1 mile Wiley Camp Trail descends from the Rogue-Umpqua Divide,and crosses Muir Creek. Wiley Camp is located at the southeast side of the creek. This trail, rated DIFFICULT, joins Buck Canyon Trail at appx. ELEV. 4800'.

ACCESS #4 MEADOW CREEK TRAIL 1044, ELEV. 4900'. Follow mileposts on State Highway 230 to mile 9.2 at the second junction with loop Road 6540. Turn left onto 6540 and go 3 miles to the junction of Road 6540/700. Turn right onto 700 and go about 1.0 mi. WATCHING CAREFULLY ON THE LEFT for the trailhead sign. This steep 1 mile trail passes Bear Camp in about 0.5 mi. through a series of meadows before joining the Buck Canyon Trail.ELEV. about 5360'. Rated DIFFICULT.

ACCESS #5 HOLE-IN-THE-GROUND TRAIL 1047, ELEV. 5200'. From State Highway 230, near milepost 9 (mile 9.2), at the northern turnoff for loop Road 6540, turn left on Road 6540 and continue 4.5 miles (at milepost 6) to the junction with Forest Road 6540/500. Turn right onto Road 500, and continue 1.5 mi. to the trailhead at the end of the road. The trail leads 0.5 mi. across Log Cr. and joins Buck Canyon Trail and Rogue Umpqua Divide Trail 1470 at the edge of a small meadow. Hole in the Ground Camp is east of the meadow just inside the trees. ELEV. about 5600'. Rated DIFFICULT.

BUCK CANYON TRAIL #1046, page 3. (See map 2)

FEATURES: The views along the way, north to south direction, include Buckneck Mtn., the knob of Devil's Slide, the Rogue-Umpqua Divide, the Foster Creek and Rogue River drainages, Mt. McLoughlin, Mt. Shasta, Buck Canyon Rim, Fish Mountain, Mt. Thielsen, the Crater Lake Rim and Union Peak. In early June when wildflowers are at their best, numerous hummingbirds feed on red horsemint at Hummingbird Meadow.

The Buck Canyon Trail ends at Hole In The Ground, a marshy meadow that at one time was a shallow, glacial lake at the head of Foster Creek. While passing through the high elevation meadows and glacial valleys, there is sometimes confusion between recreation trails and stock trails, created by summer grazing. Watch carefully for tree blazes and signs.

Most of the Buck Canyon Trail System lies within the Rogue-Umpqua Divide Wilderness Area. It is advised to obtain maps and Recreation Opportunity Guides from the Prospect, or Tiller Ranger Stations, before attempting any of these trails. "HORSE/PACK SADDLE users are encouraged to enter via ACCESS # 1, the main Buck Canyon Trailhead." (Quote: USFS Recreation Opportunity Guide)

The Rogue-Umpqua Divide Wilderness was created by the Oregon Wilderness Act of 1984. Wilderness regulations include:

PACK OUT ALL LITTER, especially foil packaging that doesn't burn.
BURY HUMAN WASTE 6 to 8 inches deep 200' or more from open water.
CAMPFIRES only in safe spots, keep small. Best to carry stoves.
CAMP IN TENT SITES, no drainage ditches, leave area as found.
MOTORIZED and MECHANICAL EQUIPMENT- prohibited in wilderness.

NATIONAL CREEK FALLS TRAIL #1053. (See map 2)

TRAIL BEGINS: -Forest Road 6530/300. ELEV. 4000'
TRAIL ENDS: -National Creek Falls. ELEV. 3760'
DISTANCE: -0.4 mile, moderate, USE: hiker only.
SEASON: -June through October.
BRING MAPS: -Prospect Ranger Dist.-Rogue River Ntl. Forest.
-USFS Rec. Opportunity Guide-National Creek Falls.

ACCESS: Just north of the Union Creek Resort, at the intersection of State Highways 62 and 230, follow mileposts on 230 to milepost 6, at the junction with Forest Road 6530. Turn right onto Road 6530 and go about 4 mi. to the junction with Road 6530/300. Turn right onto Road 300 and proceed to the National Creek Falls parking lot and trailhead.

FEATURES: This short trail drops down through a mixed conifer forest to the base of the falls. National Creek is fed by springs in Crater Lake National Park.

HISTORY: "NATIONAL CREEK, FALLS, CAMP: The date of this name is unknown; it may have been given to the creek by members of the Forest Service road building crew in 1910." (USFS quote)

BOUNDARY SPRINGS TRAIL #1057. (See map 2)

TRAIL BEGINS: -Near Crater Rim Viewpoint, Hwy. 230. ELEV. 4900'
TRAIL ENDS: -Boundary Springs, Crater Lake Park. ELEV. 5060'
DISTANCE: -About 2 miles, easy grade. USE: hiker only.
SEASON: -Usually snow-free June to October.
CONNECTING TR: -Upper Rogue Trail 1034.
BRING MAPS: -Prospect Ranger Dist. -Rogue River Ntl. Forest.
-USFS Rec. Opportunity Guide-Boundary Springs Tr.

ACCESS: Just north of Union Creek Resort, at the junction with State Highways 62 and 230, follow the mileposts northeast on 230, 18.6 miles to Crater Rim Viewpoint on the right.

Starting from the parking area, take the Upper Rogue River Trail 0.6 mi. to the junction with the Boundary Springs Trail. Turn to the left (south) onto the Boundary Springs Trail and hike about 2 miles to Boundary Springs. Along the way, the trail comes out to Lake West Road and crosses the Rogue River at a bridge. The trail resumes south immediately after crossing the bridge.

FEATURES: This trail begins a 7.2 mile link with the PCNST (Pacific Crest Trail). Hikers are advised to use special care to protect this sensitive environment....do not camp here and do not walk on the moss. Boundary Springs has been added to Crater Lake National Park, where DOGS NOT ALLOWED.

"The springs form the origin of the Upper Rogue River; named subsequent to 1905 because of their location at the boundary between Crater Lake National Park and Rogue River National Forest."
(USFS quote)

VARMINT CAMP TRAIL #1070. (See map 5 and 6)

TRAIL BEGINS: -Milepost 10 Forest Road 6205. ELEV. 3600'
TRAIL ENDS: -Forest Road 830. ELEV. 5400'
DISTANCE: -3.1 miles, moderate grades. USE: hiker/horse/mtn. bike/motorbike. Seasonal motorized closure March 1 to June 30.
SEASON: -June through October.
BRING MAPS: -USFS Prospect Ranger District, Rogue River N.F.
-USFS Recreation Opportunity Guide (this trail).

ACCESS: From the town of Prospect, Oregon, drive east on County Route 992 leading toward Butte Falls, 1.1 mile to the junction with Red Blanket Road. Follow Red Blanket Road 0.3 mile to Forest Road 6205. Turn left onto Road 6205 and continue 10.5 mi. to Varmint Camp Trailhead on the left. There is parking for 1 or 2 vehicles across the road from the trailhead. A Sign at milepost 4 of Road 6205 indicates the road is closed beyond that point December 1 to April 15.

FEATURES. From Road 6205 Trailhead, the trail climbs gradually for about 1 mi.,crosses Varmint Creek then climbs steeply for 1.5 miles through a dense conifer forest. The trail crosses a mountain meadow lined with wild onion. Look for wildflowers in mid-summer.

Caution should be exercised if using a motorcycle on this trail. The tread is narrow and rocky in places. The trail ends on Forest Road #830.

HISTORY: "Varmint Creek,Camp: A turn-of-the-century hunters' and sheepherders' camp,probably named after the presence of coyotes or other varmints." (USFS quote)

COLD SPRINGS TRAIL #1073. (See map 6)

TRAIL BEGINS:	-Forest Road 6205/100.	ELEV. 6200'
TRAIL ENDS:	-Cold Springs.	ELEV. 5940'
DISTANCE:	-2.6 miles, moderate.	
SEASON:	-May through October.	
USE:	-Hiker, horse, mountain bike, motor bike. Seasonal motorized closure March 1 to June 30.	
BRING MAPS:	-Prospect Ranger Dist.-Rogue River Ntl. Forest. -USFS Rec. Opportunity Guide-Cold Spr. Tr. 1073.	

ACCESS: From Prospect, travel east on County Route 992 leading toward Butte Falls, and go 1.1 mile to the junction with Red Blanket Road. Follow Red Blanket Road 0.3 mile to Road 6205. Turn left onto Road 6205 and go 4.0 miles to the junction with Road 6205/100. Turn left onto Road 6205/100 and go about 7 miles to the trailhead on the right. Parking space is provided directly across the road.

FEATURES: The trail begins its journey,and after about 1.0 mile reaches "Paul Bunyan's Grave" on the north side of the trail. Look for a hill with loose rocks, and a nearby metallic Forest Service sign tacked to a tree. The trail later crosses a road, and resumes directly beyond, before ending at the springs. CARRY WATER, as the springs are muddied and may be dried up.

The route is sometimes hard to follow when passing through meadows. Rock Cairns, tree blazes, and diamond-shaped markers can be followed fairly easily. Elk may be seen, or their sounds may be heard in the thickets below the trail. There is an abundance of wildflowers in season.

GEYSER SPRINGS TRAIL #1087. (See map 11)

TRAIL BEGINS:	-Forest Road 3795/300.	ELEV. 4080'
TRAIL ENDS:	-Middle Fork of the Rogue River.	ELEV. 3240'
DISTANCE:	-1.1 mile, difficult. USE: hikers only.	
SEASON:	-Summer months.	
BRING MAPS:	-Prospect Ranger Dist.-Rogue River Ntl. Forest. -USFS Rec. Opportunity Guide-Geyser Spr. Trail.	

ACCESS: From the town of Prospect, Oregon, drive east on County Road 992 leading toward Butte Falls, for 2.5 miles to the junction with Forest Route 37. Turn left onto 37 and go 2.8 miles to the junction with Forest Road 3795. Continue on 3795, 2.7 miles to Forest Road 3795/300. Follow Road 300, 1.2 miles to the trailhead on the right. Road 300 is gated from Nov. 1 to June 15.

FEATURES: After the first 1/3 mile, Geyser Springs can be seen about 25 feet below the trail. There is no established trail leading to the springs from this point, so care must be taken to get there and back. The main trail continues to the Middle Fork of the Rogue River. This is a steep trail dropping about 800 feet from the road to the river. Native rainbow and brook trout are popular with fishermen.

Geyser Springs is one of the headwater springs that feed the Middle Fork of the Rogue River.

HISTORY: The Geyser Springs Trail was once part of an old Forest Service trail system and telephone line that ran from the Imnaha Guard Station, down the Middle Fork Canyon, up to Bessie Rock Guard Station, and ended at Bessie Rock Lookout. Used for fire watch communications in the 1920's, the telephone line and much of the trail were abandoned in the 1960's. (USFS information)

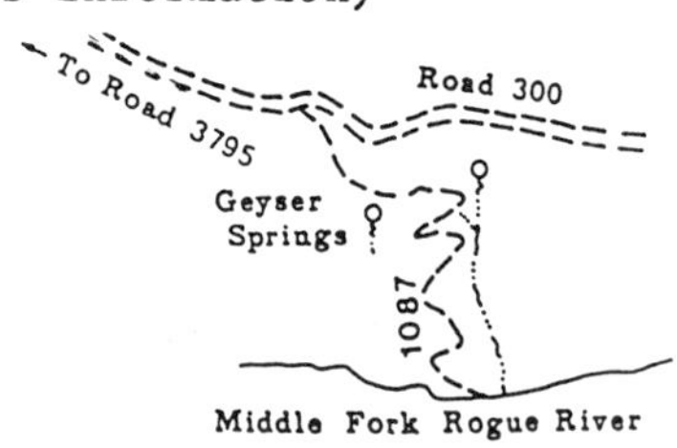

GOLDEN STAIRS TRAIL #1092 (See map 5)

TRAIL BEGINS:	-Near Forest Road 68/550.	ELEV. 3750'
TRAIL ENDS:	-Rogue-Umpqua Divide Trail 1470.	ELEV. 5350'
DISTANCE:	-4.3 mi., moderately steep, limited maintenance.	
SEASON:	-June through Oct. USE: hiker/horse/motorcycle.	
CONNECTING TR.	-Rogue-Umpqua Divide Trail 1470.	
BRING MAPS:	-Prospect Ranger Dist.-Rogue River Ntl. Forest. -USFS Rec. Opportunity Guide-Golden Stairs Trail.	

ACCESS: LOWER TRAILHEAD: From the Prospect Ranger Station (north end of Prospect Oregon), go north on State Hwy. 62, 6 miles (just beyond milepost 51), to the junction with Forest Route 68. Turn left onto 68 and follow mileposts to mile 5 at the junction with Forest Road 550. Turn right onto 550 and continue one mile to an unsigned junction. Keep left and go 2 miles, passing the junction with Road 557, and continue 0.1 mi. further to the signed trailhead on the right.

UPPER TRAILHEAD: From the junction of State Hwy. 62 and Forest Route 68, turn left and continue on 68, 2.5 miles to the junction with Forest Road 6510. Keep right onto 6510 and travel 2.0 miles to the junction with Forest Road 6510/500. Turn left onto Road 500 and travel about 4.0 miles to the junction with Roads 700 and 770. Continue straight ahead onto Rd.700, 1.1 mi. to Yellowjacket Camp. The Rogue Umpqua Divide Trail passes by this point. Follow this trail 1.0 mile west to the upper end of Golden Stairs Trail.

FEATURES: The lower end of the trail begins through stands of fir before continuing along the southern, exposed ridge of Falcon Butte. Along the way, there are good views of the Rogue River, Elk Creek and Woodruff Creek drainages. Further on toward the Rogue-Umpqua Divide, the face of Elephant Head and the slopes of Abbott Butte will be seen. The upper end of the trail junctions with the Rogue-Umpqua Divide Trail about 1.0 mile west of Forest Road 6510/700. NO WATER

HISTORY: Golden Stairs Trail was "named in part from the Abbott brothers alleged gold mine in the area." (USFS quote)

ROGUE-UMPQUA DIVIDE TRAIL #1470. (See maps 5,1B and 2)

TRAIL BEGINS:-Junction of Forest Routes 68 and 30 at Rogue-Umpqua Divide, at milepost 30 on Route 68.
TRAIL ENDS: -Three Lakes Camp, Forest Road 3703.
DISTANCE: -31.4 miles USE: hiker/horse. SEASON: summer/fall.
BRING MAPS: -USFS Rogue-Umpqua Divide, Boulder Creek and Mt. Thielsen Wildernesses.
-USFS Tiller, Diamond Lake and Prospect Ranger Districts-Umpqua and Rogue River National Forests.

FEATURES: This National Recreation Trail is the primary route through the Rogue-Umpqua Divide Wilderness. The trail offers exceptional views both east and west as it weaves across the crest of the divide. To the west, lies the irregular and deeply dissected terrain of the Umpqua Drainage;while to the east the traveler sees the broad, open Rogue Basin, with the peaks of the high Cascades rising above. In addition to the fine vistas,the divide features a spectacular display of wildflowers in its many meadows from mid-June until mid-August.

The Divide Trail begins from the southern end of the wilderness. In places, the trail parallels the old CCC road to Abbott Butte. Due to a steep and narrow section of trail, horse users are advised to take the old road at one point and loop back into the trail, avoiding a potential hazard.

The trail passes below Abbott Butte Lookout and descends to a small pond below a rock cliff called Elephant Head. The old lookout is still standing, but it is unsafe to climb up to the building.

Traveling east, the trail is joined by Golden Stairs Trail #1092, three miles beyond Abbott Butte. This steep trail leads to the Rogue River National Forest Road #6800-550. One mile past this junction, the trail enters Yellowjacket Camp. From here,the trail follows an old skid road for 1/2 mile. A live creek crosses the trail just below the road. The trail then climbs the south slope of Anderson Mountain and opens to a gigantic sub-alpine meadow. Here,Sandstone trail #1436 joins the divide trail from the Umpqua side. From the Rogue side of the divide,Anderson Camp Trail #1075 reaches the ridgetop and joins the divide trail.

From Anderson Mountain, the Divide Trail travels northerly on the crest of a rocky ridge, offering fine views of Crater Lake Rim and Mt. McLoughlin to the east; Highrock Mountain to the west and Abbott Butte to the southwest. Pup Prairie Trail #1434 intersects the Divide Trail just before the trail meets Road 6515-530 at its junction with Road 6515. Here, a spring can be found in the meadow south of this junction. Road 6515-530 becomes the route for the Divide Trail for about 1.5 miles to the junction of Acker Divide Trail #1437. At this intersection the road leads another 1/2 mile to Hershberger Lookout. The Divide Trail however, continues north at this junction, along the route known as the Log Pile Trail. Fish Lake Trail #1570 intersects the Rogue-Umpqua Divide Trail 3/4 mile down this section of trail.

About 1/4 mile further, the Rocky Rim Trail #1572 intersects to the west. The Divide Trail then passes through a saddle onto the eastern face of Weaver Mountain where vistas open to the north and east. The trail then descends to the edge of an ancient shallow glacial lake, now a marshy meadow called Hole-in-the-ground. After passing along the southeast edge of the meadow, the trail forks. The Divide Trail continues on the northerly fork, crossing the meadow to Hole-in the Ground Camp. Here, Buck Canyon Trail #1046 intersects and the Divide Trail heads north for a strenuous one mile climb to Road #3700-870.

This road, at the end of Fish Creek Valley serves as a connecting route between segments of the Divide Trail. To return to the Rogue-Umpqua Divide Trail, follow this road for about 1 mile to Happy Camp. 1/10 of a mile further down the road, the trail continues off to the left of the road. Take this trail to the intersection with the Whitehorse Meadow Trail #1477, and proceed northeast on this trail down the valley. About 3/4 of a mile down the valley, the Whitehorse Meadow Trail turns right and climbs out of the valley. The Divide Trail continues down the valley. This segment of trail passes the Fish Creek Shelter before it climbs out of the valley and crosses Road #3700-870.

The Divide Trail continues up the ridge with some steep stretches and then down the east slope, across Forest Route #37, and on to Buck Camp. Clear Camp lies about 1 mile further down the trail, and the Rogue-Umpqua Divide Trail terminates at THREE LAKES CAMP, on Forest Road #3703. (From Tiller Ranger Dist. Recreation Guide)

ACCESS TO ROGUE-UMPQUA DIVIDE TRAIL.

SOUTHERN END OF ROGUE-UMPQUA DIVIDE TRAIL.-Abbott Butte Trailhead.

From the town of Prospect, go north on Hwy. 62 just beyond milepost 51 at the junction with Forest Route 68. Turn left onto 68 and go 13 miles to the Rogue-Umpqua Divide at the junction with Forest Route 30. The trailhead is on the right.

VIA GOLDEN STAIRS TRAIL #1092.

North of Prospect on Hwy. 62, just beyond milepost 51, turn left onto Forest Route 68 and follow mileposts to mile 5 at the junction with Forest Road 550.Turn right and go 1 mi. to an(unsigned) junction. Keep left and go 2 miles, passing the junction with Rd. 557, and continue 0.1 mile further to the signed trailhead on the right. This steep trail continues 4.3 miles to the Rogue-Umpqua Divide Trail, about 1 mile west of Forest Road 6510-700.

YELLOWJACKET CAMP.

North of Prospect on Hwy. 62, just beyond milepost 51, turn left on Forest Route 68 and go about 2.5 miles to Forest Road 6510. Turn right and follow 6510, 2 miles to Road 6510/500. Follow Road 500 about 4 miles to the junction of Roads 700 and 770. Continue straight ahead onto Road 700, 1.1 mi. to Yellowjacket Camp.

VIA ANDERSON CAMP TRAIL #1075.

North of Prospect on Hwy. 62, just beyond milepost 51, turn left onto Forest Route 68 and go about 2.5 miles to Forest Road 6510. Turn right and follow 6510, 5.8 miles to Forest Road 6515. Turn left onto 6515 and go 6.3 miles, looking carefully for the trailhead on the left. Anderson Camp Trail reaches the Rogue-Umpqua Divide Trail after 3/4 mile. To reach Anderson Mountain Summit, turn left (south) to a sign posted at a short, faint trail to the summit.

VIA HERSHBERGER ROAD.

North of Prospect on Hwy. 62, just beyond milepost 51, turn left onto Forest Route 68 and go about 2.5 miles to Forest Road 6510. Turn right and follow 6510, 5.8 miles to Forest Road 6515. Turn left onto 6515 and go 9.6 miles to the junction of Roads 525 and 530. A spring is located in the meadow south of this junction, along the east bank of Flat Creek. The trail follows along Road 530 for about 1.5 miles before continuing as a trail to points north.

-continued

ACCESS TO ROGUE-UMPQUA DIVIDE TRAIL-continued.

VIA HOLE-IN-THE-GROUND TRAIL #1047.
North of Union Creek Resort, at the junction of Hwys. 62 and 230, follow mileposts on 230 to mile 9.1 (the northern end of loop Rd. 6540). Turn left and go about 4.8 miles (at milepost 6) to the junction with Forest Road 6540/500. Turn right onto Road 500 and go 1.5 miles to the trailhead at the end of the road. ELEV. 5200' Trail 1047 travels along Log Creek and joins Rogue-Umpqua Divide Trail at the edge of a small glacial meadow. Hole-in-the-Ground Camp is east of the meadow, just inside the trees. The junction with Buck Canyon Trail #1046 appears at this camp ELEV. 5600'.

TO WHERE THE DIVIDE TRAIL CROSSES FOREST ROUTE 37.
Follow mileposts on State Highway 230 to mi. 12.1 at the junction with Forest Road 6560. Turn left onto Road 6560 and go 4 miles to the Rogue-Umpqua Divide, where the route number becomes Route 37. Follow Route 37, 0.4 miles further and look carefully for a sign far to the left, indicating the Divide Trail leading southwest.On the right side of Route 37,look just beyond for a road track from where the Divide Trail leads northeast to Three Lakes Camp.

ALONG FISH CREEK VALLEY ROAD 870.
Continue 0.1 mi. further on Route 37 to the junction with Forest Road 800. Turn left onto Road 800 and go 3 miles to Fish Creek Valley Road 870. Turn left onto Road 870 and go 0.9 mile to where the Divide Trail crosses left from Road 37 and right toward the Fish Creek Shelter.

Fish Creek Valley Road continues about 3 miles to where the Divide Trail merges from the right (from Fish Creek Valley) to follow Road 870, about 1.1 mi. to its end. A sign reads: "Hole-in-the-ground 1 mile, Hershberger Lookout 5 miles, Abbott Butte 19 miles".

FROM THREE LAKES ROAD 3703.
North of Union Creek Resort, follow mileposts on Hwy. 230 to mile 20.6 Turn left onto Three Lakes Road 3703 and go 5.7 mi. to the junction of Road 3703/400. Turn left on Road 400 and go 0.2 mile to a parking area at the west end of the lake. Follow blazes on an old road, 0.8 mi. to the beginning of the trail.

The Rogue-Umpqua-Divide Trail 1470 lies within the Rogue-Umpqua Divide Wilderness, created by the Oregon Wilderness Act of 1984.

WILDERNESS REGULATIONS INCLUDE:

-PACK OUT ALL LITTER, especially foil packaging that doesn't burn.

-BURY HUMAN WASTE 6 to 8 inches deep, 200 feet or more from open water.

-CAMPFIRES only in safe spots, keep small. It is best to carry stoves.

-CAMPING: Pitch your tent so no drainage ditch is required. Replace rocks and other materials removed from sleeping areas.

-MOTORIZED and MECHANICAL equipment, including bicycles, are prohibited in the wilderness.

(EXCERPTS: "New Wilderness on the Umpqua National Forest" brochure)

As You Hike Under The Forest Canopy These Guys Will dispute Your Passage.

ROCKY RIM TRAIL #1572. (See map 1B)

TRAIL BEGINS: -UPPER TRAILHEAD: Rogue Umpqua Divide Trail 1470, 1 mile north of Hershberger Mtn. ELEV. 5680'

TRAIL ENDS: -LOWER TRAILHEAD: Beaver Swamp Trailhead, Umpqua Forest Road 2840/400 near Fish Lake. ELEV. 4000'

DISTANCE: -6.8 miles, moderate. USE: hiker/horse.

SEASON: -Upper end snow-free July to October.

CONNECTING TR.: -Rogue-Umpqua Divide Trail 1470.
-Rocky Ridge Trail 1571, (partially abandoned).

BRING MAPS: -Tiller Ranger District-Umpqua National Forest.
-USFS -Rogue Umpqua Divide, Boulder Creek and Mt. Thielsen Wildernesses.
-USFS Recreation Opportunity Guide Rocky Rim Tr.

ACCESS: -UPPER END: North of Prospect on Hwy. 62 just beyond milepost 51, turn left onto Forest Route 68 and go about 2.5 miles to Forest Road 6510. Turn right and follow 6510, 5.8 miles to Forest Road 6515. Turn left onto 6515 and go 9.6 miles to the junction of Roads 525, 530 and the Rogue-Umpqua Divide Trail 1470.A spring is located in the meadow south of this junction along the east bank of Flat Creek. Follow Road 530 about 1.5 miles to where the Divide Trail continues. Take the Divide Trail 1 mile north to the beginning of Rocky Rim Trail.

FEATURES: This description uses only the 4 mile portion of Rocky Rim Trail from its upper end near Hershberger Mountain to the junction with the Rocky Ridge Trail and return, a very attractive day hike. From the Rogue-Umpqua Divide Trail, Rocky Rim Trail travels northwest through timber and subalpine meadows before meeting the narrow backbone of Rocky Ridge. The trail features a birdseye view of Fish Lake, the Castle Creek drainage, and of the high Cascade Mountains. Wildflowers usually are in great numbers, well into the summer months.

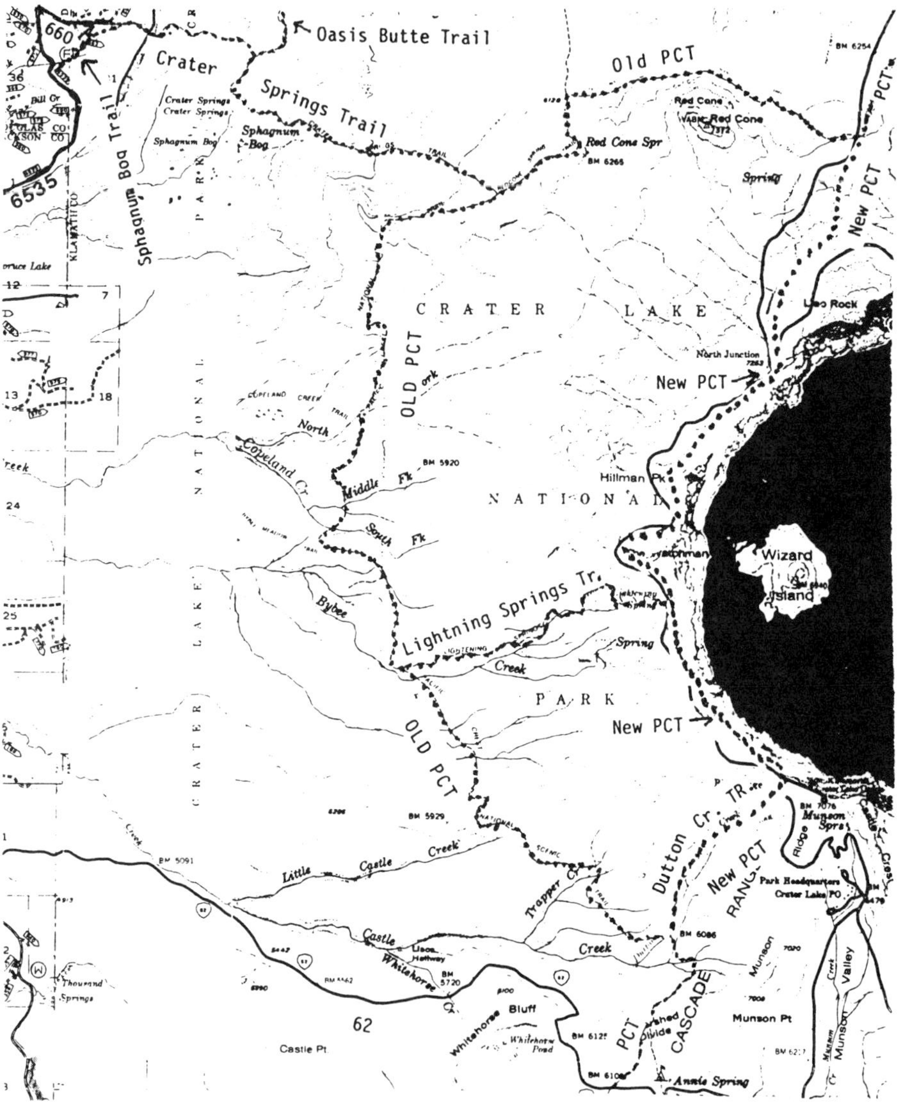
Oasis Butte Trail
Crater Springs Trail
Sphagnum Bog Trail
Old PCT
New PCT
Red Cone
Red Cone Spr
Spring
660
6535
Crater Springs
Sphagnum Bog
CRATER LAKE NATIONAL PARK
OLD PCT
Leo Rock
North Junction
Copeland Cr
North
Middle Fk
South Fk
Hillman Pk
Watchman
Wizard Island
Lightning Springs Tr.
Bybee
Creek
Spring
Dutton Cr. TR.
Munson Spr
Ridge
Park Headquarters
Crater Lake PO
Little Castle Creek
Castle Creek
Trapper Cr
Whitehorse Cr
Whitehorse Bluff
Castle Pt.
62
CASCADE
PCT
Munson Pt
Annie Spring
Munson Valley
Thousand Springs
BM 5920
BM 5929
BM 5091
BM 6086
BM 5720
BM 6125
BM 6106

CRATER LAKE NATIONAL PARK BACKCOUNTRY USE REGULATIONS.

BACKCOUNTRY USE PERMITS ARE REQUIRED FOR ALL OVERNIGHT STAYS. The only exception is for overnight hikers who enter on the Pacific Crest Trail and exit the PCT at the opposite boundary. Free permits are available at entrance stations, information and visitor centers, from park rangers (after hours) or by mail. OTHER REGS:

1. CAMPING AND CAMPFIRES Open campfires allowed where not specifically prohibited.. Use only dead and down wood. No cutting or damaging living or standing vegetation, or collecting wood above 6900 ft. Use established fire rings at existing sites. In un-designated sites, remove all signs of fire by scattering rocks and churning the soil. Prior to leaving the campsite, make sure the fire is out and cold.
   CAMPING AND OPEN FIRES are prohibited between Rim Drive and Crater Lake; on Phantom Ship; Wizard Island; on Mt. Scott or its summit trails; within any meadow; within one mile of any paved road, nature trail or developed area; within 1/4 mile of Boundary Springs or Sphagnum Bog; within 100 ft. of any water source, trail or other camping party except when using a designated campsite.
2. PARTY SIZE(overnight trips) Limit 8 persons, 12 head of stock.
3. STAY ON TRAILS: NO HIKING OR CLIMBING INSIDE THE RIM except on the Cleetwood Trail.
4. PETS ARE NOT ALLOWED ON ANY PARK TRAIL, NOR ANYWHERE ELSE IN THE BACKCOUNTRY.
5. FIREARMS, bicycles, and motorized vehicles ARE NOT PERMITTED IN THE BACKCOUNTRY.
6. HORSES/PACK ANIMALS permitted only on designated trails. Horse Regulation handouts are available at park visitor centers.
7. SANITATION: Pack out all litter and leave clean campsite. Use privies where available, otherwise make your toilet in a shallow slit trench and cover when finished, away from camp and over 100 feet from any water source. BOIL OR TREAT ALL WATER.
8. PROTECTION FROM BEARS: Suspend food items from a tree branch, at least 10 ft. above ground and 4 ft. horizontally from the trunk. Store and prepare food away from sleeping areas. Food is defined as any packaged, bottled or canned consumables, drinks, toiletries, perfumes, soaps, etc. (Excerpts "Crater Lake Backcountry Use" leaflet).

UNION PEAK TRAIL, CRATER LAKE NATIONAL PARK. (See map 7)

TRAIL BEGINS: -Pacific Crest Trail, about 3 miles southwest of State Highway 62. ELEV. 6550'
TRAIL ENDS: -Union Peak summit. ELEV. 7709'
DISTANCE: -About 2.5 miles, moderate to steep grades.
USE: -Hikers only.
SEASON: -Usually snow-free July through September.
CONNECTING TR. -Pacific Crest National Scenic Trail.
BRING MAPS: -USFS Pacific Crest Trail-Oregon Central Portion.
-CRATER LAKE map/brochure-National Park Service.

ACCESS: Just north of Union Creek Resort, at the intersection of State Hwys. 230 and 62, travel northeast on 62, 15.7 miles to a point where the Pacific Crest Trail (PCNST) crosses the highway. ELEV. about 6200'. After parking, go southwest on the PCNST about 3 miles to the junction with the Union Peak Trail. Follow the Union Peak Trail about 2.5 miles to the summit of Union Peak. CARRY WATER.

To the south you can see Mt. McLoughlin. Diamond Peak, Mt. Bailey and Mt. Thielsen are to the north. The Crater Lake Rim, with its lofty peaks, appears in the northeast.

NOTE: PLEASE OBSERVE CRATER LAKE NATIONAL PARK BACKCOUNTRY USE REGULATIONS LISTED AT THE BEGINNING OF THIS CHAPTER.

HISTORY: "UNION PEAK (7709 feet), located in the southwest corner of the park, was so-named during the Civil War by Northern sympathizers in the Rogue River Valley."
(USFS quote)

DUTTON CREEK TRAIL- CRATER LAKE NATIONAL PARK. (See map 7)
(Southern leg of a Pacific Crest Trail alternate route)

TRAIL BEGINS:	-Pacific Crest Trail (PCNST).	ELEV. 6100'
TRAIL ENDS:	-Park Headquarters Road, 200 feet south of its junction with the Rim Drive.	ELEV. 7100'
DISTANCE:	-2.5 miles one way. Steep grades.	
SEASON:	-Usually snow-free July through September.	
CONNECTING TRAIL:	-Pacific Crest National Scenic Trail.	
BRING MAPS:	-USGS Crater Lake West, 7.5' series, 1985. -Pacific Crest Trail, Oregon Central Portion. -CRATER LAKE map/brochure-National Park Service.	

ACCESS: LOWER TRAILHEAD: North of Union Creek Resort at the junction of State Highways 62 and 230, go 15.7 miles on Hwy. 62 to where the Pacific Crest Trail crosses the highway. Park at this location and hike north, 1.7 miles to the junction with the lower end of the Dutton Cr. Tr.(the southern leg of the new PCT alternate route). After leaving this older section of the PCT, the Dutton Creek Trail leads 2.5 miles to its upper trailhead on Park Headquarters Road near West Rim Drive.

UPPER TRAILHEAD: From the south entrance station of Crater Lake National Park, travel beyond the Park Headquarters, and continue north to within 200 feet of the junction with the West Crater Lk. Rim Drive. Dutton Creek Trail leads downhill left (southwest).

From the upper trailhead,the PCT alternate route crosses West Rim Drive and follows 6 miles along the west rim of Crater Lake.After crossing the East Rim Drive at North Junction, the route descends from Llao Rock and, after 2 miles, reaches the intersection where this alternate route meets the older section of the PCT.

HISTORY: Captain Clarence E. Dutton commanded a U.S. Geological Survey party to sound the depth of Crater Lake from their boat, the Cleetwood. Their deepest wire soundings indicated the lake depth at 1996 feet, amazingly close to sonar measurements of 1932 feet officially recorded in 1959. (From "Crater Lake National Park" brochure) PLEASE SEE BEGINNING OF THIS CHAPTER FOR BACKCOUNTRY USE REGULATIONS IN CRATER LAKE PARK.

LIGHTNING SPRINGS TRAIL. (See map 7)

TRAIL BEGINS: -Crater Lake Rim Drive. ELEV. 7170'
TRAIL ENDS: -Pacific Crest Trail. ELEV. 5850'
DISTANCE: -4 miles, steep grades.
SEASON: -Usually snow-free July through September.
CONNECTING TR. -Pacific Crest National Scenic Trail.
BRING MAPS: -USGS Crater Lake West, 7.5' series, 1985.
-USFS Pacific Crest Trail-Oregon Central Portion.
-CRATER LAKE map/brochure-National Park Service.

ACCESS: The Lightning Springs Trail begins from the west portion of Crater Lake Rim Drive, about 2.3 miles northwest of Rim Village. (This point can also be reached from Highway 238 at the junction with the North Rim Access Road. Take the North Rim Access Road to the Crater Lake Rim Drive and turn right for about 3.5 miles to Lightning Springs Trailhead.)

FEATURES: The trail switchbacks sharply downhill, reaching Lightning Springs in less than 1 mile. Water is available here, but should be boiled before drinking. From the springs, a stream follows the trail as it continues to the Pacific Crest Trail (PCNST) near Bybee Creek. Travelling south on the PCNST leads 6.3 miles to State Highway 62. BACKCOUNTRY USE REGULATIONS IN CRATER LAKE PARK ARE LISTED AT THE BEGINNING OF THIS CHAPTER.

Build Campfires only in safe places, and make small fires.

CHAPTER 12 - DIAMOND LAKE AREA

MT. THIELSEN TRAIL #1456. (See map 1A)

TRAIL BEGINS:	-State Highway 138 near milepost 81.	ELEV. 5400'
TRAIL ENDS:	-Mt. Thielsen Summit.	ELEV. 9182'
DISTANCE:	-4.9 miles. more difficult.	
SEASON:	-Summer and fall; hiker,horse. Winter skiing.	
CONNECTING TR:	-Spruce Ridge Trail 1458, Pacific Crest Trail.	
BRING MAPS:	-USFS Recreation Guide, Diamond Lake Ranger Dist. -Mt. Thielsen Wilderness information-USFS Diamond Lake, Chemult, Crescent Ranger Districts. -USFS Pacific Crest Trail-Central Oregon Portion. -USGS "Diamond Lake" and "Mount Thielsen", 7.5' series 1985.	

ACCESS: Near the southeast corner of Diamond Lake, State Highways 230 and 138 intersect. From this point, go 1.5 miles north on 138 to Mt. Thielsen Trailhead on the right (east) side of the road between mileposts 81 and 82.

FEATURES: The trail leads upwards 1.6 miles to the junction with Spruce Ridge Trail 1458, and 1.3 miles further to the Pacific Crest Trail.

After crossing the Pacific Crest Trail, a 2 mile scramble begins a steep climb along a ridge to the east side of the summit pinnacle. The route up to the pinnacle must be well chosen to allow for proper hand and foot placements. This portion is steep. The use of a climber's rope is not absolutely necessary, but could be set in place as guidance and support to others in your party who may need it. Views from the summit extend north to Mt. Hood and south to Mt. Shasta.

HISTORY: Mt. Thielsen has been referred to as the "Lightning Rod of the Cascades," and was named for Hans Thielsen, a prominent railroad engineer and builder. The peak is one of several old volcanoes formed by lava flow about 2 million years ago when geologic forces folded and fractured the High Cascades. (USFS Information)

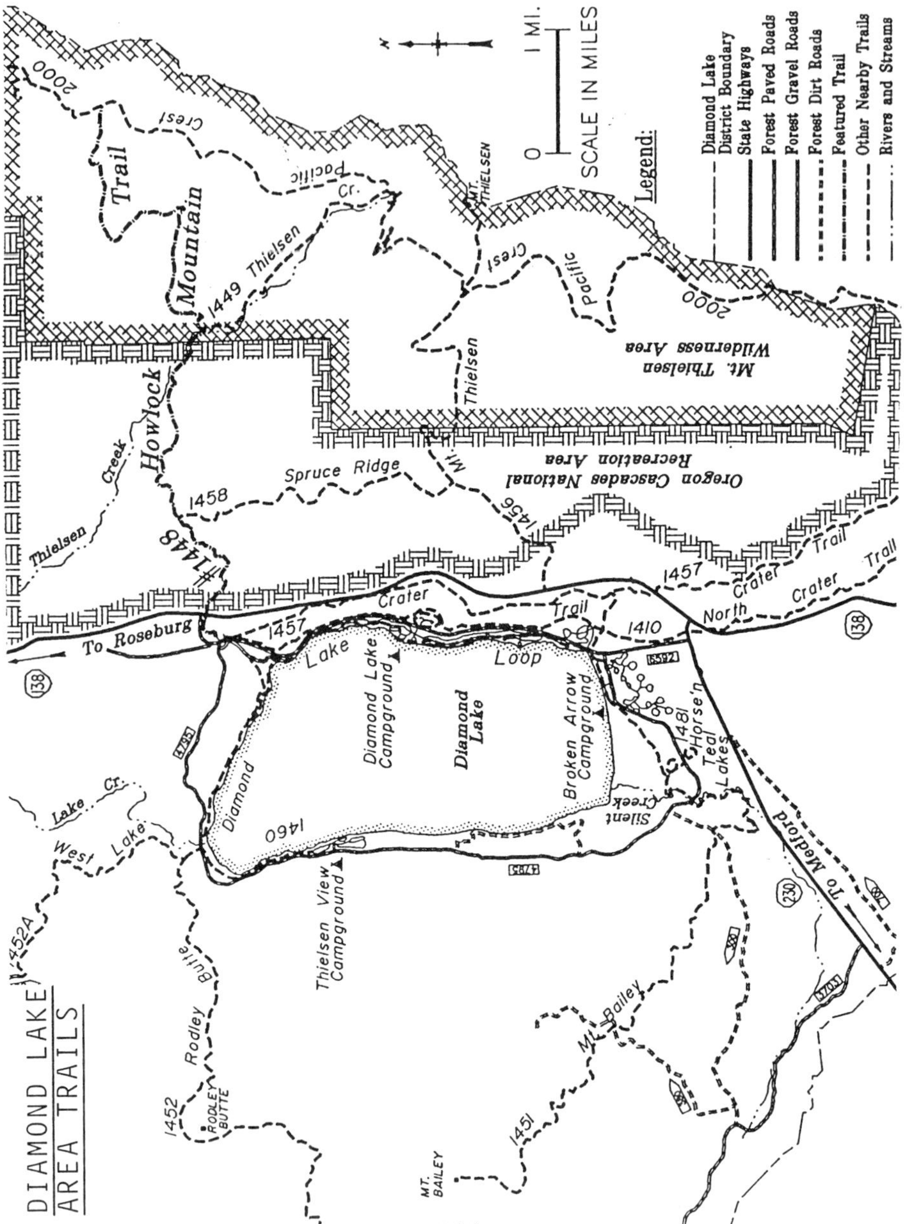

DIAMOND LAKE AREA TRAILS

HOWLOCK MTN. TRAIL #1448. (See map 1A)

TRAIL BEGINS: -Forest Road 4795 near Diamond Lake. ELEV. 5390'
TRAIL ENDS: -Pacific Crest Trail (PCNST). ELEV. 7220'
DISTANCE: -7 miles, difficult. USE: hiker/horse/skiers.
SEASON: -Hikers, July through September. Winter skiing.
CONNECTING TR. -Spruce Ridge Trail 1458, Thielsen Creek Trail 1449 and Pacific Crest National Scenic Trail.
BRING MAPS: -USFS Recreation Guide, Diamond Lake Ranger Dist.
-Mt. Thielsen Wilderness information-USFS Diamond Lake, Chemult, Crescent Ranger Districts.
-USFS Pacific Crest Trail-Oregon Central Portion.

ACCESS: Just north of the Union Creek Resort at the junction with Highways 62 and 230, follow mileposts on 230, 23.9 mi. to the junction with State Hwy. 138. Turn left and go north on 138, 4.3 miles to the junction of Road 4795, the north entrance to Diamond Lake Recreation Area. Turn south onto Road 4795 and go 0.3 mile to the Howlock Mtn. Trailhead parking area on the left.

FEATURES: From the Howlock Mtn. Trailhead, the Spruce Ridge Trail is 1.2 miles, Timothy Meadows about 3 mi., Thielsen Creek Trail 3.5 miles(the last source of water along the Howlock Mtn. Trail), and Pacific Crest Trail 7 miles. This point on the Pacific Crest Trail is nearly 1 mile northwest of and 1000 feet lower elevation than Howlock Mountain.

From the upper Howlock Mtn. Trailhead, Windego Pass is 19 miles north along the PCNST and the PCNST Trailhead on Hwy. 138 is 11.0 miles south.

The views of Howlock Mountain, Mt. Thielsen, Mt. Bailey and of open meadows are outstanding. A loop hike using the Howlock Mtn. Trail 1448 can be made by hiking right (south) along the Pacific Crest Trail 3 miles to the Thielsen Creek Trail junction. Turn right onto Thielsen Creek Trail 1449 and go about 2 1/4 miles to the Howlock Mountain Trail. Keep left and follow the Howlock Mtn. Trail 3 1/2 miles back to its trailhead. The total loop distance is nearly 16 miles.

THIELSEN CREEK TRAIL #1449. (See map 1A)

TRAIL BEGINS: -(LOWER END): Howlock Mtn. Trail. ELEV. 5600'
TRAIL ENDS: -(UPPER END): Pacific Crest Trail. ELEV. 6500'
DISTANCE: -2.1 miles, more difficult. USE: hiker and horse in summer and fall. Winter skiing.
CONNECTING TR. -Howlock Mtn. Trail 1448 and Pacific Crest Trail.
BRING MAPS: -USFS Recreation Guide, Diamond Lake Ranger Dist.
-Mt. Thielsen Wilderness information USFS Diamond Lake, Chemult, Crescent Ranger Districts.
USFS Pacific Crest Trail-Oregon Central Portion.

ACCESS: Follow the directions to Howlock Mtn. Trailhead on the previous page. Take the Howlock Mtn. Trail 3.5 mi. to the LOWER END of the Thielsen Creek Trail. Turn right and go 2.1 miles southeast to the Pacific Crest Trail.

From the upper Thielsen Creek Trailhead, Windego Pass is 22 miles north along the PCNST and the North Crater Trailhead on Hwy. 138 is 8 miles south.

FEATURES: Thielsen Creek Camp is along the upper end of the Thielsen Creek Trail about 1/8 mile below the Pacific Crest Trail. Water is available. A 16 mile loop trip back to the Howlock Mtn. Trailhead could be made by using the Thielsen Creek Trail, taking the Pacific Crest Trail 3 miles north to the Howlock Mtn. Trail, then turning left and following Howlock Mtn. Trail 7 miles back to its trailhead.

Always take extra clothing along. You may need some dry things to put on.

MT. BAILEY TRAIL #1451. (See maps 1A or 3)

TRAIL BEGINS: -Forest Road 4795/300. ELEV. 5200'
TRAIL ENDS: -Mt. Bailey summit. ELEV. 8363'
DISTANCE: -5 miles, moderate grades. USE: hiker only.
SEASON: -Hikers July to October.
BRING MAPS: -Diamond Lake Ranger Dist.-Umpqua Ntl. Forest.
-USFS Rec. Opportunity Guide-Mt. Bailey Trail.
-USGS Diamond Lake, 7.5' series, 1985.

ACCESS #1. From the southeast corner of Diamond Lake, go about 2 miles west on Road 4795 to the junction of Road 4795/300. Turn left onto Road 300 and go 0.4 mile to the trailhead parking lot. Mt. Bailey Trail begins on the right of the parking area. ELEV. about 5200'.

ACCESS#2. INTERCEPTS THE MT. BAILEY TRAIL, 2-1/4 MILES HIGHER ON THE MOUNTAIN SLOPES, ELEV. ABOUT 6075'. Near milepost 21 on State Highway 230, find the junction with Forest Road 3703. Turn onto Road 3703 and travel northwest, about 2 miles to the junction with Forest Road 4795/300. Turn right onto 300 and go about 0.1 mi. to Forest Road 4795/380 on the left. Road 380 is narrow, rocky and undriveable. It is a 1.5 mile hike up Road 380 to the point where Mt. Bailey Trail crosses and climbs to the summit.

FEATURES: No technical ability is required to reach the summit. The last 0.5 mi. is quite steep and rocky and may be too difficult for small children. Mt. Thielsen and Diamond Lake are in the foreground. To the north you can see Mt. Jefferson, Three Fingered Jack, Mt.Washington, the Three Sisters, Broken Top, Diamond Peak, Bachelor Butte and nearby Cowhorn Mountain.

To the south you can see the Crater Lake Rim, Union Peak, Mt. McLoughlin and Mt. Shasta.

Rogue River National Recreation Trail

PACIFIC CREST TRAIL ACCESS, FOREST ROAD 2025. (See map 27)

SEASON: -Usually snow-free July through October.
BRING MAPS: -USFS Rogue River and Klamath National Forests.
-USFS Pacific Crest Trail-Oregon Southern Portion.

ACCESS: From the the town of Ruch, Oregon, follow mileposts south on Upper Applegate Road to mile 9.3, at the junction with Beaver Creek Road (Forest Route 20). Turn left onto 20 and follow mileposts to mile 14.1 at the junction with Forest Road 2025.

Turn right onto 2025 and follow mileposts to:
-Mile 4.3 Pacific Crest Trail crosses the road, look for signs.
-Mile 5.1 Pacific Crest Trail crosses the road at the junction with Forest Road 40-S-01. Look for signs.

Forest Road 2025 can also be reached via Forest Route 20 from the east, but portions of the road could be bumpy and not recommended for passenger cars.

FEATURES: Watch carefully for trail signs, as road spurs and other evidence of timber harvesting can add confusion. For water sources along the trail, check with Star Ranger Station near milepost 7 on Upper Applegate Road.

ALWAYS READ THE POSTED SIGNS AT THE TRAILHEAD.

PACIFIC CREST TRAIL ACCESS, FOREST ROUTE 22. (See maps 20 and 28)

SEASON: -Usually snow-free July to October. Wildflowers in abundance throughout the summer months.

BRING MAPS: -USFS Rogue River and Klamath National Forests.
-USFS Pacific Crest Trail-Oregon Southern Portion.

ACCESS: From Talent, Oregon, at the intersection of Talent Avenue and Main Street, go south on Main St., which becomes Wagner Creek Road in about 1 mile. Follow mileposts on Wagner Creek Road to the following mileage points:

- -Mile 4.5 Pavement ends.
- -Mile 7.1 Bald Mt. Road junction, keep left.
- -Mile 9.1 Wagner Gap (three-way junction) keep left on Forest Route 22.

Continue on Forest Route 22, approx. 8 miles to the junction with Forest Route 20 on the Siskiyou Crest. Turn right on Forest Route 20 and go 0.1 mi. to the junction of Forest Roads 2040 and 40S16. Look to the left where the Pacific Crest Trail crosses 40S16.

FEATURES: Forest Route 22 is unpaved, and there are some curves at its lower elevations. It is best to be cautious. Otherwise, this road provides a good access to the Pacific Crest Trail as it continues along the Siskiyou crest. For other access points along Forest Route 20, see details on the following page.

PACIFIC CREST TRAIL ACCESS-ALONG FOREST ROUTE 20 and Hwy. 99 (Maps 24,27,28)

SEASON: -Usually snow-free by late July at higher elevations, (Mt. Ashland and Dutchman Peak areas).

BRING MAPS: -USFS Pacific Crest Trail-Oregon Southern Portion.
-USFS Rogue River and Klamath National Forests.
-BLM Medford District, Pacific Crest Trail Log.

ACCESS: From Interstate Highway 5,Ashland Exit 14, continue 9 miles to Mt. Ashland Exit 6 leading to a junction with Old Highway 99 South. Keep right and go 0.6 mile to a -hiker trail- sign on the right indicating the Pacific Crest Trail leading west toward Mt. Ashland and California. Continue 0.1 mile to Mt. Ashland Access Road, and follow this road to mile readings:

Mile 7.0 PCNST crosses the road at the National Forest Boundary, FROM THIS POINT THE ROAD BECOMES FOREST ROUTE 20.
Mile 11.1 Grouse Gap, PCNST parallel to road on the left(south).
Mile 16.1 Junction with Forest Roads 40S16 and 40S20, look left to where the PCNST crosses.
Mile 16.9 PCNST crosses Route 20 at Siskiyou Gap.
Mile 19.9 Wrangle Gap, Jnc. Road 2030, PCNST on right (north).
Mile 20.1 PCNST crosses Route 20.
Mile 21.9 Track on left (south) leads about 0.1 mile to Sheep Camp Springs.
Mile 22.3 Jackson Gap. To reach the PCNST turn left onto Road 40S01 and go 0.6 mile to where the PCNST crosses.
Mile 23.7 (Appx.) Junction with Forest Road 2025. To reach the PCNST, turn left and go 4.3 miles to where the PCNST crosses.

FEATURES: Food and a pay telephone are located at Callahan's Restaurant on Old Highway 99S just east of Interstate 5 Mt. Ashland exit. Route 20 between Grouse Gap and Road 2025 may be too rough for passenger cars. Water is scarce along this portion of the trail.ORVs including bicycles-NOT ALLOWED on the PCT.

PACIFIC CREST TRAIL ACCESS-PILOT ROCK ROAD. (See map 29)

SEASON: -Usually snow-free by early May.
BRING MAPS: -USFS Pacific Crest Trail-Oregon Southern Portion.
-BLM Medford District-Pacific Crest Trail Log.

ACCESS: From Ashland Exit 14, continue southeast on Interstate Hwy. 5, 9 miles to Mt. Ashland Exit 6. The off-ramp leads to a junction with Old Highway 99 South. Keep to the right at this junction and go 1.9 miles to the junction with Pilot Rock Road 40-2E-33. ALONG THE WAY, THE PACIFIC CREST TRAIL FOLLOWS OLD HIGHWAY 99S FOR A DISTANCE OF 1/2 MILE SOUTH OF THE FREEWAY OVERPASS. LOOK ON THE LEFT FOR A TRAIL SIGN NAILED TO A TREE WHERE THE PCNST LEAVES THE ROAD AND HEADS TOWARD PILOT ROCK.

Turn left (east) onto Pilot Rock Road using your odometer to note the following Pacific Crest Trail (PCNST) crossings:

Mile 1 PCNST crosses road in a saddle, look for trail signs.
Mile 2.1 Keep left downhill at a junction. (A right turn would lead 0.8 mile to the base of Pilot Rock and an access to the PCNST.)
Mile 2.9 Road junction, stay uphill to the right.
Mile 3.8 Road junction, stay right.
Mile 3.9 PCNST crosses at the crest of a ridge near a road gate in a recent logging area. Look for trail signs. From this point, the PCNST LEADS RIGHT passing the base of Pilot Rock and reaches Old Highway 99S in about 5.8 miles. The PCNST LEADS LEFT (northeast) to State Hwy. 66 (Greensprings Hwy.) in 11 mi., passing the slopes of Soda Mtn. and Hobart Bluff. CARRY WATER.

HISTORY: "PILOT ROCK, a volcanic plug so named because of its prominence as a landmark to early travelers on the Oregon-California Trail. Although the chute on the north face of the rock can be scaled without special equipment, climbers should be cautious of loose rock." (USFS quote)

PACIFIC CREST TRAIL ACCESS, BALDY CREEK ROAD 40-3E-5.(Maps 22,29)

SEASON: -Usually snow-free late May to October.

BRING MAPS: -USFS Pacific Crest Trail-Oregon Southern Portion.
-BLM Transportation Map-Medford District-Klamath Resource Area.
-BLM Medford District-Pacific Crest Trail Log.

ACCESS: From Ashland Interstate Highway 5 Exit 14, travel 14.8 miles (southeast) on State Highway 66. Turn right onto Tyler Creek Road and go 1.4 miles to the junction with Baldy Creek Road 40-3E-5. Take 40-3E-5, 5.7 miles to the crest of a ridge at the junction with Road 40-3E-30. The PCNST crosses the road (40-3E-5) just before reaching a cattle guard.

TURNING RIGHT (SOUTH) onto the PCNST leads 9.4 mi. to Interstate Hwy. 5 (passing Porcupine Mtn. at mile 2.6 and Pilot Rock at mile 5.3)

TURNING LEFT (NORTH) onto the PCNST leads 7.4 mi. to Hwy 66 (passing the western slopes of Soda Mountain at mile 1.5 and crossing Soda Mountain Road near mile 3.0).

FEATURES: The Baldy Creek Road provides access to the Pacific Crest National Scenic Trail, southwest of Soda Mountain Lookout, at the near mid-point of the Highway 66-Interstate Highway 5 section of the trail. CARRY WATER when hiking in this area. The Pacific Crest Trail passes through BLM and private lands. Watch carefully for the trail as it travels through areas of timber harvesting. Numerous roads and cattle trails can add to the confusion. Wildflowers are abundant from May to July.

PACIFIC CREST TRAIL ACCESS, STATE HIGHWAY 66.

SEASON: -Usually snow-free late May through October. Wildflowers abundant May to July.

BRING MAPS: -USFS Pacific Crest Trail-Oregon Southern Portion.
-BLM Transportation Map -Medford District -Klamath Resource Area.
-BLM Medford District-Pacific Crest Trail Log.

USE: CLOSED TO MOTORIZED/MECHANICAL VEHICLES, INCLUDING BICYCLES.

ACCESS: From Interstate Hwy. 5, Ashland Exit 14, follow the mileposts east on State Hwy. 66, 15.7 miles to the highway summit at Soda Mtn. Road. The Pacific Crest Trail crosses Hwy. 66 just beyond.

From this point the trail leads RIGHT, south and west, 16.8 miles to Interstate Highway 5. Hobart Bluff, Soda Mountain Road, Soda Mountain, and Pilot Rock are landmarks along the way.

Leading from the LEFT of Highway 66, the PCNST travels 4.6 miles to Little Hyatt Reservoir then approx. 1.5 miles further to Hyatt Prairie Road.

FEATURES: In this area of the Pacific Crest Trail, there are views of the Rogue River Valley, Mt. Shasta in northern California and the Klamath Basin. The trail passes through mixed private and BLM administered lands. Watch for trail insignias. The trail may be hard to follow due to timber harvesting, cattle trails, and numerous roads. CARRY DRINKING WATER, as on-route supplies are very limited. Check with Ashland Ranger Station or Medford BLM office for exact locations.

HISTORY: "State Highway 66.......Known locally as the Greensprings Highway, this road parallels the 'Old Applegate Trail' which was used during the 1840's by pioneers who branched off the main Oregon Trail at Fort Hall Idaho and crossed the sagebrush desert of northern Nevada." (USFS quote)

PACIFIC CREST TRAIL ROAD ACCESS POINTS-cont.
FOREST MAP: Pacific Crest Trail-Oregon Southern Portion.

HYATT LAKE RESERVOIR. (See map 22)
From Interstate Hwy. 5, Ashland Exit 14, follow mileposts east on State Hwy. 66, 17.5 mi.to the junction with East Hyatt Lake Road. Turn left onto this road and travel 3.1 mi.north to the south end of Hyatt Lake at the junction with West Hyatt Lake Road. A hikers camp at nearby Hyatt Lake Campground provides showers. Hyatt Lake Resort (across the lake) has food, phone and a maildrop.

The Pacific Crest Trail crosses the above road junction and leads southwest 1.5 mi. to Little Hyatt Lake, and 4.6 miles further to Greensprings Hwy 66. Leading northeast from Hyatt Lake, the trail goes along the east shore of Howard Prairie Lake and points north.

KENO ACCESS ROAD 39-7E-31. (See map 23)
From Interstate Hwy. 5, Ashland Exit 14,travel east on State Hwy. 66, 0.6 mi.to the junction with Dead Indian Memorial Road (County Route 722).Turn left onto this Route and follow mileposts to mile 18.5 at the junction with Keno Access Road 39-7E-31. Turn right onto 39-7E-31 and go 5.0 miles to where the Pacific Crest Trail crosses. Hiking northeast from this point, leads 3 miles to Big Springs at Griffin Pass and points north. Hiking southwest leads 3 miles to the southern shore of Howard Prairie Lake and BLM Road 38-4E-32. Willow Lake Campground is located 1.8 miles northwest along this road, on the southwest shore Of Howard Prairie Lake.

GRIFFIN PASS, ROAD 2520. (See map 23)
From Interstate Hwy. 5, Ashland Exit 14,travel east on State Hwy, 66, 0.6 mi. to the Junction with Dead Indian Memorial Rd. (County Route 722).Turn left onto this route and follow mileposts to mile 23.7 at the junction with Forest Road 2520. Turn right onto 2520 and continue 4.0 mi. to Griffin Pass, where the Pacific Crest Tr. crosses. 600 feet further on Road 2520 leads to a faint trail on the left leading to a spring (metal storage container). The water needs to be treated. Hiking northeast, the PCNST climbs to the eastern slopes of Old Baldy Mountain and on to Dead Indian Memorial Road. Hiking southwest,the trail descends to Keno Access Rd. and on toward Howard Prairie Lake and other points south.

PACIFIC CREST TRAIL ROAD ACCESS POINTS.-cont.
FOREST MAP: Pacific Crest Trail-Oregon Southern Portion.

OLD BALDY MOUNTAIN. ROAD 2520/600. (See map 23)
From Interstate Hwy. 5, Ashland Exit 14, travel east on Hwy. 66, 0.6 mi. to the junction with Dead Indian Memorial Road. Turn left onto this road and go 23.7 mi. to Road 2520, on the right. Turn onto Road 2520 and go 2.4 mi. to the junction with Road 2520/640. Turn left onto Road 640 and go 0.6 mi. and merger with Road 600. Follow Road 600, passing junctions with Roads 680 and 650, 1.0 mi. to Roads end (where a log blocks a Jeep track leading to the summit of Old Baldy Mountain, a good sidetrip.)
-There are no signs giving directions to the Pacific Crest Trail. From the above log at roads end,follow a faint path 200 feet east to the PCNST. It would be well to mark the path for your return trip to Road 600. Turning right onto the PCNST leads past a Forest service gate, 2.0 mi. to Griffin Pass and points south. Turning left onto the PCNST leads downhill 1.7 miles to where Burton Flat Road crosses and 1.9 mi. further to Dead Indian Mem. Road.

DEAD INDIAN MEMORIAL ROAD: (See map 23)
From Interstate Hwy. 5, Ashland Exit 14,follow State Hwy. 66, 0.6 mi. to Dead Indian Memorial Road. Turn left onto this road and go 27.2 mile to a PCNST parking area on the right. The PCNST leads south, 3.6 mi. to Old Baldy Mtn. and southern points. The PCNST leads North 11 mi.,passing Brown Mtn. Shelter, Rd.700,west slopes of Brown Mtn., and High Lakes Trail Jnc. before reaching Hwy.140.

STATE HIGHWAY 140. (See map 16)
From WHITE CITY, follow mileposts east on Hwy. 140 to mile 32.5 at the Pacific Crest Trail Summit Parking Area on the left. The PCNST South from Highway 140 crosses the Highlakes Trail in 0.5 mile, travels along the western slopes of Brown Mtn. It then passes the forks of Little Butte Creek,the Brown Mtn.Trail junction, Road 700 at the 9.2 mile point, Brown Mtn. Shelter and 2.0 mile further to Dead Indian Memorial Road.

The PCNST north from highway 140 enters Sky Lakes Wilderness in 2.0 mi., and crosses Mt. McLoughlin Trail in another 1.5 mile. It then continues through Sky Lakes Wilderness and Crater Lake Park.

PACIFIC CREST TRAIL ROAD ACCESS POINTS -cont.
FOREST MAP: Pacific Crest Trail, Oregon Central Portion.

STATE HIGHWAY 62, NEAR ANNIE SPRING. (SEE MAP ON PAGE 160)
North of Union Creek Resort at the junction of State Highways 230 and 62,go 15.7 mi.northeast on Hwy.62 to where the PCNST crosses. This point is 0.8 mile west of Crater Lake Park south entrance.

The PCNST SOUTH FROM HIGHWAY 62 passes Union Peak before continuing through Sky Lakes Wilderness, with good views of many lakes and Mt. McLoughlin just north of State Highway 140.

GOING 1.7 miles NORTH on the PCT leads to a junction with DUTTON CREEK TRAIL, The route for pack stock/hiker continues 15.2 miles to a Pacific Crest Trail Parking Area on North Rim Access Road, and 9 mi. more to Highway 138. A SHORTER, HIKER ONLY SCENIC ROUTE co-locates with the DUTTON CREEK TRAIL, 2.5 miles to Park Headquarters Road at Rim Village. The Alternate PCT continues about 6.0 miles, skirting the west rim of the lake to North Rim Drive. After crossing North Rim Drive,the trail descends about 2.5 miles along the west slopes of Llao Rock to rejoin the original section of the PCT at the PCT parking area on North Rim Access Road. It is 9.0 trail miles further to State Highway 138.

STATE HIGHWAY 138. (See map 1A or 3)
From the southeast corner of Diamond Lake,at the intersection of Highways 230 and 138, travel 4 mi. southeast on Hwy.138 to where the Pacific Crest Trail crosses the highway.This crossing is 3/4 mile east of the north entrance to Crater Lake National Park.

IF TRAVELING SOUTH through Crater Lake National Park, please see the previous description.

The Pacific Crest Trail NORTH FROM HIGHWAY 138 passes the junctions of North Crater Trail 1410, Mt. Thielsen Trail 1456,Thielsen Creek Trail 1449 and Howlock Mtn.Trail 1448. These 4 trails offer sidetrips to Diamond Lake Resort.

TRAIL PARK PERMITS

JANUARY 1, 1998 is the beginning of a 2 year trial period when Trail Park Passes are required to park at certain trailheads on the Rogue River National Forest and most trailheads on the Siskiyou National Forest, to generate funds for much needed maintenance work on trails and trailheads. Passes are required to park at or within 1/4 mile of designated trailheads.

Day passes cost $3.00 and annual passes sell for $25.00 and are available at Forest Service offices and selected commercial outlets. Golden Age and Golden Access Passport holders may purchase passes at a 50% discount. Trail maintenance volunteers may qualify for a free annual pass. Trail passes are honored at all designated Trail-Park trailheads in Oregon and Washington.

Forest officers will place fee envelopes on vehicles that are in non-compliance and will allow trail users the opportunity to pay the day pass fee or purchase a annual pass through the mail to avoid the $30 fine.

The Rogue River National Forest has a list of designated trailheads, available upon request. Please refer to "WHERE TO GET INFORMATION AND PERMITS" listed on page 6 of this book.

ALPHABETICAL INDEX OF TRAILS

ALPHABETICAL INDEX OF TRAILS, cont.

ALPHABETICAL INDEX OF TRAILS, cont.

ALPHABETICAL INDEX OF TRAILS PAGE

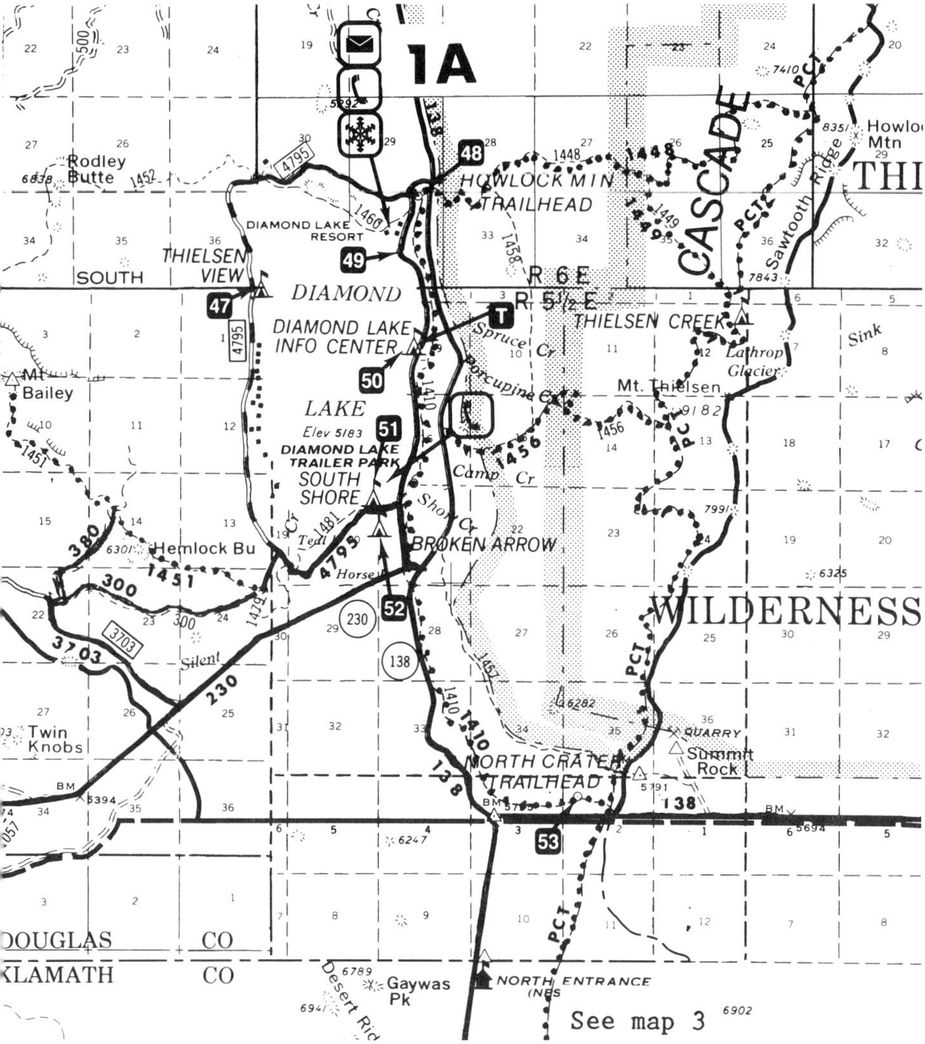

1A
Rodley Butte
HOWLOCK MTN TRAILHEAD
DIAMOND LAKE RESORT
THIELSEN VIEW
SOUTH
DIAMOND
DIAMOND LAKE INFO CENTER
LAKE
Elev 5183
DIAMOND LAKE TRAILER PARK
SOUTH SHORE
BROKEN ARROW
Mt Bailey
Hemlock Bu
Teal L
Horse L
Silent
Twin Knobs
CASCADE
Howlock Mtn
THI
Sawtooth Ridge
R 6 E
R 5 1/2 E
THIELSEN CREEK
Spruce Cr
Porcupine Cr
Camp Cr
Short Cr
Lathrop Glacier
Mt. Thielsen
9182
Sink
WILDERNESS
QUARRY
Summit Rock
NORTH CRATER TRAILHEAD
PCT
DOUGLAS CO
KLAMATH CO
Desert Ridge
Gaywas Pk
NORTH ENTRANCE (NPS)
See map 3

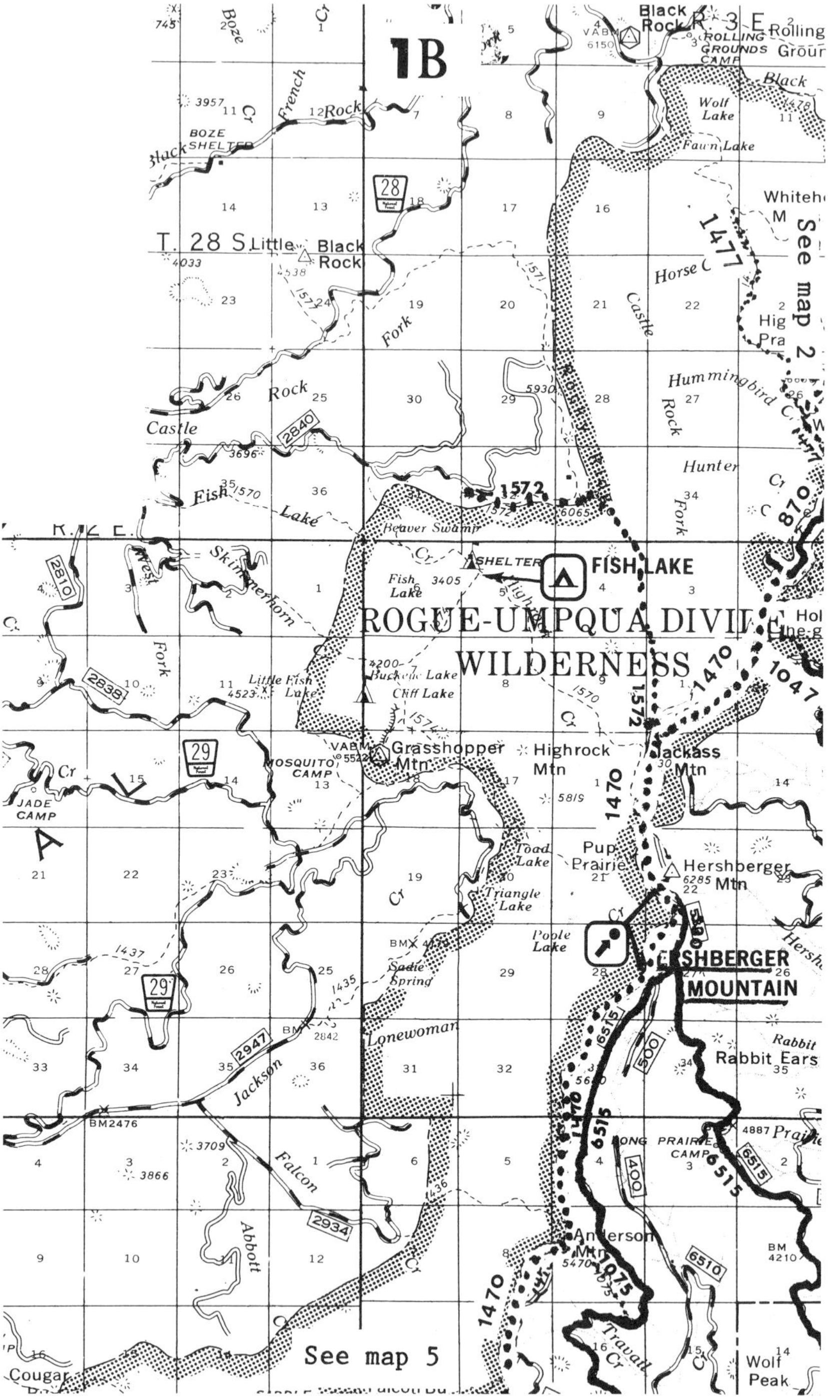
1B
Black Rock
R. 3 E.
Rolling Grounds Camp
Wolf Lake
Fawn Lake
Boze Shelter
French
Rock
T. 28 S.
Little Black Rock
Horse Cr
Castle
Fork
Hummingbird Cr
Rocky Rim
Hunter
See map 2
Fish Lake
Beaver Swamp
Skimmerhorn
West Fork
Shelter
FISH LAKE
ROGUE-UMPQUA DIVIDE
WILDERNESS
Little Fish Lake
Buckeye Lake
Cliff Lake
Grasshopper Mtn
Highrock Mtn
Jackass Mtn
Mosquito Camp
Jade Camp
Toad Lake
Pup Prairie
Hershberger Mtn
Triangle Lake
Poole Lake
HERSHBERGER MOUNTAIN
Sadie Spring
Lonewoman
Rabbit Ears
Jackson
Long Prairie Camp
Falcon
Abbott
Anderson Mtn
Travail Cr
Wolf Peak
Cougar
See map 5

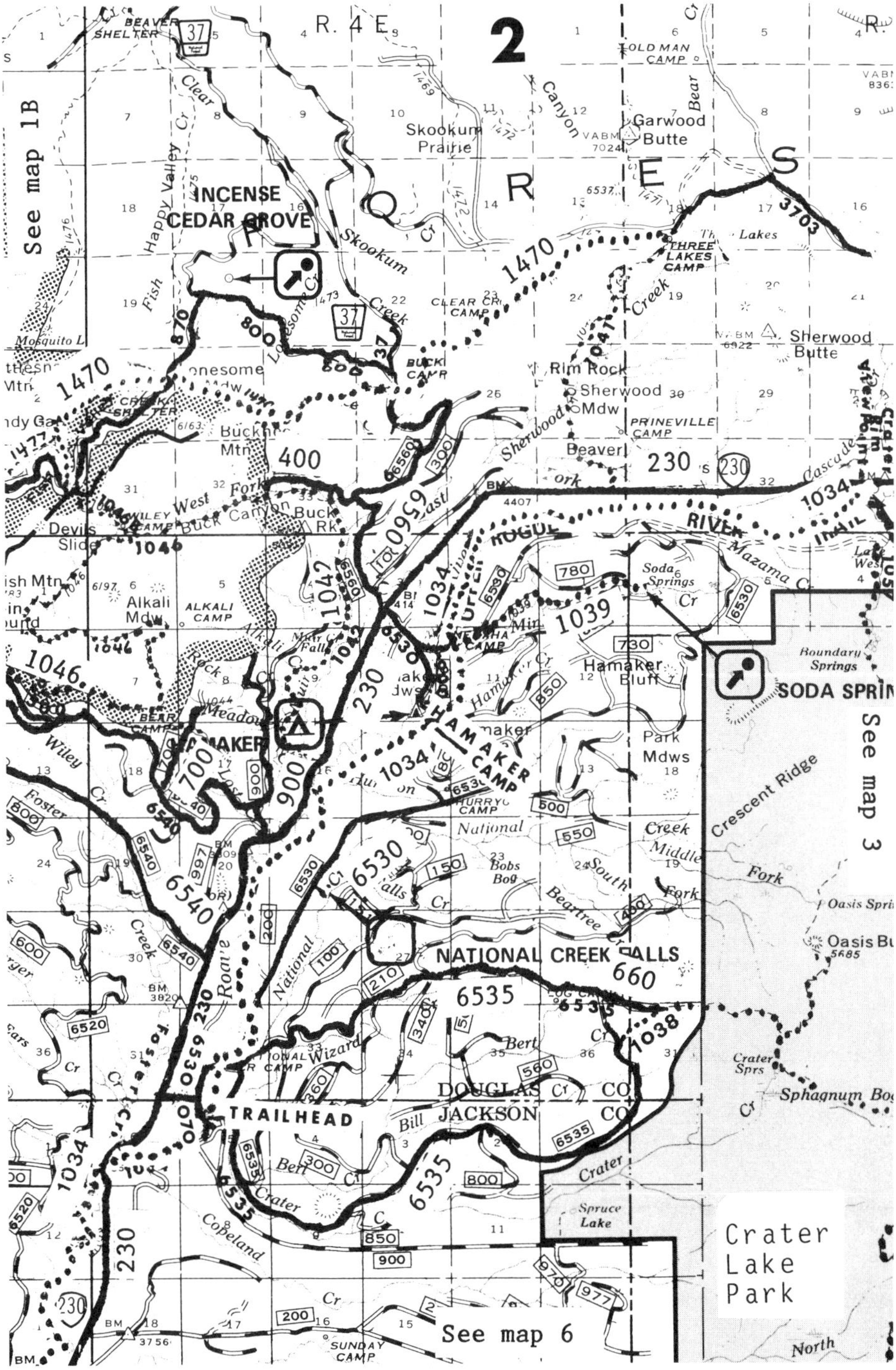
2
R. 4 E.
See map 1B
See map 3
See map 6
Crater Lake Park
INCENSE CEDAR GROVE
BEAVER SHELTER
OLD MAN CAMP
Garwood Butte
Skookum Prairie
Canyon
Bear
Happy Valley Cr
Clear Cr
Skookum Creek
Lonesome Cr
CLEAR CR CAMP
BUCK CAMP
THREE LAKES CAMP
Three Lakes
Sherwood Butte
Rim Rock
Sherwood Mdw
PRINEVILLE CAMP
Beaver
Buck Mtn
West Fork
Buck Canyon
Buck Rk
Devils Slide
WILEY CAMP
Alkali Mdw
ALKALI CAMP
Alkali Cr
Rock Cr
BEAR CAMP
Meadow
HAMAKER CAMP
Hamaker Bluff
Hamaker Cr
Soda Springs
SODA SPRINGS
Boundary Springs
ROGUE RIVER TRAIL
Mazama Cr
Cascade
Park Mdws
Crescent Ridge
Middle Fork
South Fork
Oasis Spring
Oasis Butte
National Cr
Bobs Bog
Beartree Cr
NATIONAL CREEK FALLS
HURRYCANE CAMP
Crater Sprs
Sphagnum Bog
Wizard
DOUGLAS CO
JACKSON CO
TRAILHEAD
Bert Cr
Bill Cr
Crater Cr
Copeland
Spruce Lake
SUNDAY CAMP
Foster Cr
Wiley Cr
Roane
North
1470
1034
1039
1046
1038
230
6530
6535
6540
6560
3703

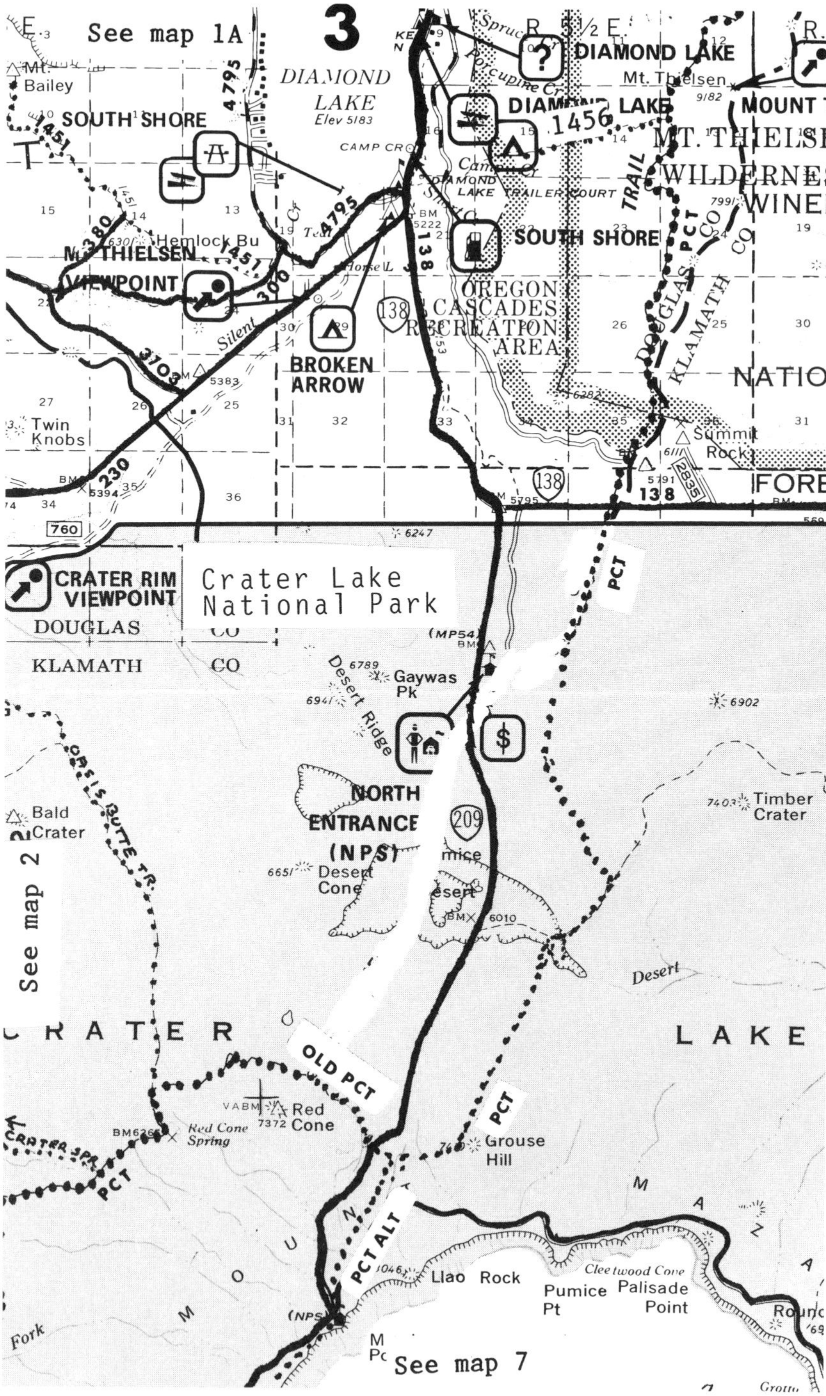
3
See map 1A
DIAMOND LAKE
Elev 5183
DIAMOND LAKE
DIAMOND LAKE
1456
MOUNT T
Mt. Thielsen
MT. THIELSE
WILDERNES
WINEM
TRAIL
PCT
DOUGLAS CO
KLAMATH CO
NATIO
FORE
Mt. Bailey
SOUTH SHORE
4795
1451
CAMP CR
DIAMOND LAKE TRAILER COURT
SOUTH SHORE
380
Hemlock Bu
Mt. THIELSEN VIEWPOINT
300
138
OREGON CASCADES RECREATION AREA
BROKEN ARROW
3703
Silent
Twin Knobs
Summit Rock
230
760
2835
CRATER RIM VIEWPOINT
Crater Lake National Park
DOUGLAS CO
KLAMATH CO
(MP54)
Gaywas Pk
Desert Ridge
NORTH ENTRANCE (NPS)
209
Pumice Desert
Desert Cone
Bald Crater
Timber Crater
OASIS BUTTE TR.
See map 2
CRATER
LAKE
Desert
OLD PCT
PCT
Red Cone
Red Cone Spring
CRATER SPR.
Grouse Hill
MAZAMA
MOUNT
PCT ALT
Llao Rock
Pumice Pt
Cleetwood Cove
Palisade Point
Fork
(NPS)
See map 7
Grotto

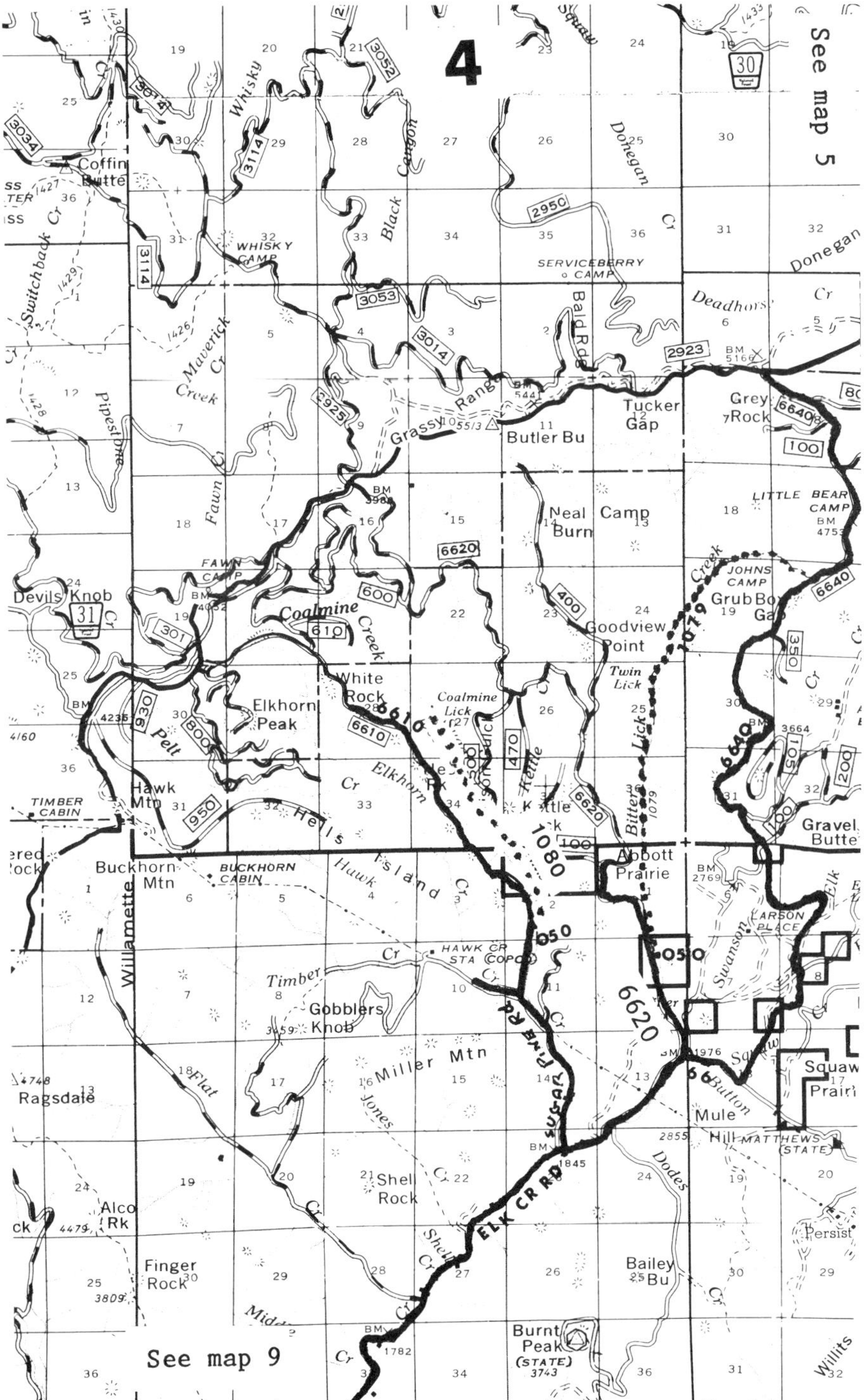
4
See map 5
See map 9
Coffin Butte
Switchback Cr
Whisky Cr
Whisky Camp
Black Canyon
Donegan Cr
Serviceberry Camp
Bald Rdg
Deadhorse Cr
Maverick Cr
Pipestone Cr
Fawn Cr
Grassy Range
Butler Bu
Tucker Gap
Grey Rock
Little Bear Camp
Neal Camp Burn
Fawn Camp
Devils Knob
Coalmine Creek
Goodview Point
Johns Camp
Grub Box Gap
Twin Lick
Bitter Lick Creek
White Rock
Elkhorn Peak
Coalmine Lick
Pelt Cr
Hawk Mtn
Timber Cabin
Elkhorn Cr
Kettle Cr
Hells Island Cr
Gravel Butte
Abbott Prairie
Buckhorn Mtn
Buckhorn Cabin
Hawk Cr
Larson Place
Swanson
Willamette
Hawk Cr Sta (COPCO)
Timber Cr
Gobblers Knob
Miller Mtn
Sugar Pine Rd
Squaw Prairie
Ragsdale
Flat Cr
Jones Cr
Button
Mule Hill
Matthews (State)
Dodes Cr
Shel Rock
Alco Rk
Elk Cr Rd
Persist
Finger Rock
Shell Cr
Bailey Bu
Burnt Peak (State) 3743
Willits
Middle Cr
3034
3014
3114
3052
3053
2950
2923
2925
6640
100
6620
600
610
31
301
350
400
630
800
6610
470
500
1079
1080
950
1050
105
200
30

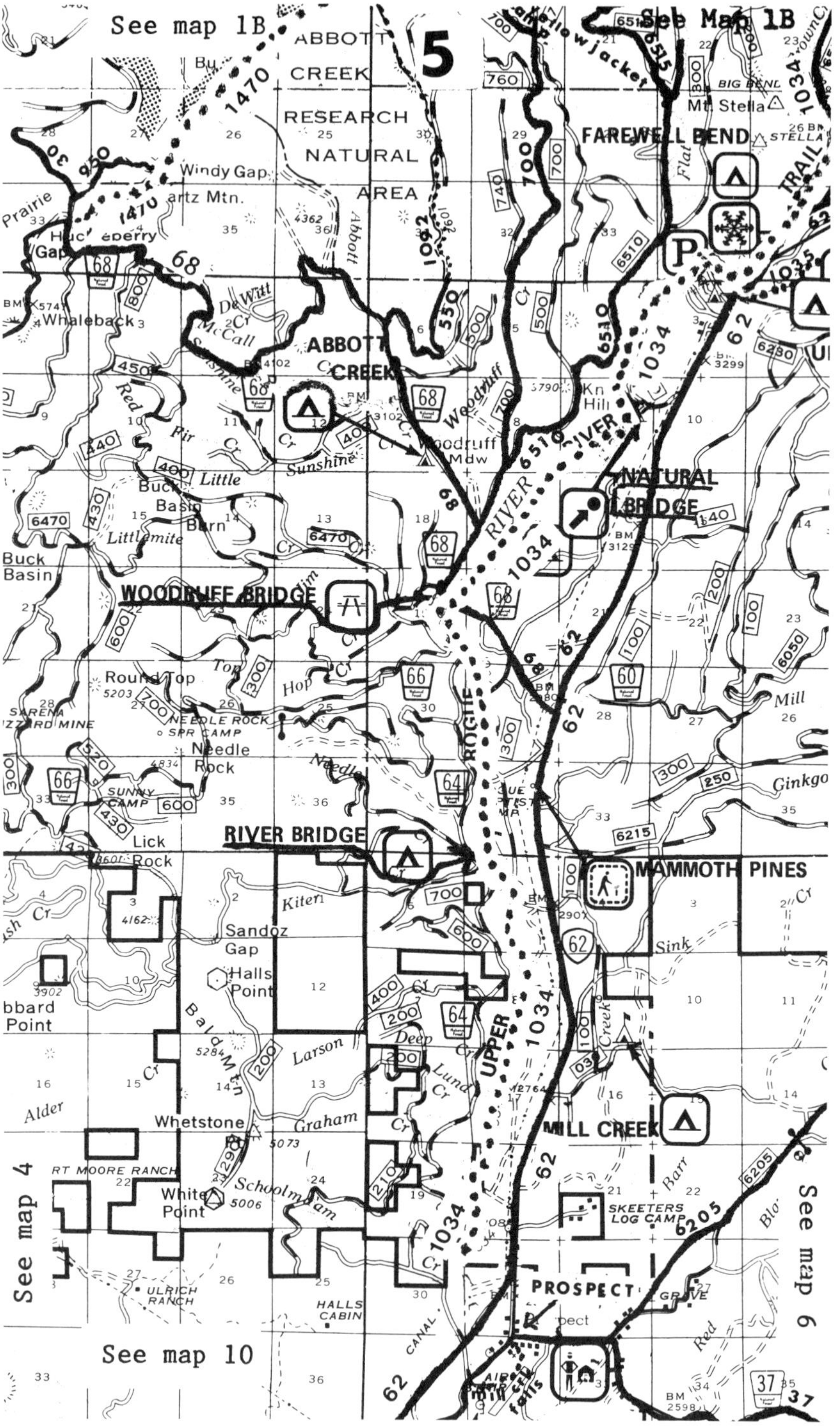
5
See map 1B
See Map 1B
See map 4
See map 6
See map 10
ABBOTT CREEK RESEARCH NATURAL AREA
Windy Gap
Huckleberry Gap
Whaleback
Mt. Stella
STELLA
BIG BEND
FAREWELL BEND
TRAIL
Yellowjacket
ABBOTT CREEK
De Witt Cr
McCall
Sunshine Cr
Woodruff Mdw
Woodruff
NATURAL BRIDGE
Little
Buck Basin
Burn
Littlemite
WOODRUFF BRIDGE
RIVER
ROGUE
UPPER
Round Top
SARENA
NEEDLE ROCK
SPR CAMP
Needle Rock
SUNNY CAMP
Lick Rock
RIVER BRIDGE
MAMMOTH PINES
Sandoz Gap
Halls Point
Bald Mtn
Larson
Deep Cr
Lund Cr
Alder
Whetstone Pt
Graham
Schoolmarm
White Point
RT MOORE RANCH
ULRICH RANCH
HALLS CABIN
MILL CREEK
SKEETERS LOG CAMP
PROSPECT
GROVE
CANAL
Mill
Ginkgo
Sink
Creek
Barr
Red
Abbott
Flat
1470
950
30
68
800
450
440
400
430
6470
600
300
700
66
520
290
200
210
64
100
1034
62
6510
6515
760
740
500
550
1092
6230
1035
140
60
6050
6215
250
6205
37

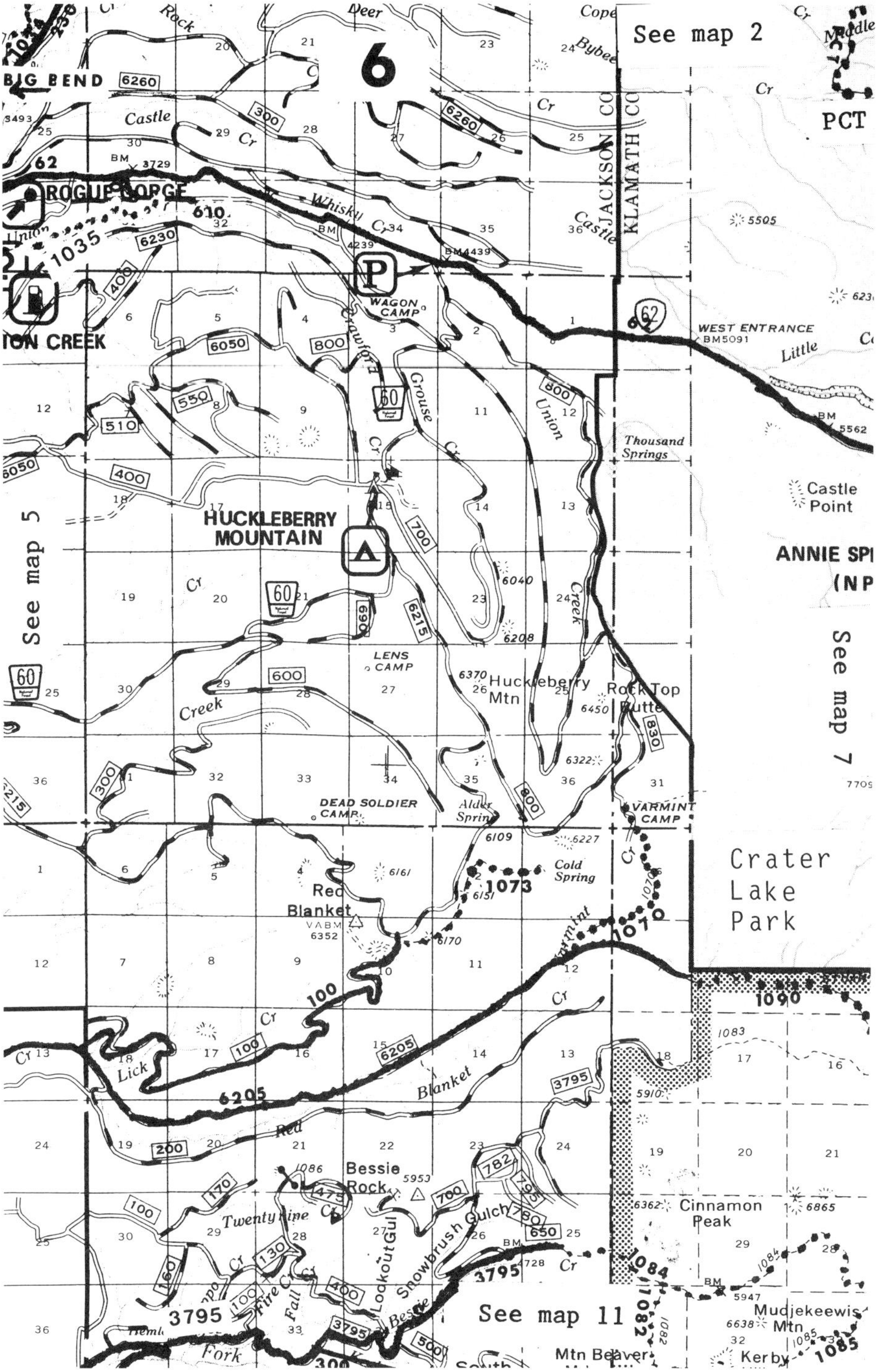
6
See map 2
See map 5
See map 7
See map 11
BIG BEND
ROGUE GORGE
ION CREEK
PCT
HUCKLEBERRY MOUNTAIN
Huckleberry Mtn
WAGON CAMP
LENS CAMP
DEAD SOLDIER CAMP
VARMINT CAMP
WEST ENTRANCE
Thousand Springs
Castle Point
ANNIE SP
(NP
Rock Top Butte
Alder Spring
Cold Spring
Red Blanket
Bessie Rock
Cinnamon Peak
Mudjekeewis Mtn
Mtn Beaver
Kerby
Crater Lake Park
JACKSON CO
KLAMATH CO
Snowbrush Gulch
Lookout Gul
Twenty Nine Cr
Lick Cr
Union Creek
Grouse Cr
Crawford Cr
Whisky Cr
Castle Cr
Rock Cr
Deer Cr
Bybee Cr
Blanket Cr
Red Blanket
Fire Cr
Fall Cr
Bessie Cr
Fork
1035
1073
1070
1090
1083
1084
1082
1085
6260
6230
6050
6205
6215
3795
62

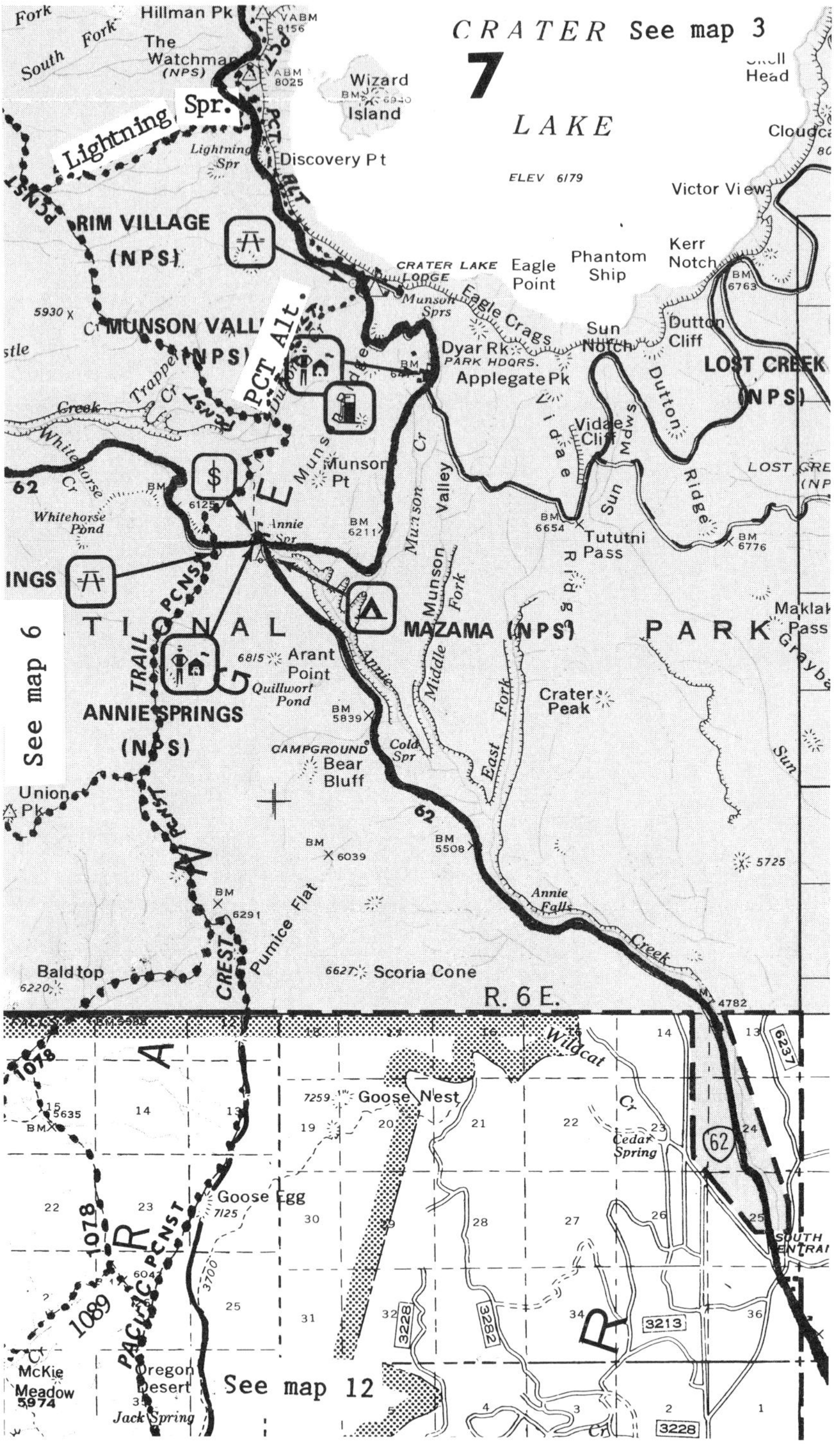
CRATER LAKE
7
See map 3
ELEV 6179
Hillman Pk
The Watchman (NPS)
Wizard Island
Lightning Spr.
Discovery Pt
RIM VILLAGE (NPS)
CRATER LAKE LODGE
Munson Sprs
Eagle Crags
Eagle Point
Phantom Ship
Kerr Notch
Victor View
Skell Head
Cloudcap
PCT Alt.
MUNSON VALLEY (NPS)
Dyar Rk
PARK HDQRS.
Applegate Pk
Sun Notch
Dutton Cliff
Dutton Ridge
LOST CREEK (NPS)
Vidae Cliff
Vidae Ridge
Munson Pt
Annie Spr
Whitehorse Pond
Tututni Pass
MAZAMA (NPS)
NATIONAL PARK
Maklaks Pass
Arant Point
Quillwort Pond
ANNIE SPRINGS (NPS)
Crater Peak
CAMPGROUND
Bear Bluff
Cold Spr
Union Pk
Pumice Flat
Annie Falls
Annie Creek
Baldtop
Scoria Cone
PACIFIC CREST TRAIL
R. 6 E.
Wildcat Cr
Goose Nest
Cedar Spring
Goose Egg
SOUTH ENTRANCE
McKie Meadow
Oregon Desert
Jack Spring
See map 6
See map 12

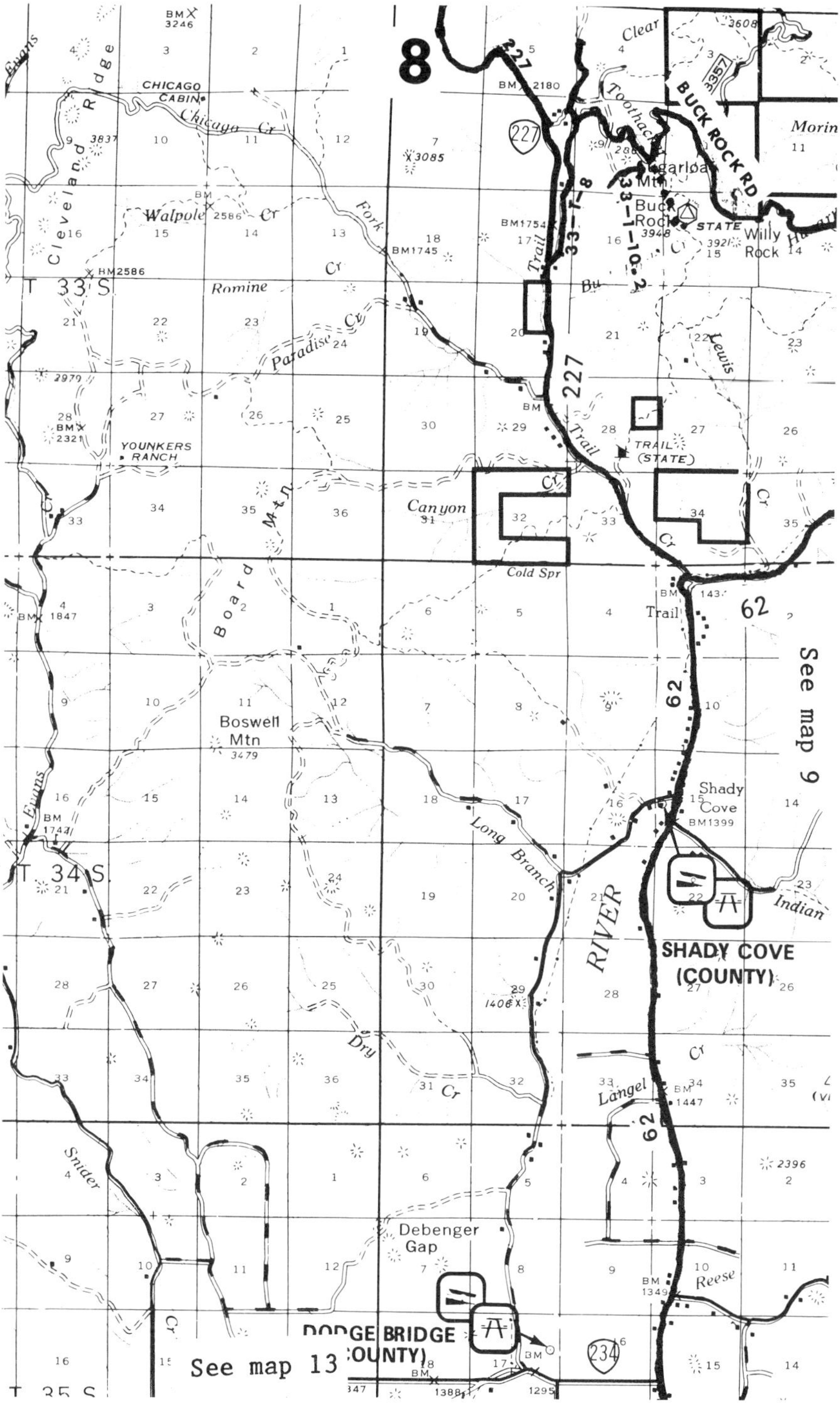
8
Chicago Cabin
Chicago Cr
Cleveland Ridge
Walpole Cr
Romine Cr
Paradise Cr
Fork Cr
Younkers Ranch
Board Mtn
Canyon Cr
Cold Spr
Clear Cr
Toothache Cr
Sugarloaf Mtn
Buck Rock
STATE
Willy Rock
Lewis
TRAIL (STATE)
BUCK ROCK RD
3357
227
33-1-8
33-1-10.2
T 33 S.
T 34 S.
T 35 S.
62
See map 9
Boswell Mtn
3479
Long Branch
RIVER
Shady Cove
BM1399
Indian
SHADY COVE (COUNTY)
Dry Cr
Langel Cr
Evans Cr
Snider Cr
Debenger Gap
DODGE BRIDGE (COUNTY)
Reese
234
See map 13

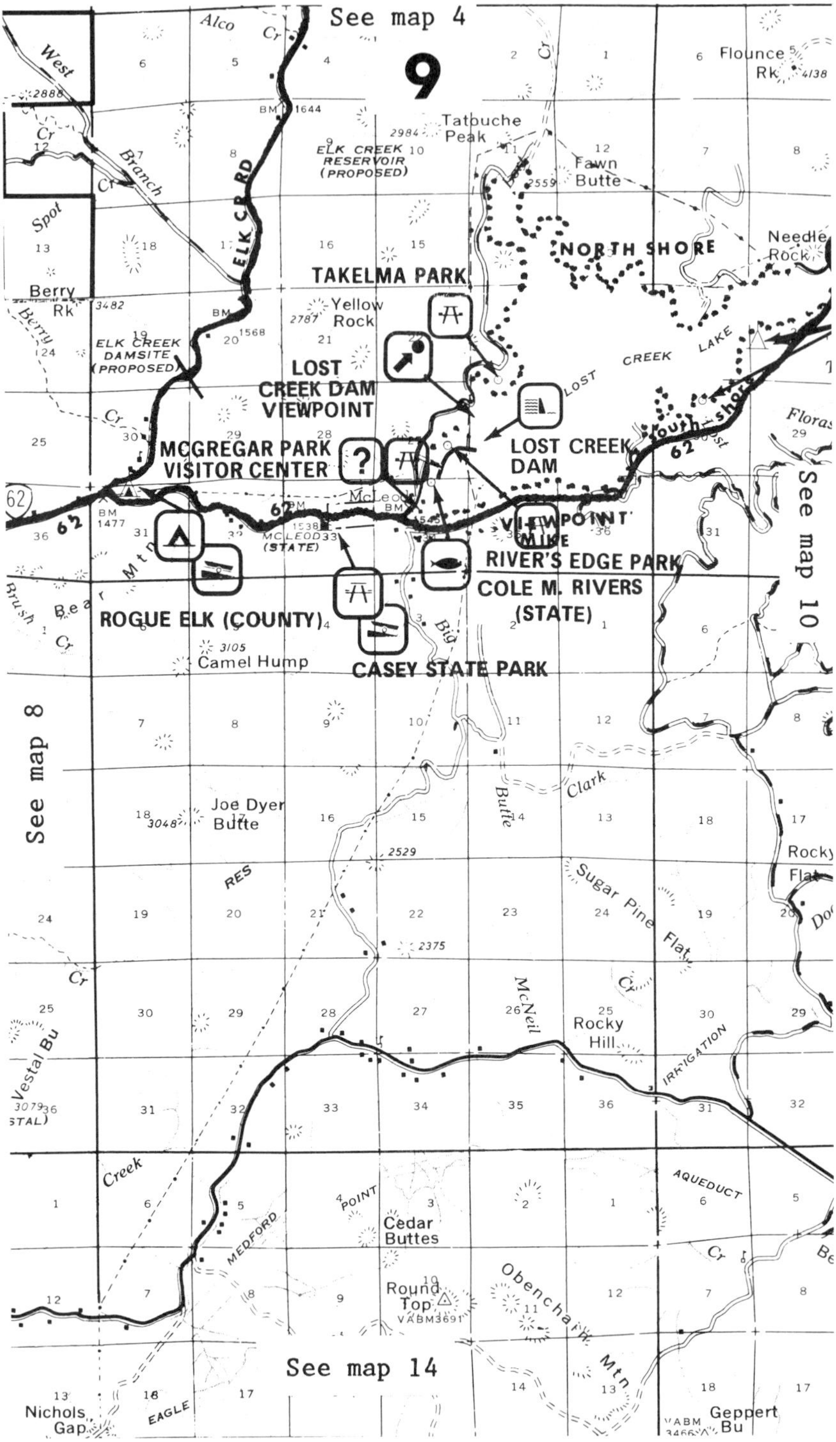

See map 4
9
See map 8
See map 10
See map 14
TAKELMA PARK
LOST CREEK DAM VIEWPOINT
McGREGAR PARK VISITOR CENTER
NORTH SHORE
LOST CREEK LAKE
LOST CREEK DAM
VIEWPOINT MIKE
RIVER'S EDGE PARK
COLE M. RIVERS (STATE)
ROGUE ELK (COUNTY)
McLEOD (STATE)
CASEY STATE PARK
ELK CREEK RESERVOIR (PROPOSED)
ELK CREEK DAMSITE (PROPOSED)
ELK CR RD
Tatouche Peak
Fawn Butte
Flounce Rk
Needle Rock
Yellow Rock
Berry Rk
Camel Hump
Joe Dyer Butte
Sugar Pine Flat
Rocky Hill
Rocky Flat
Cedar Buttes
Round Top
Obenchain Mtn
Nichols Gap
Geppert Bu
Vestal Bu
Bear Mtn
McNeil
Clark
Butte
Big
MEDFORD POINT
EAGLE
IRRIGATION
AQUEDUCT
RES
62

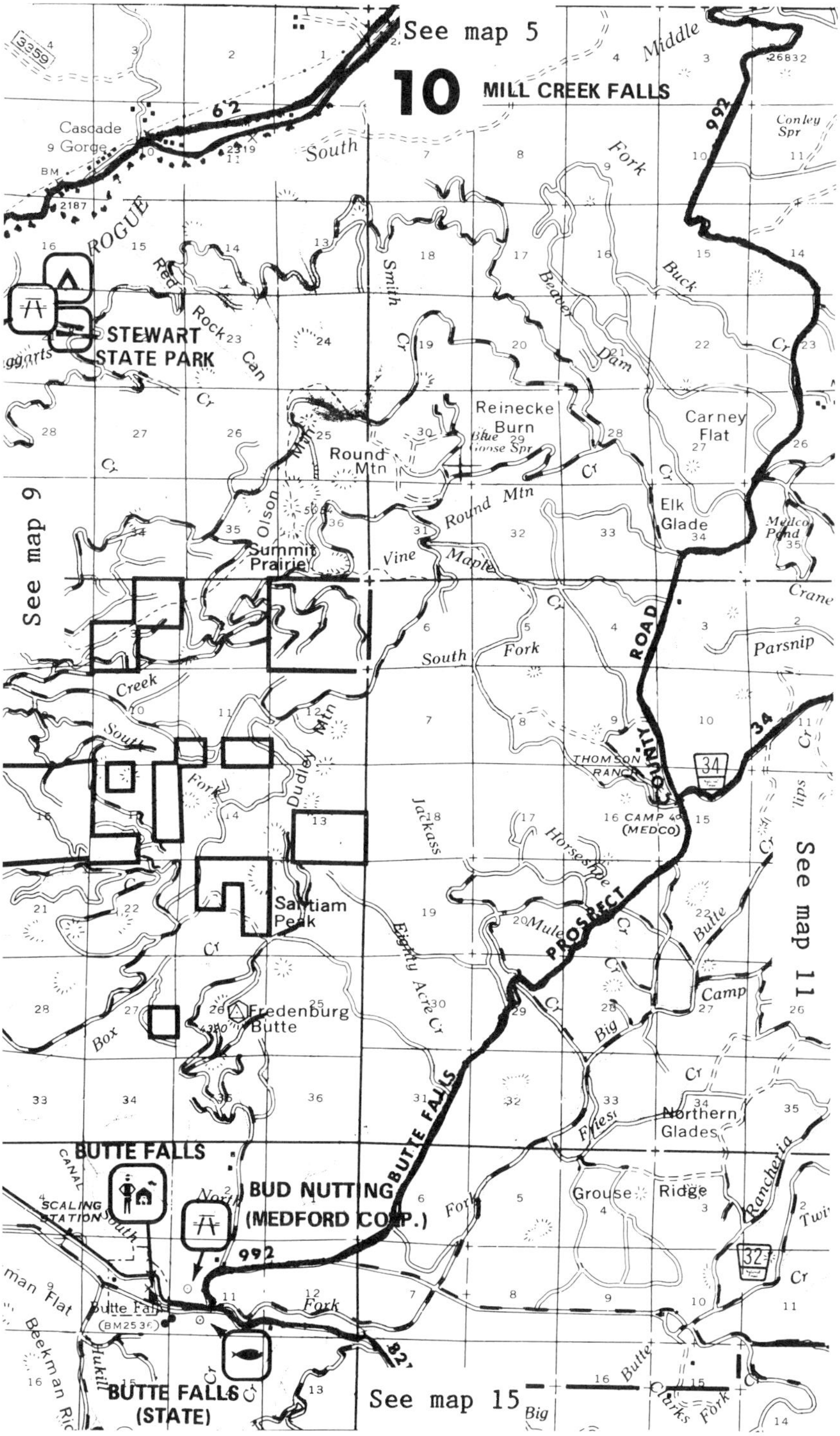
10
MILL CREEK FALLS
See map 5
See map 9
See map 11
See map 15
Cascade Gorge
ROGUE
STEWART STATE PARK
Red Rock Can Cr
South Fork
Middle Fork
Smith Cr
Beaver Dam Cr
Buck Cr
Conley Spr
Reinecke Burn
Blue Goose Spr
Round Mtn
Carney Flat
Elk Glade
Medco Pond
Olson Mtn
Summit Prairie
Vine Maple Cr
Round Mtn Cr
Crane
Parsnip
Creek
South Fork
Dudley Mtn
Jackass
THOMSON RANCH
CAMP 4 (MEDCO)
COUNTY ROAD
PROSPECT
BUTTE FALLS
Horseshoe
Mule Cr
Saltiam Peak
Eighty Acre Cr
Fredenburg Butte
Box
Big Cr
Camp
Butte
Northern Glades
Friese
Grouse Ridge
Rancheria
BUTTE FALLS
SCALING STATION
CANAL
BUD NUTTING (MEDFORD CORP.)
North Fork
Butte Falls
Beekman
Hukill
BUTTE FALLS (STATE)
Clarks Fork
Big Butte
992
62
34
32
821

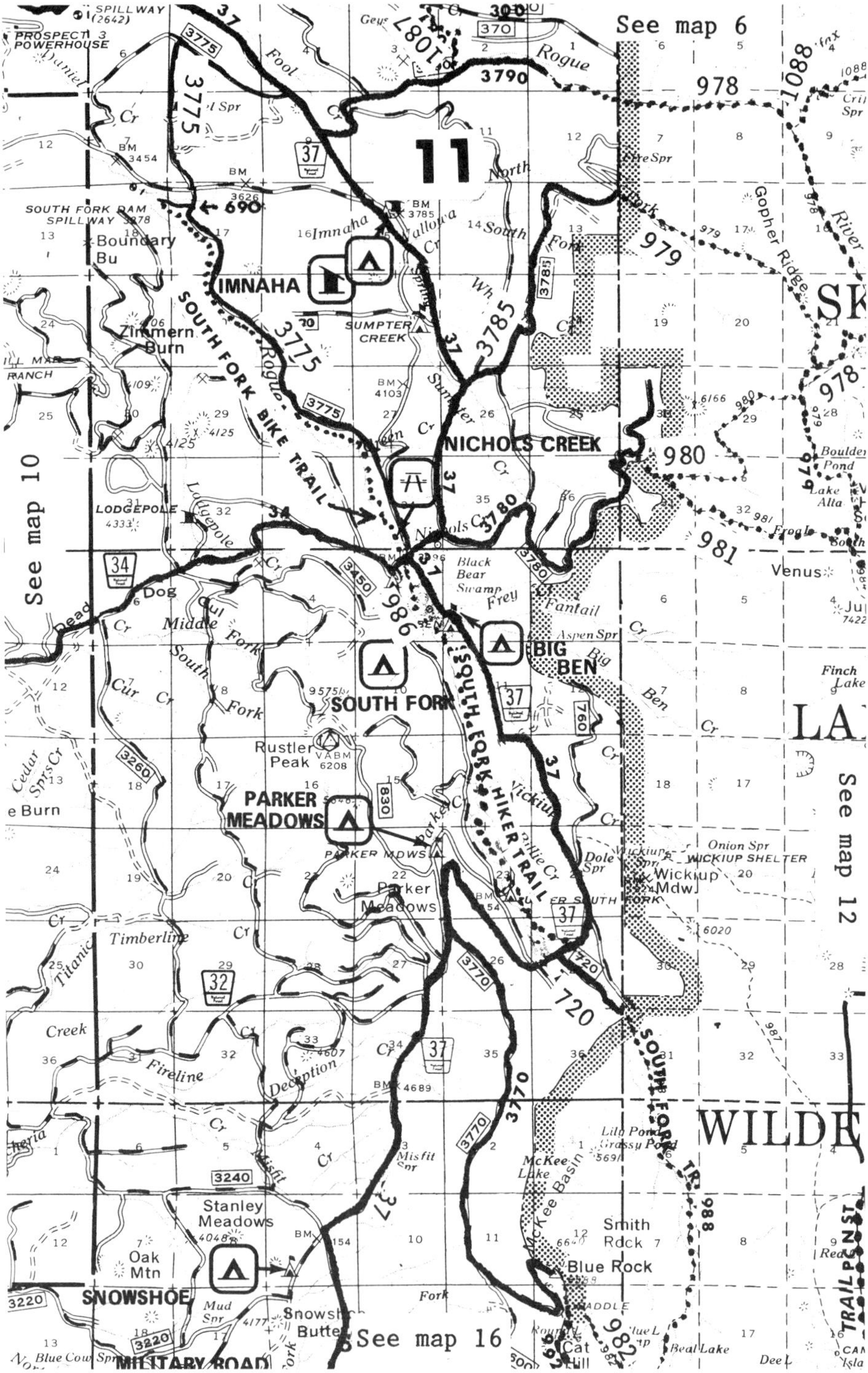

11
See map 6
See map 10
See map 12
See map 16
IMNAHA
SUMPTER CREEK
NICHOLS CREEK
BIG BEN
SOUTH FORK
PARKER MEADOWS
SNOWSHOE
SOUTH FORK BIKE TRAIL
SOUTH FORK HIKER TRAIL
SOUTH FORK TR. 988
MILITARY ROAD
PROSPECT 3 POWERHOUSE
SPILLWAY (2642)
SOUTH FORK DAM SPILLWAY 3878
Boundary Bu
Zimmern Burn
LODGEPOLE 4333
Rustler Peak
Parker Meadows
Stanley Meadows 4048
Oak Mtn
Snowshoe Butte
Black Bear Swamp
Aspen Spr
Dole Spr
Onion Spr
WICKIUP SHELTER
Wickiup Mdw
McKee Lake
McKee Basin
Lily Pond
Grassy Pond
Smith Rock
Blue Rock
Cat Hill
Gopher Ridge
Boulder Pond
Lake Alta
Venus
Finch Lake
Misfit Spr
Mud Spr
Blue Cow Spr
Timberline
Fireline
Deception
Rogue
North Fork
WILDE
LA
SK
TRAIL PCNST

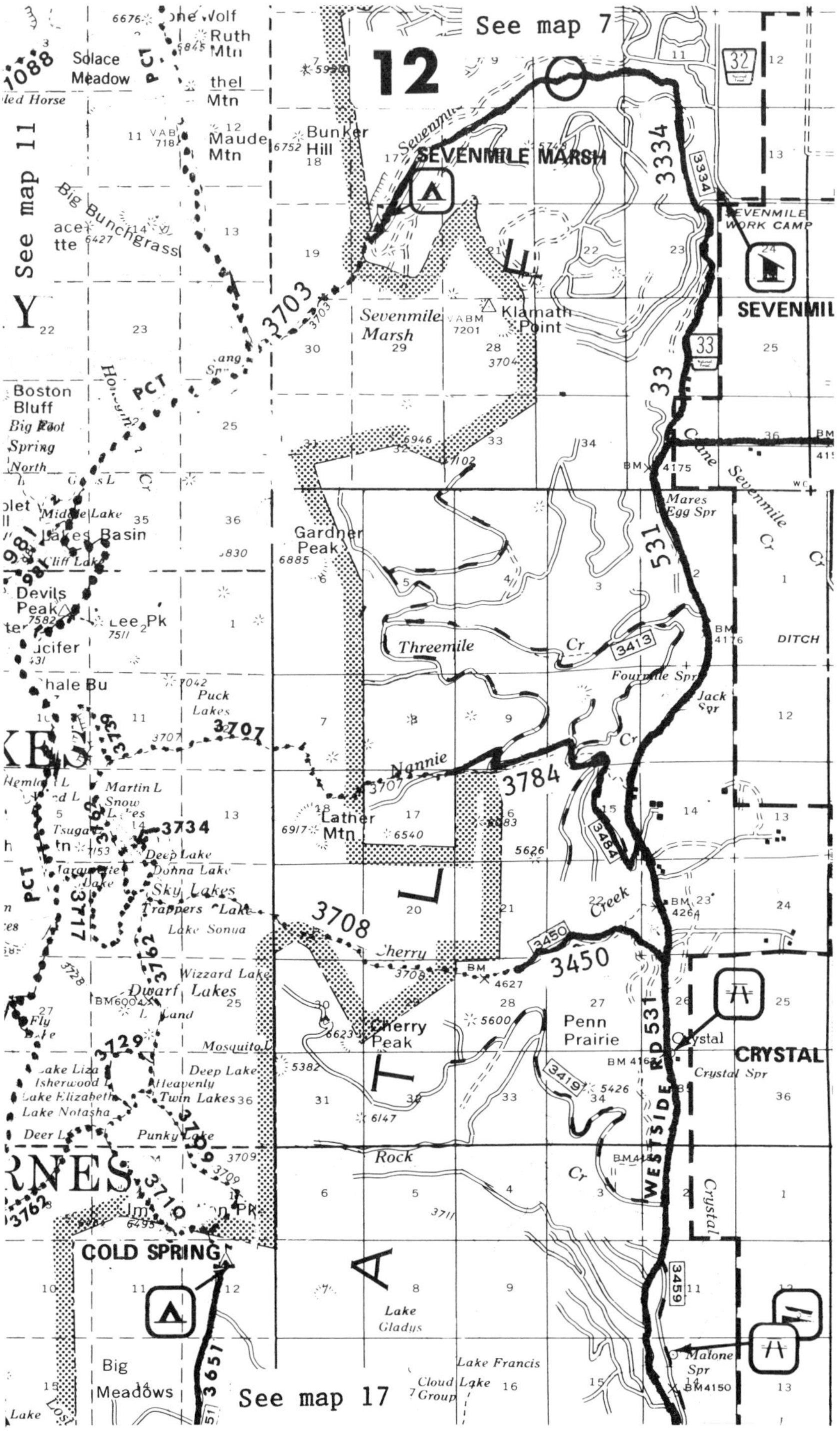
See map 7
12
See map 11
See map 17
Solace Meadow
Ruth Mtn
Maude Mtn
Bunker Hill
SEVENMILE MARSH
Sevenmile Marsh
Klamath Point
SEVENMILE WORK CAMP
SEVENMIL
Big Bunchgrass
Boston Bluff
Middle Lake
Lakes Basin
Cliff Lake
Devils Peak
Lee Pk
Gardner Peak
Threemile Cr
Fourmile Spr
Jack Spr
Mares Egg Spr
Sevenmile Cr
DITCH
Puck Lakes
Nannie Cr
Lather Mtn
Martin L
Snow Lakes
Deep Lake
Donna Lake
Sky Lakes
Trappers Lake
Lake Sonya
Wizzard Lake
Dwarf Lakes
Cherry Creek
Cherry Peak
Penn Prairie
Crystal
CRYSTAL
Crystal Spr
Mosquito L
Deep Lake
Heavenly Twin Lakes
Lake Notasha
Punky Lake
Rock Cr
COLD SPRING
Big Meadows
Lake Gladys
Lake Francis
Cloud Lake Group
Malone Spr
WESTSIDE RD 531
PCT
3334
33
531
3703
3704
3707
3708
3413
3784
3484
3450
3419
3734
3729
3710
3709
3762
3717
3459
3651
BM 4175
BM 4176
BM 4264
BM 4150
BM 4627

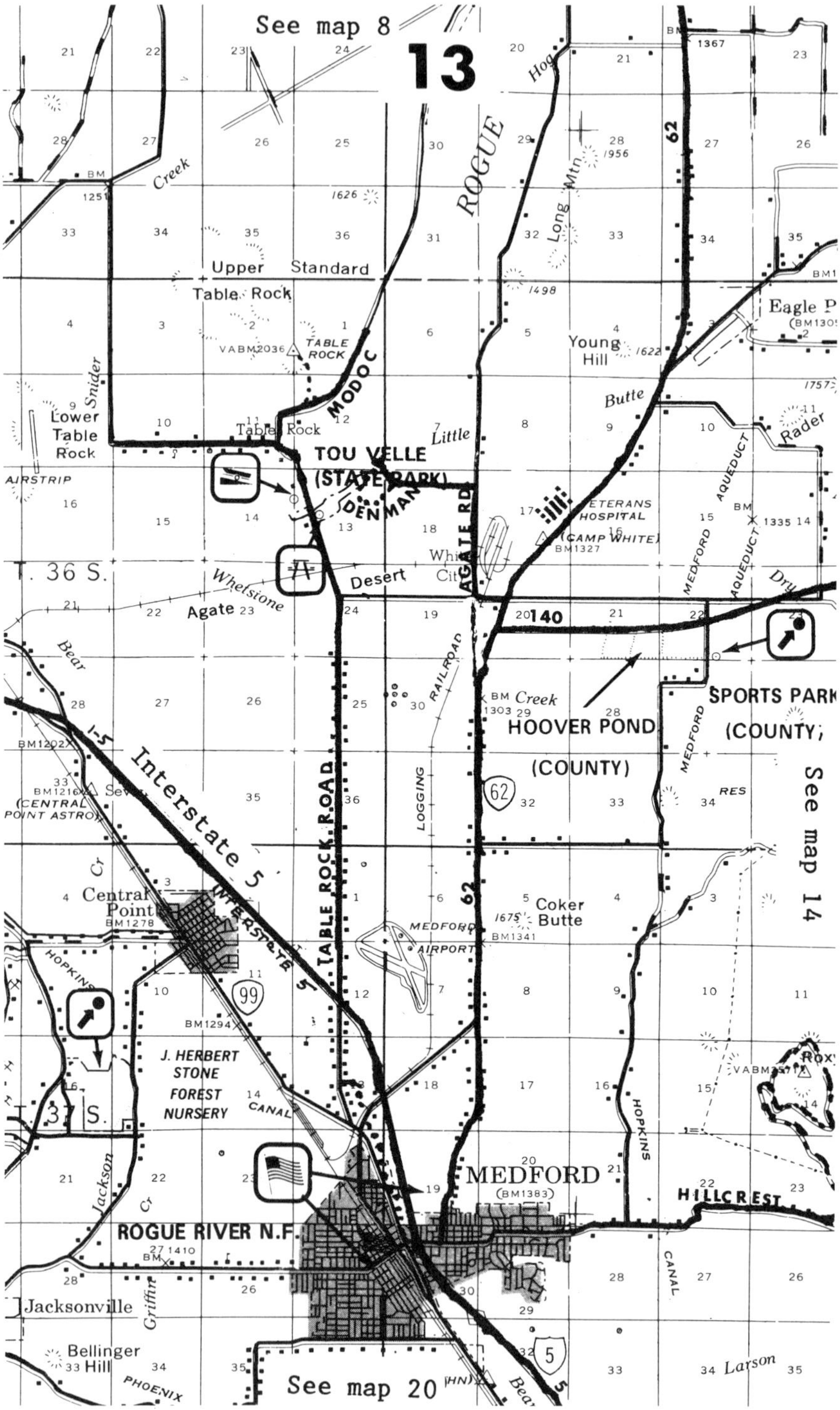

See map 8
13
ROGUE
Creek
Upper Standard
Table Rock
TABLE ROCK
VABM2036
MODOC
Long Mtn
Young Hill
Butte
Lower Table Rock
Snider
AIRSTRIP
Table Rock
TOU VELLE (STATE PARK)
DENMAN
Little
AGATE RD
VETERANS HOSPITAL (CAMP WHITE)
MEDFORD AQUEDUCT
Rader
Eagle P
T. 36 S.
Whetstone
Agate
Desert
White City
140
62
Bear
Creek
HOOVER POND (COUNTY)
SPORTS PARK (COUNTY)
See map 14
I-5
Interstate 5
(CENTRAL POINT ASTRO)
TABLE ROCK ROAD
LOGGING RAILROAD
MEDFORD
RES
Central Point
Coker Butte
MEDFORD AIRPORT
HOPKINS
99
J. HERBERT STONE FOREST NURSERY
CANAL
T. 37 S.
Jackson Cr
ROGUE RIVER N.F.
MEDFORD
HILLCREST
CANAL
Jacksonville
Griffin
Bellinger Hill
PHOENIX
See map 20
Larson
5

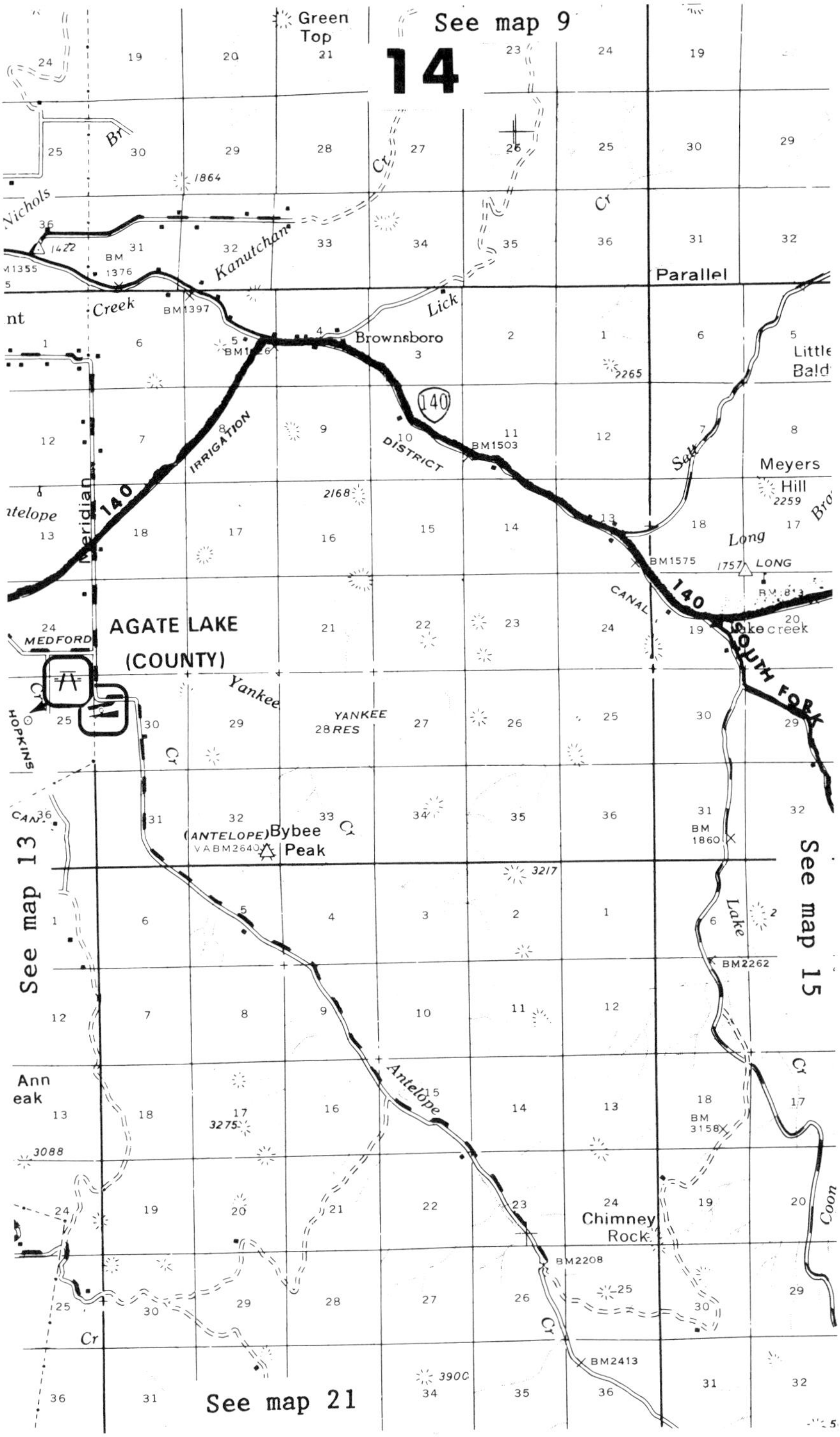
14
See map 9
See map 13
See map 15
See map 21
Green Top
Nichols
Br
Kanutchan
Creek
Cr
Lick
Parallel
Brownsboro
140
IRRIGATION
DISTRICT
CANAL
Salt
Meyers Hill
2259
Little Bald
Long
LONG
Lake creek
SOUTH FORK
Meridian
AGATE LAKE
(COUNTY)
MEDFORD
HOPKINS
Yankee
YANKEE
RES
(ANTELOPE) Bybee Peak
VABM2640
3217
Lake
Antelope
Chimney Rock
Coon
1864
1422
BM 1376
BM1397
BM1503
BM1575
2168
2265
1757
BM 1860
BM2262
BM 3158
BM2208
BM2413
3275
3088
3900

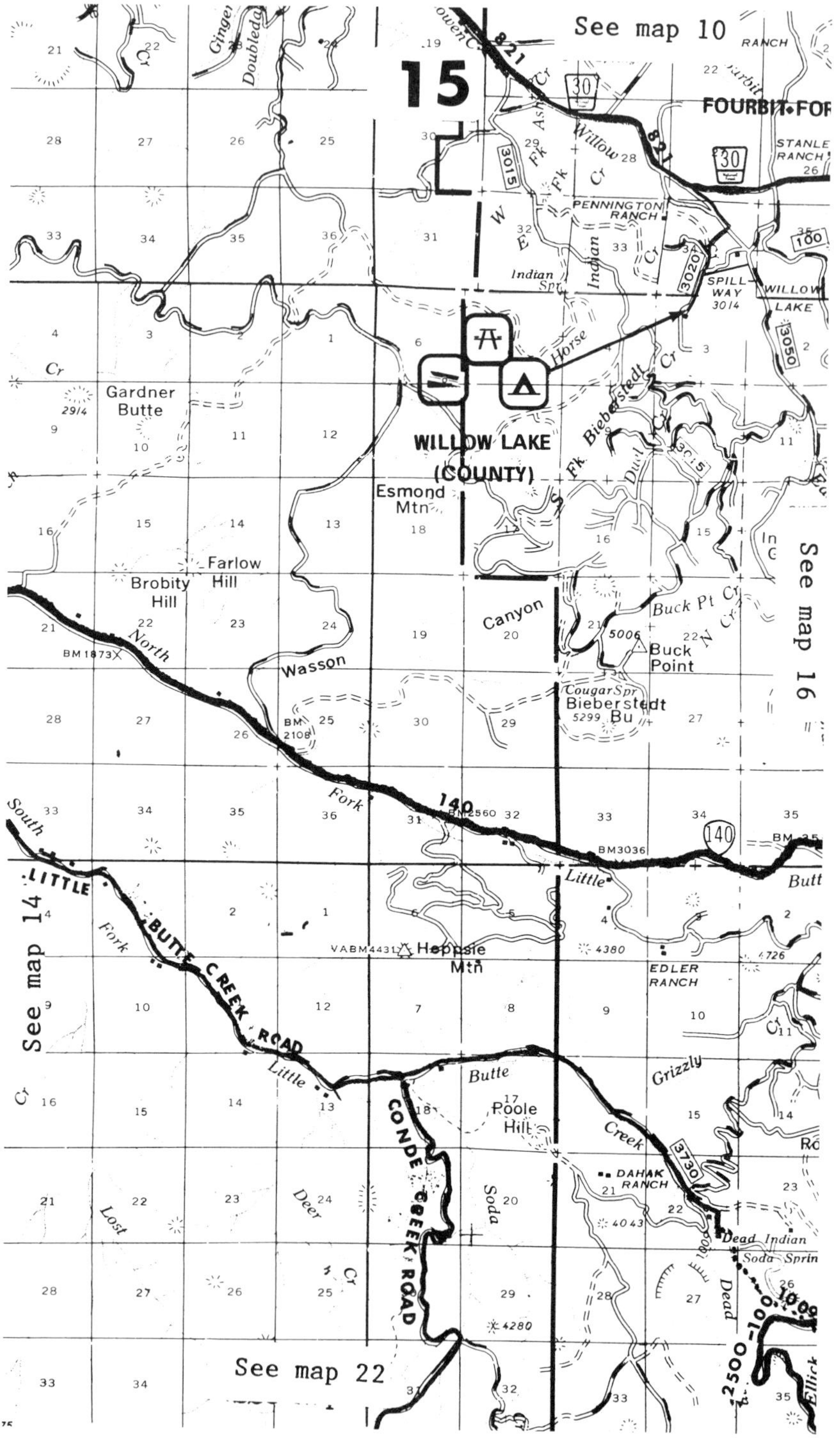

15
See map 10
See map 14
See map 16
See map 22
WILLOW LAKE
(COUNTY)
FOURBIT•FOR
STANLE
RANCH
PENNINGTON
RANCH
SPILL
WAY
3014
WILLOW
LAKE
Gardner
Butte
Esmond
Mtn
Brobity
Hill
Farlow
Hill
Buck
Point
Biebersteidt
Bu
Cougar Spr
Indian Spr
Heppsie
Mtn
Poole
Hill
EDLER
RANCH
DAHAK
RANCH
Dead Indian
Soda Sprin
LITTLE BUTTE CREEK ROAD
CONDE CREEK ROAD
North Fork
South Fork
Little Butte Creek
Wasson
Canyon
Grizzly
Buck Pt Cr
Willow Cr
Horse
Soda
Deer
Lost
Dead
BM 1873
BM 2108
BM 2560
BM 3036
VABM 4431
821
140

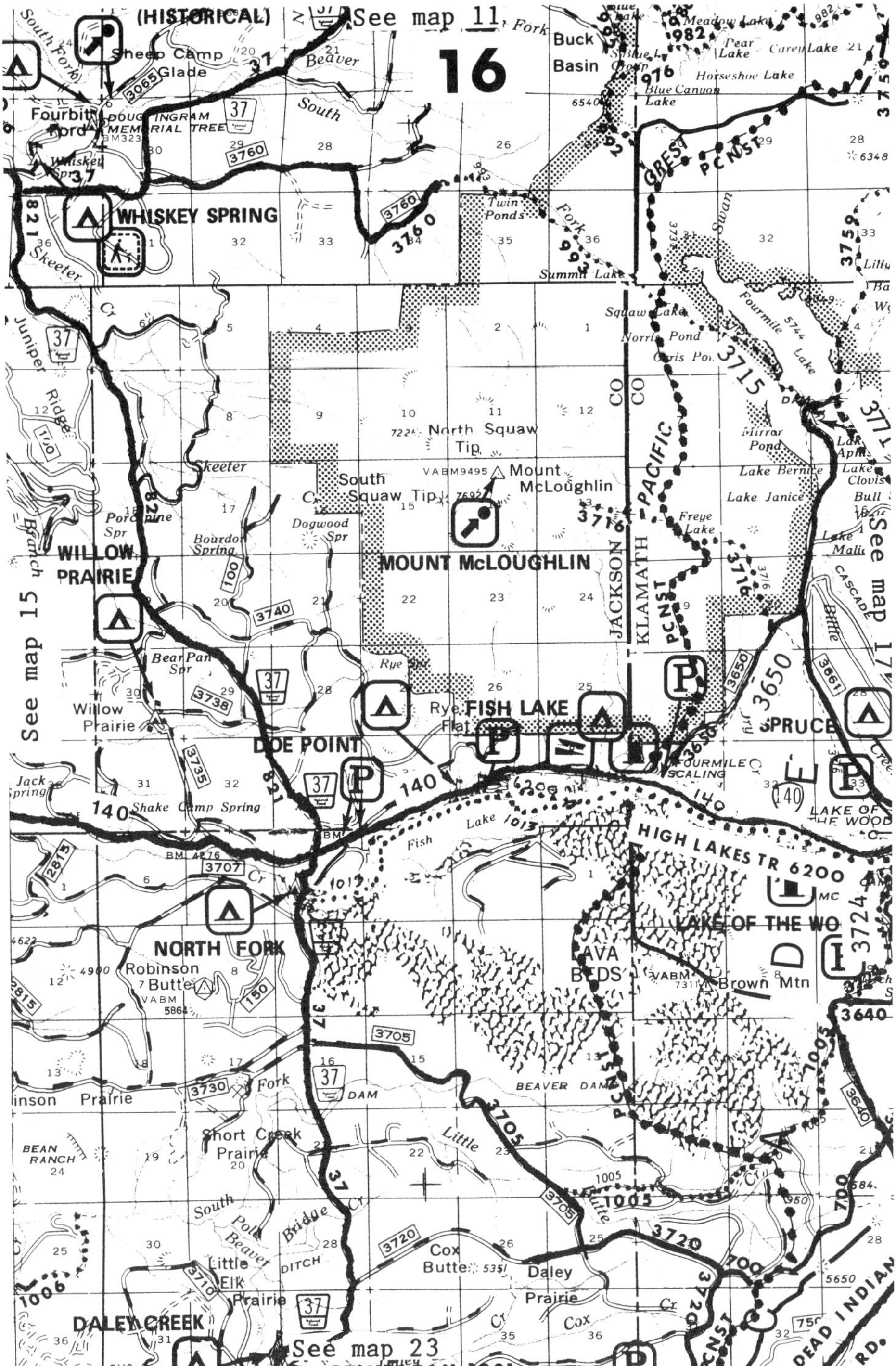
16
(HISTORICAL)
See map 11
See map 15
See map 17
See map 23
Sheep Camp Glade
Fourbit Ford
DOUG INGRAM MEMORIAL TREE
WHISKEY SPRING
Buck Basin
Meadow Lake
Pear Lake
Carey Lake
Horseshoe Lake
Blue Canyon Lake
CREST
PCNST
Twin Ponds
Summit Lake
Squaw Lake
Norris Pond
Fourmile Lake
Mirror Pond
Lake Bernice
Lake Janice
Freye Lake
North Squaw Tip
Mount McLoughlin
South Squaw Tip
MOUNT McLOUGHLIN
Dogwood Spr
Bourdon Spring
Porcupine Spr
Juniper Ridge
Skeeter Cr
WILLOW PRAIRIE
Bear Pan Spr
Willow Prairie
Rye Spr
Rye Flat
FISH LAKE
DOE POINT
JACKSON CO
KLAMATH CO
PACIFIC
SPRUCE
FOURMILE SCALING
LAKE OF THE WOODS
Jack Spring
Shake Camp Spring
Fish Lake
HIGH LAKES TR 6200
LAKE OF THE WO
LAVA BEDS
Brown Mtn
NORTH FORK
Robinson Butte
Robinson Prairie
BEAVER DAM
Short Creek Prairie
BEAN RANCH
Little Elk Prairie
Cox Butte
Daley Prairie
DALEY CREEK
BEAVER DAM 2001
DEAD INDIAN RD.
CASCADE
3065
3760
3715
3716
3740
3738
3735
3707
3705
3730
3720
3710
3650
3661
3640
3724
140
37
821
1005
1006
700
993
976
982

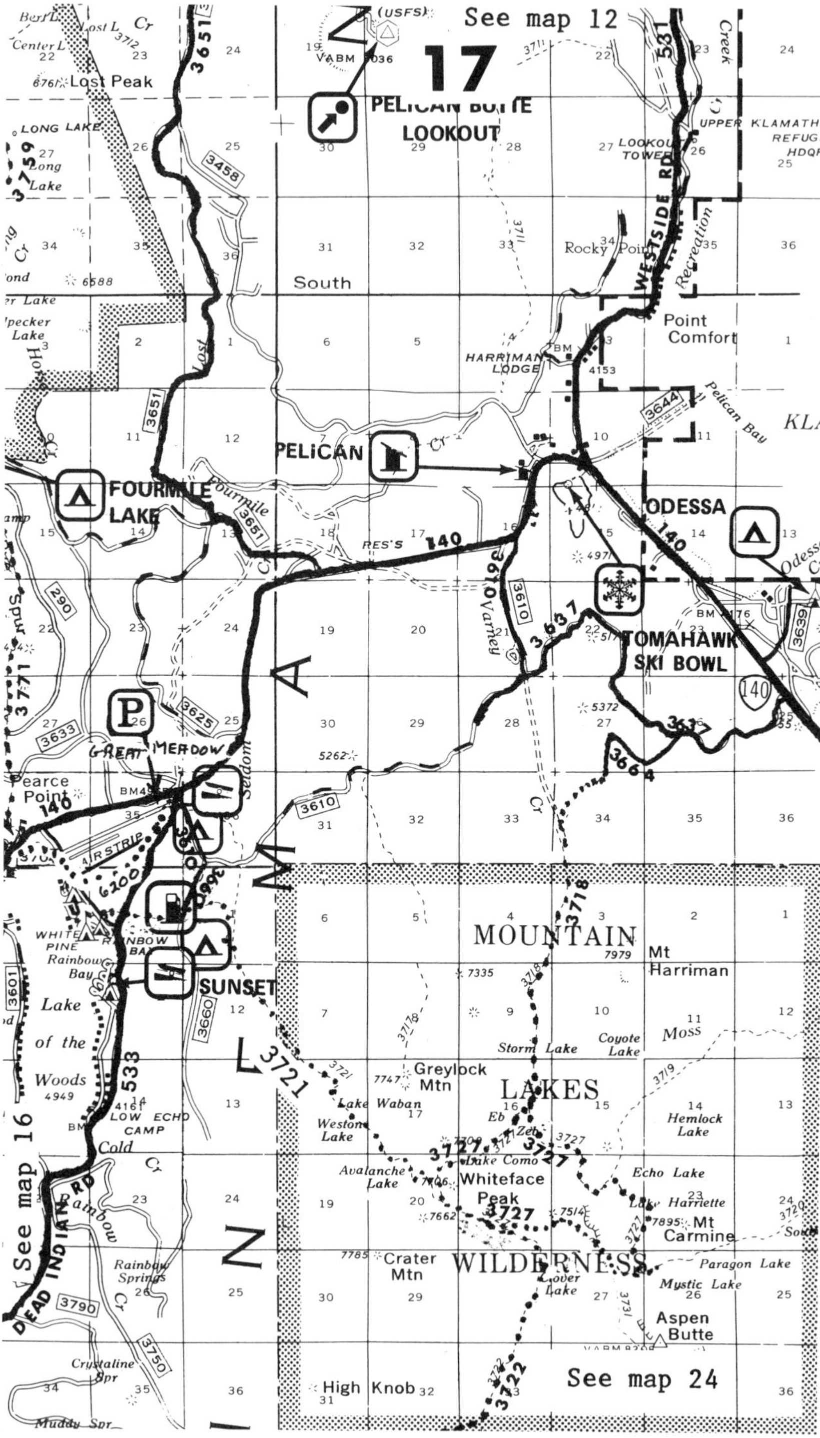

17
See map 12
See map 16
See map 24
PELICAN BUTTE LOOKOUT
(USFS)
Lost Peak
Long Lake
UPPER KLAMATH REFUGE HDQRS
LOOKOUT TOWER
WESTSIDE RD
Recreation
Rocky Point
South
Point Comfort
HARRIMAN LODGE
Pelican Bay
PELICAN
FOURMILE LAKE
Fourmile
RES'S
ODESSA
Odessa Cr
TOMAHAWK SKI BOWL
Varney Cr
Seldom Cr
GREAT MEADOW
Pearce Point
AIR STRIP
WHITE PINE
RAINBOW BAY
Rainbow Bay
SUNSET
Lake of the Woods
LOW ECHO CAMP
Cold Cr
Rainbow Cr
Rainbow Springs
Crystaline Spr
Muddy Spr
DEAD INDIAN RD
MOUNTAIN LAKES WILDERNESS
Mt Harriman
Storm Lake
Coyote Lake
Moss
Greylock Mtn
Lake Waban
Weston Lake
Hemlock Lake
Lake Como
Avalanche Lake
Whiteface Peak
Echo Lake
Lake Harriette
Mt Carmine
Crater Mtn
Paragon Lake
Clover Lake
Mystic Lake
Aspen Butte
High Knob
140
533
531
3651
3458
3644
3610
3637
3639
3664
3625
3633
3771
3759
290
6200
3601
3660
3721
3718
3719
3727
3722
3720
3731
3790
3750

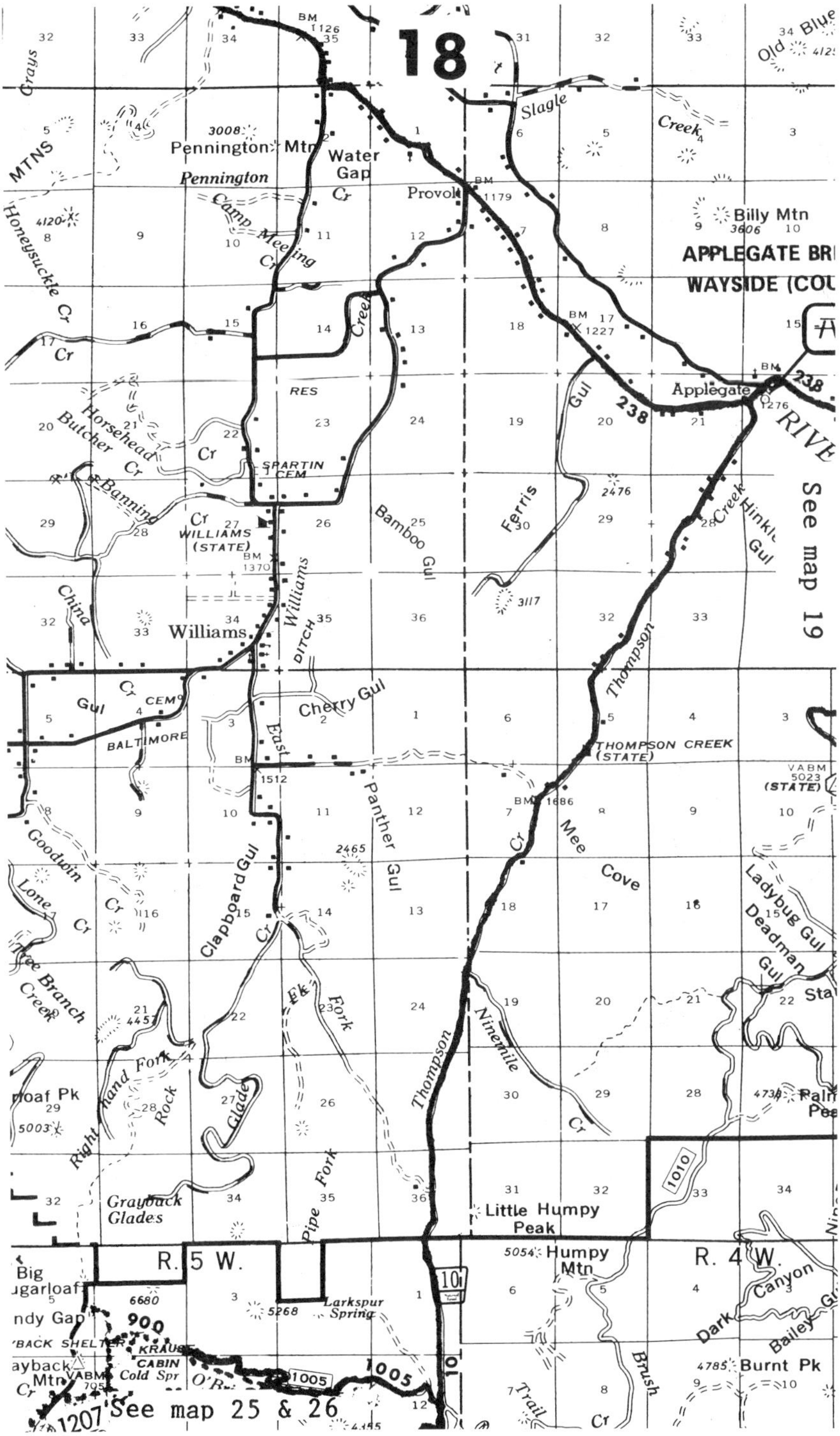

18
Grays
MTNS
Honeysuckle Cr
Pennington Mtn
3008
Pennington
Camp Meeting Cr
Water Gap Cr
Provolt
BM 1179
BM 1126
Slagle Creek
Old Blue
4125
Billy Mtn
3606
APPLEGATE BR
WAYSIDE (COU
4120
BM 1227
Applegate
BM 1276
238
RIVE
Creek
RES
SPARTIN CEM
Horsehead Cr
Butcher Cr
Banning Cr
WILLIAMS (STATE)
BM 1370
Bamboo Gul
Ferris Gul
2476
Hinkle Gul
See map 19
3117
China
Williams
Williams
DITCH
Thompson
Gul Cr
CEM
BALTIMORE
Cherry Gul
East
BM 1512
THOMPSON CREEK (STATE)
VABM 5023 (STATE)
Panther Gul
BM 1686
Mee Cove
Goodwin Cr
Lone Cr
Clapboard Gul
2465
Cr
Ladybug Gul
Deadman Gul
Tree Branch Creek
Fk
Fork
Ninemile Cr
Thompson
4457
Right Hand Fork
Rock
Glade
Sugarloaf Pk
5003
4738
Palmer Peak
Pipe Fork
Grayback Glades
1010
Little Humpy Peak
5054
Humpy Mtn
R. 5 W.
R. 4 W.
Big Sugarloaf
6680
5268
Larkspur Spring
Sandy Gap
900
GRAYBACK SHELTER
KRAUS CABIN
Cold Spr
Grayback Mtn
VABM 705
O'Br
1005
1005
10
10
Dark Canyon
Bailey
4785
Burnt Pk
Brush Cr
Trail
1207
See map 25 & 26
4155

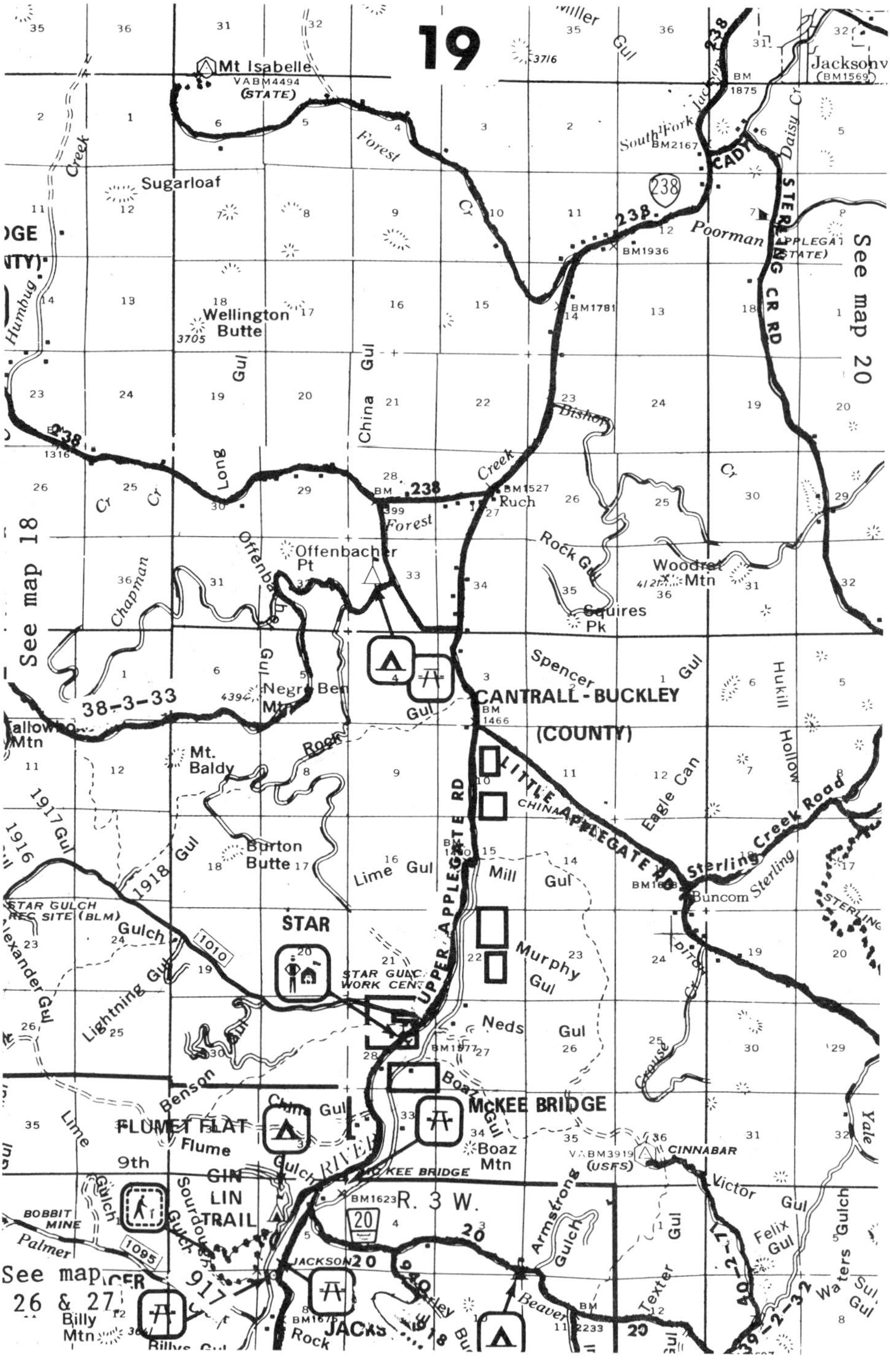

19
Mt Isabelle
VABM4494
(STATE)
Jacksonv
BM1875
Sugarloaf
Forest Cr
South Fork Jackson
CADY
238
STERLING CR RD
Daisy Cr
Poorman
APPLEGATE (STATE)
See map 20
BM2167
BM1936
BM1781
Wellington Butte
3705
3716
Humbug Creek
Long Gul
China Gul
Bishop
Creek
Ruch
BM1527
Cr
238
1316
Forest
Offenbacher Pt
Offenbacher Gul
Chapman Cr
Rock Gul
Woodrat Mtn
Squires Pk
See map 18
Negro Ben Mtn
4394
38-3-33
Tallowbo Mtn
Spencer Gul
CANTRALL - BUCKLEY (COUNTY)
BM 1466
Hukill Hollow
Mt. Baldy
Rock Gul
LITTLE APPLEGATE RD
CHINA
Eagle Can
Sterling Creek Road
1917 Gul
1916
1918 Gul
Burton Butte
Lime Gul
UPPER APPLEGATE RD
Mill Gul
Sterling
Buncom
STERLING
STAR GULCH REC SITE (BLM)
Alexander Gul
Gulch
1010
STAR
STAR GULCH WORK CENTER
Murphy Gul
Ditch Cr
Lightning Gul
Neds Gul
Crouse
BM1577
Benson
Boaz Gul
McKEE BRIDGE
China Gul
FLUMET FLAT
Flume
9th
Lime Gulch
Boaz Mtn
VABM3919 (USFS)
CINNABAR
Victor Gul
Yale
RIVER
McKEE BRIDGE
GIN LIN TRAIL
Sourdough Gulch
BM1623
R. 3 W.
20
Armstrong Gulch
Texter Gul
Felix Gul
Gulch
Waters Gul
BOBBIT MINE
Palmer
1095
917
JACKSON
20
See map 26 & 27
Billy Mtn
Billys Gul
BM1676
Rock
JACKS
Beaver
BM 2233
40-2-1
39-2-32

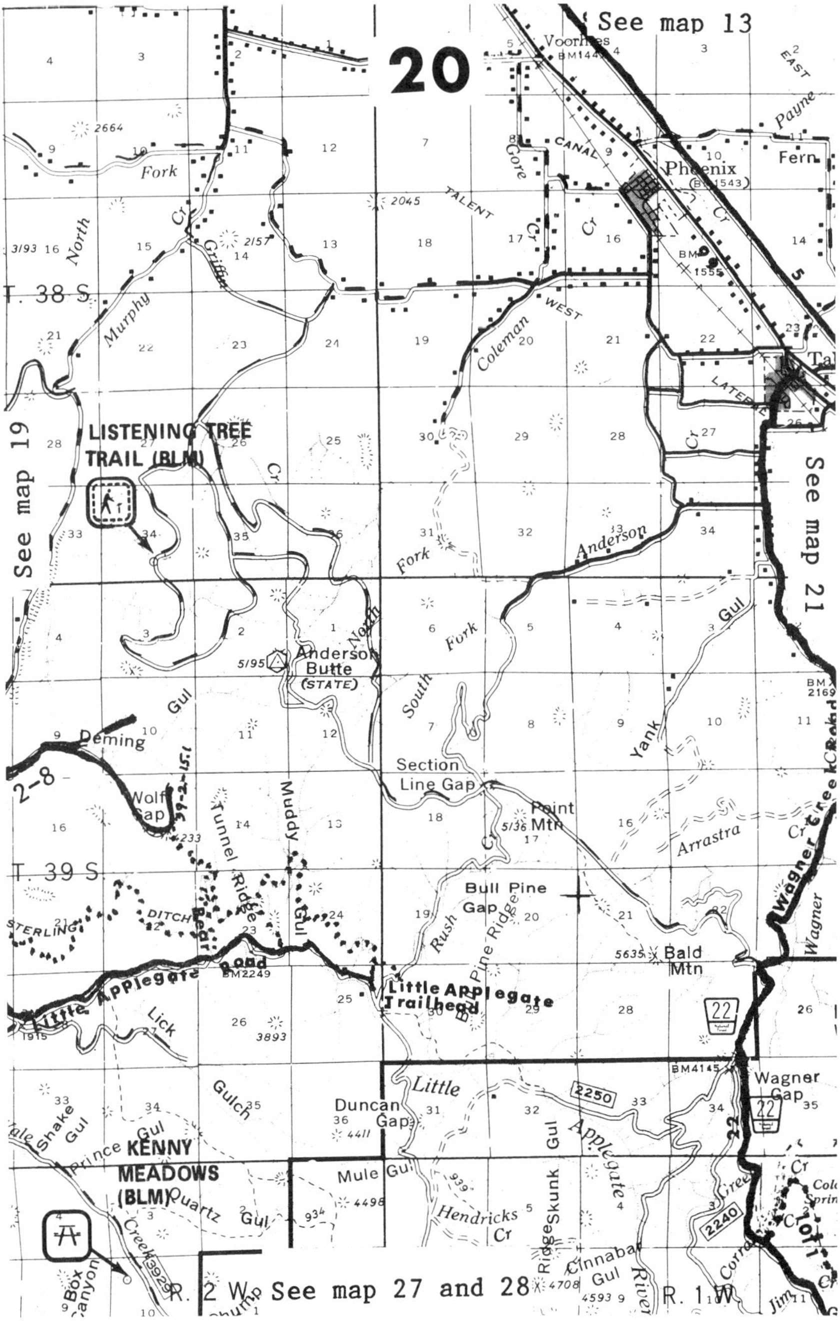

20
See map 13
See map 19
See map 21
See map 27 and 28
Voorhies
Phoenix
Fern
Payne
EAST
CANAL
TALENT
WEST
LATERAL
Gore Cr
Coleman
North Fork
Murphy Cr
Griffin
T. 38 S.
T. 39 S.
LISTENING TREE TRAIL (BLM)
Anderson
Anderson Butte (STATE)
North Fork
South Fork
Section Line Gap
Deming Gul
Wolf Gap
Tunnel Ridge
Muddy Gul
Point Mtn
Yank Gul
Arrastra Cr
Wagner Creek Road
Wagner
Bull Pine Gap
Rush Cr
Pine Ridge
Bald Mtn
STERLING DITCH
Bear
Little Applegate Road
Little Applegate Trailhead
Lick Gul
Little Applegate River
Duncan Gap
Wagner Gap
Shake Gul
Prince Gul
KENNY MEADOWS (BLM)
Quartz Gul
Gulch
Mule Gul
Hendricks Cr
Skunk Gul
Ridge
Cinnabar Gul
Box Canyon Creek
R. 2 W.
R. 1 W.
2250
2240
22
1011

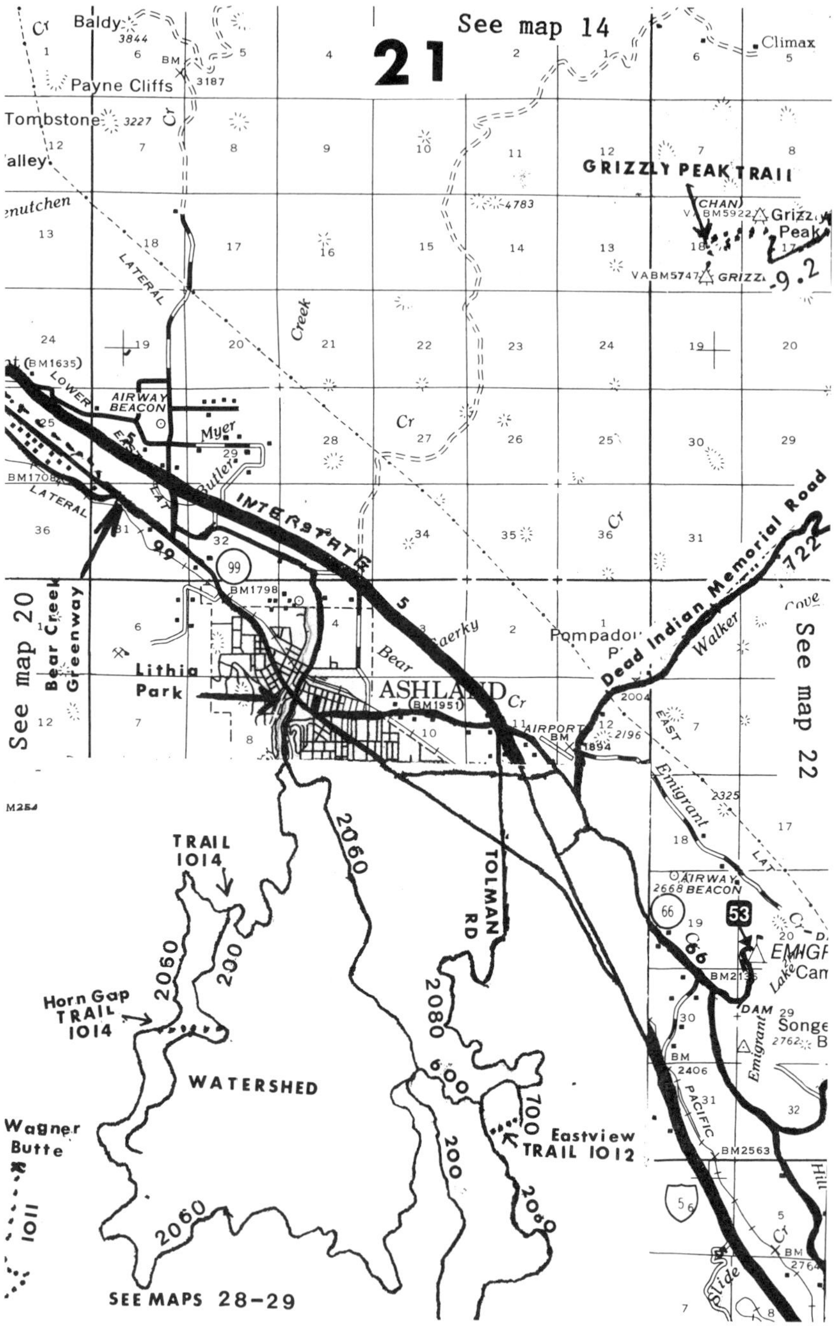
21
See map 14
See map 20
See map 22
SEE MAPS 28–29
GRIZZLY PEAK TRAIL
9.2
Baldy
3844
Payne Cliffs
Tombstone
3227
Climax
Grizzly Peak
INTERSTATE 5
99
Bear Creek Greenway
Lithia Park
ASHLAND
Dead Indian Memorial Road
722
Walker
Pompadour
AIRPORT
AIRWAY BEACON
Myer
Butler
LOWER
LATERAL
Emigrant
66
53
TRAIL 1014
Horn Gap TRAIL 1014
2060
200
TOLMAN RD
2080
600
700
Eastview TRAIL 1012
WATERSHED
Wagner Butte
1011
PACIFIC
Slide Cr
Songer

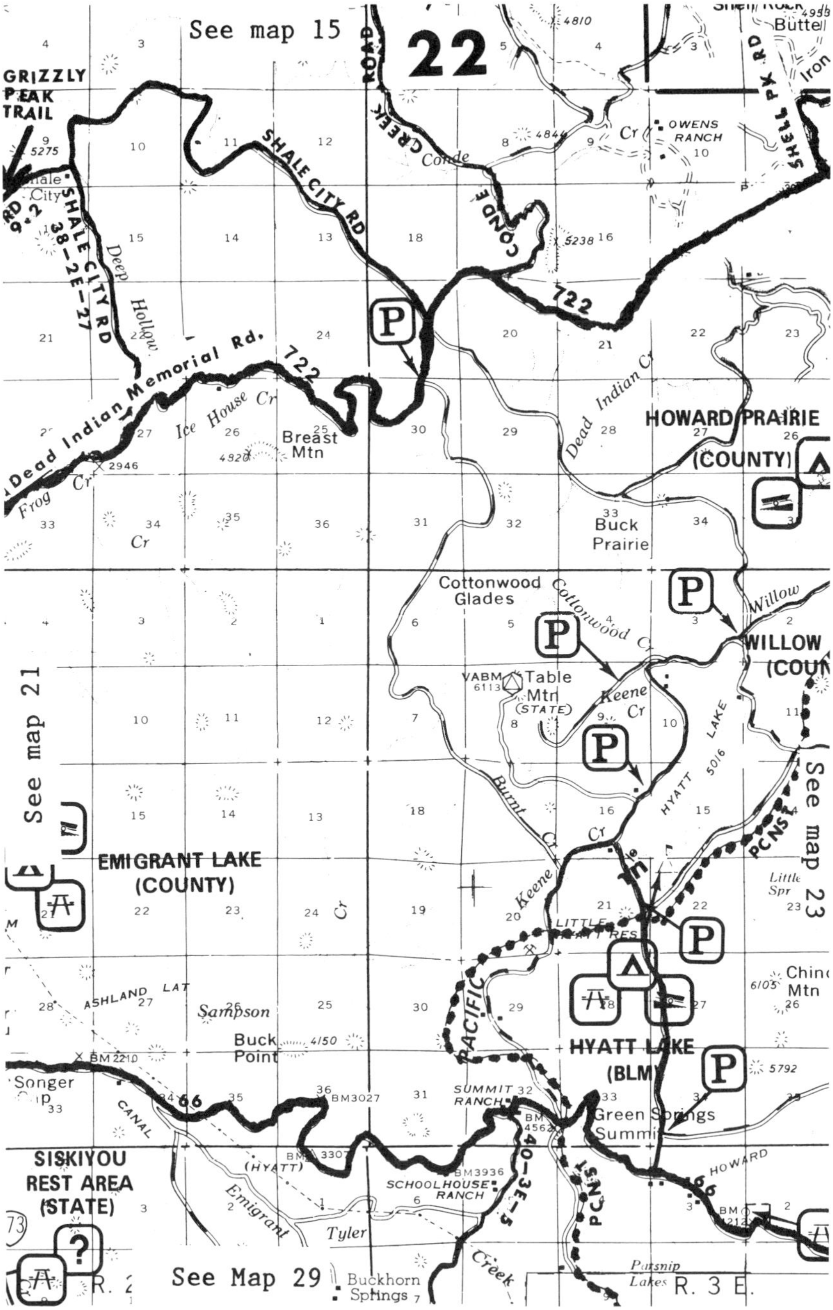
22
See map 15
See map 21
See map 23
See Map 29
GRIZZLY PEAK TRAIL
SHALE CITY RD
SHALE CITY RD 38-2E-27
CREEK ROAD
CONDE
Conde
SHELL PK RD
Shell Rock Butte
OWENS RANCH
Deep Hollow
Dead Indian Memorial Rd.
722
Ice House Cr
Breast Mtn
Frog Cr
Dead Indian Cr
HOWARD PRAIRIE (COUNTY)
Buck Prairie
Cottonwood Glades
Cottonwood Cr
WILLOW
Willow
VABM 6113
Table Mtn (STATE)
Keene Cr
HYATT LAKE 5016
Burnt Cr
PCNST
Little Spr
EMIGRANT LAKE (COUNTY)
LITTLE HYATT RES
PACIFIC
Chinc Mtn
ASHLAND LAT
Sampson
Buck Point
HYATT LAKE (BLM)
Songer Gap
66
CANAL
SUMMIT RANCH
Green Springs Summit
40-3E-5
SISKIYOU REST AREA (STATE)
(HYATT)
SCHOOLHOUSE RANCH
HOWARD
Emigrant
Tyler
Creek
Buckhorn Springs
Parsnip Lakes
R. 3 E.

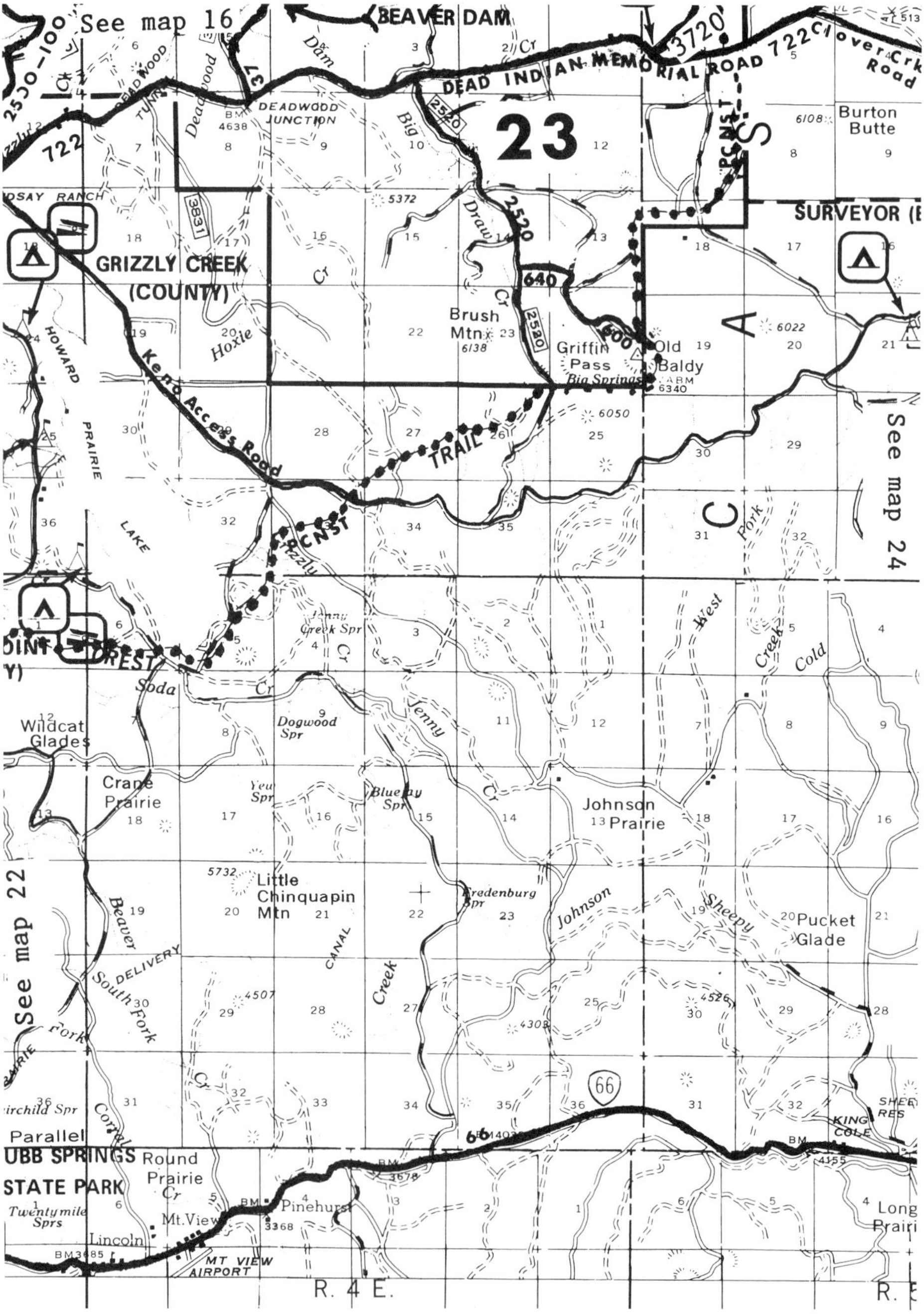

See map 16
BEAVER DAM
DEAD INDIAN MEMORIAL ROAD 722
Clover Crk Road
3720
2520
23
DEADWOOD JUNCTION
Deadwood
Dam
Big
Burton Butte
SURVEYOR
PCNST
GRIZZLY CREEK (COUNTY)
HOWARD PRAIRIE LAKE
Keno Access Road
Hoxie
Brush Mtn
6138
Draw
640
600
Griffin Pass
Big Springs
Old Baldy
6340
6050
6022
5372
TRAIL
See map 24
West Fork
Grizzly
Jenny Creek Spr
Soda Cr
Wildcat Glades
Dogwood Spr
Jenny Cr
Cold Creek
Crane Prairie
Yew Spr
Bluejay Spr
Johnson Prairie
5732
Little Chinquapin Mtn
Fredenburg Spr
Johnson
Sheepy
Pucket Glade
See map 22
Beaver
DELIVERY
South Fork
CANAL
Creek
4507
4526
4303
66
Fairchild Spr
Parallel
HUBB SPRINGS STATE PARK
Round Prairie
Twentymile Sprs
Mt.View
Lincoln
Pinehurst
3678
3368
BM3685
MT VIEW AIRPORT
KING COLE
SHEEP RES
4155
Long Prairie
R. 4 E.

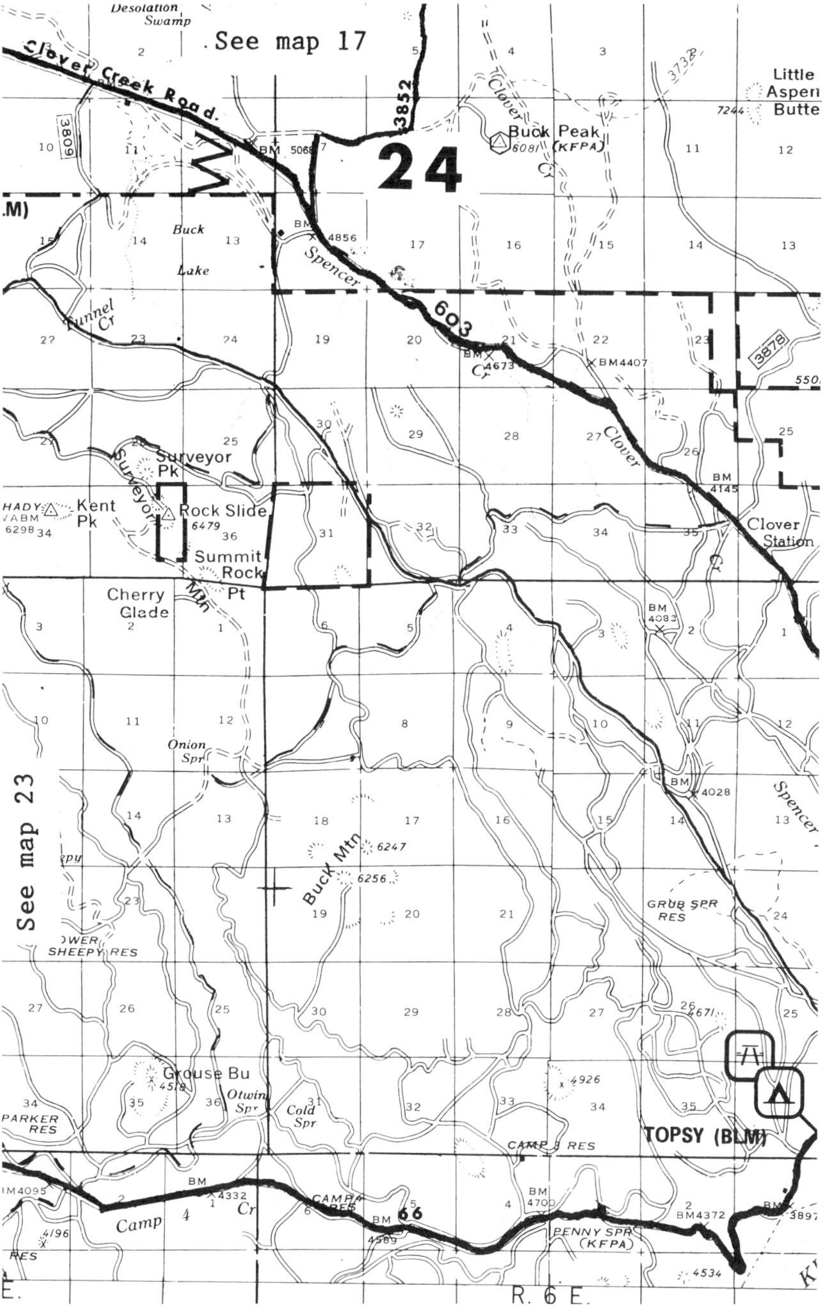
See map 17
Clover Creek Road
24
603
66
See map 23
Desolation Swamp
Buck Peak (KFPA)
Little Aspen Butte
Buck Lake
Spencer
Clover Cr
Surveyor Pk
Kent Pk
Rock Slide
Summit Rock
Cherry Glade
Surveyor Mtn
Clover Station
Onion Spr
Buck Mtn
GRUB SPR RES
SHEEPY RES
Grouse Bu
Otwin Spr
Cold Spr
PARKER RES
CAMP 3 RES
TOPSY (BLM)
Camp Cr
PENNY SPR (KFPA)
R. 6 E.

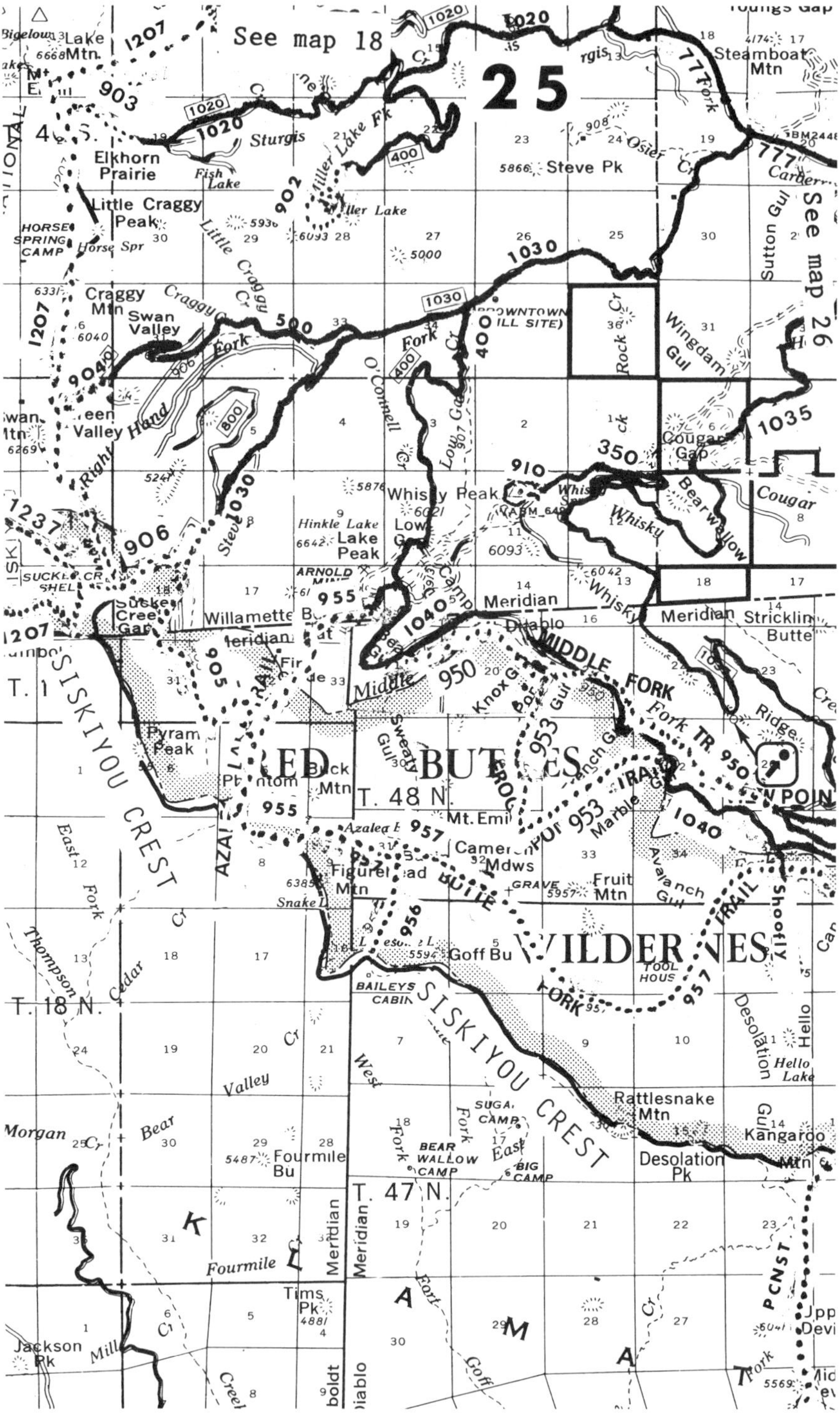

See map 18
25
See map 26
Lake Mtn.
Elkhorn Prairie
Fish Lake
Sturgis
Miller Lake Fk
Miller Lake
Little Craggy Peak
HORSE SPRING CAMP
Horse Spr
Little Craggy Cr
Steve Pk
Osier Cr
Steamboat Mtn
Craggy Mtn
Swan Valley
Craggy Cr
Fork
Rock Cr
Wingdam Gul
Sutton Gul
Cougar Gap
Cougar
Green Valley
Right Hand
O'Connell Cr
Low Gap
Whisky Peak
Whisky
Bearwallow
Hinkle Lake
Lake Peak
ARNOLD MINE
Sucker Cree Gap
Willamette
Meridian
Diablo
Stricklin Butte
SISKIYOU CREST
RED BUTTES
WILDERNESS
MIDDLE FORK
Pyram Peak
Phantom
Buck Mtn
T. 48 N.
Mt. Emily
Cameron Mdws
Figurehead Mtn
Snake L
GRAVE
Fruit Mtn
Marble Gul
Avalanche Gul
Shoofly
Goff Bu
TOOL HOUSE
BAILEYS CABIN
Desolation
Hello Lake
East Fork
Thompson
Cedar Cr
T. 18 N.
Valley Cr
West Fork
SUGAR CAMP
BEAR WALLOW CAMP
BIG CAMP
Rattlesnake Mtn
Kangaroo Mtn
Desolation Pk
Morgan
Bear Cr
Fourmile Bu
T. 47 N.
Meridian
Fourmile
Tims Pk
Jackson Pk
Mill
Creek
PCNST
K L A M A T

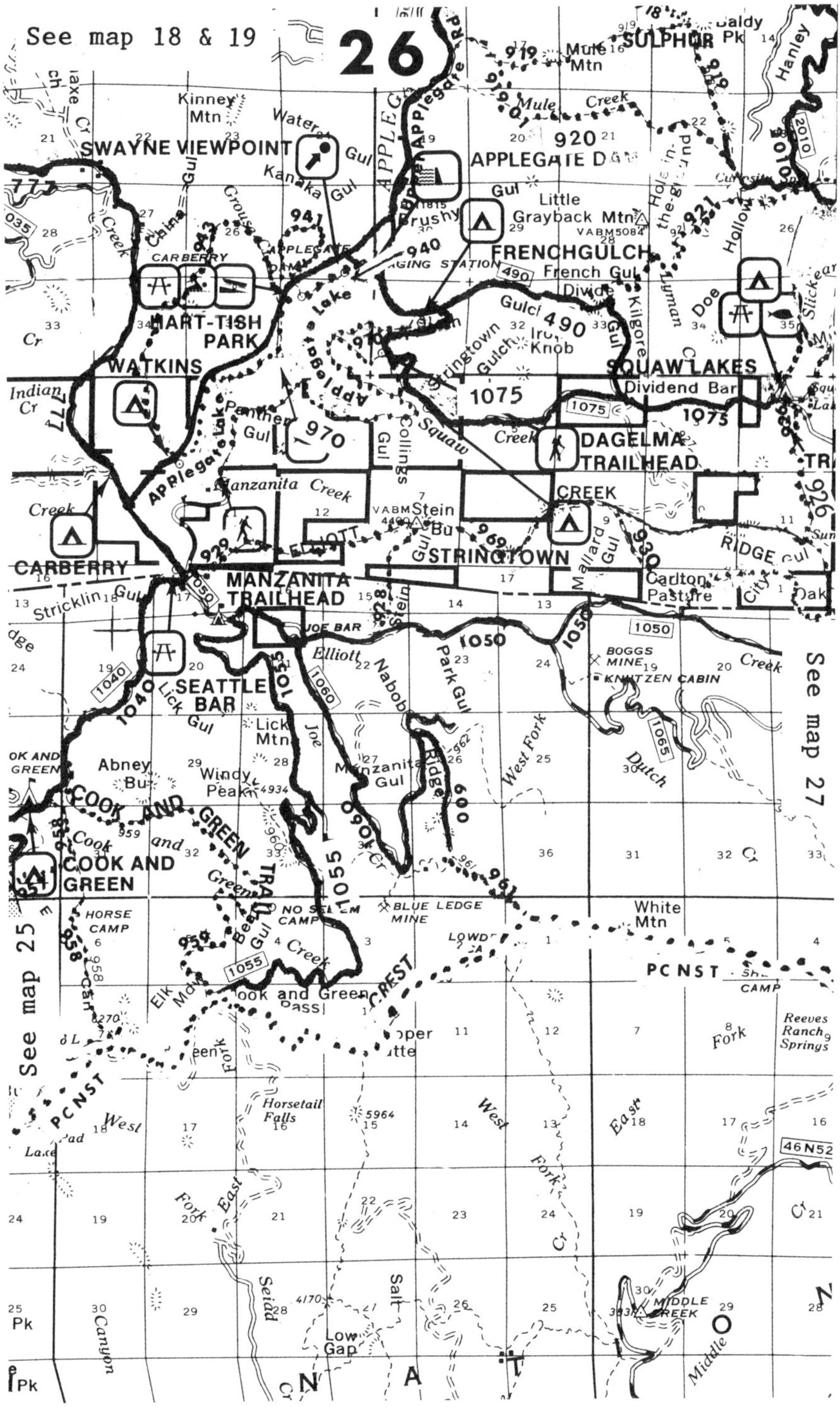

See map 18 & 19
26
SWAYNE VIEWPOINT
APPLEGATE DAM
Kinney Mtn
Mule Mtn
SULPHUR
Baldy Pk
Mule Creek
Little Grayback Mtn
FRENCHGULCH
French Gul
Divide
Iron Knob
CARBERRY
HART-TISH PARK
WATKINS
Applegate Lake
SQUAW LAKES
Dividend Bar
DAGELMA TRAILHEAD
CREEK
STRINGTOWN
MANZANITA TRAILHEAD
Manzanita Creek
Stein Bu
Carlton Pasture
JOE BAR
SEATTLE BAR
Lick Mtn
Windy Peak
Abney Bu
BOGGS MINE
KNUTZEN CABIN
COOK AND GREEN TRAIL
COOK AND GREEN
HORSE CAMP
BLUE LEDGE MINE
White Mtn
PCNST
Cook and Green Pass
CREST
Reeves Ranch Springs
Horsetail Falls
Low Gap
MIDDLE CREEK
See map 25
See map 27

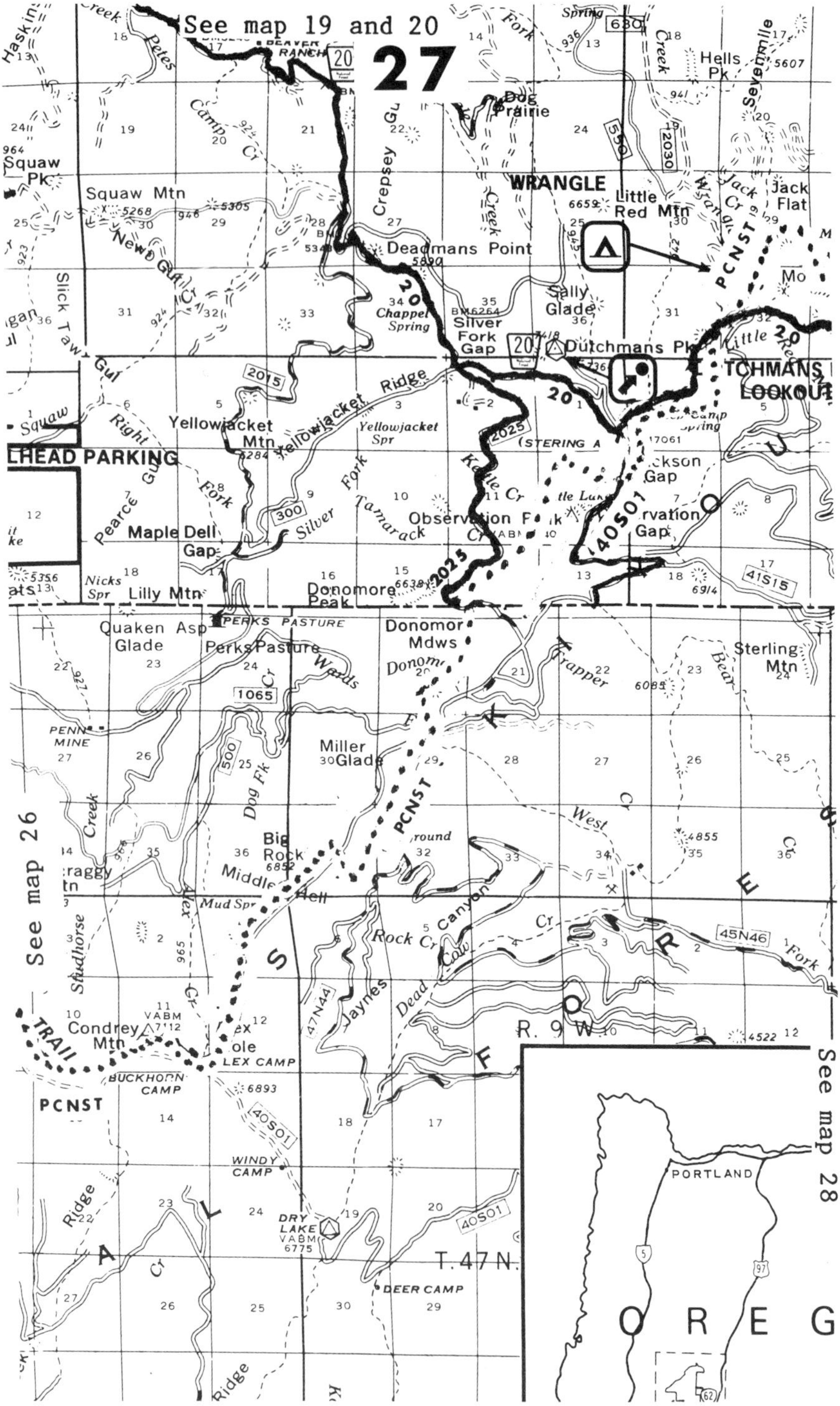
See map 19 and 20
27
See map 26
See map 28
Squaw Pk
Squaw Mtn
Dog Prairie
WRANGLE
Little Red Mtn
Hells Pk
Jack Flat
Deadmans Point
Chappel Spring
Silver Fork Gap
Sally Glade
Dutchmans Pk
Yellowjacket Mtn
Yellowjacket Ridge
Yellowjacket Spr
Maple Dell Gap
Observation Peak
Lilly Mtn
Donomore Peak
Quaken Asp Glade
Perks Pasture
Donomore Mdws
Sterling Mtn
PENN MINE
Miller Glade
Big Rock
Condrey Mtn
LEX CAMP
BUCKHORN CAMP
PCNST
WINDY CAMP
DRY LAKE VABM 6775
DEER CAMP
R. 9 W.
T. 47 N.
PORTLAND
O R E G

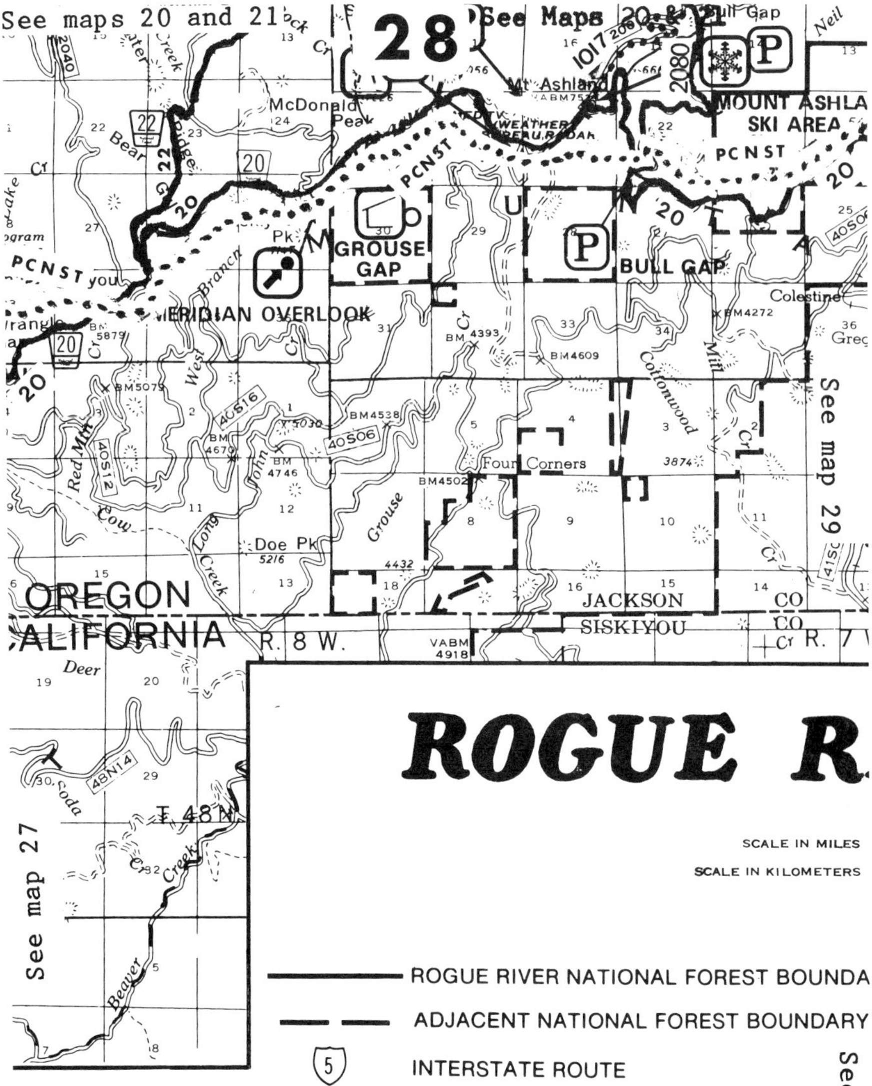

ROGUE R

SCALE IN MILES

SCALE IN KILOMETERS

ROGUE RIVER NATIONAL FOREST BOUNDA

ADJACENT NATIONAL FOREST BOUNDARY

5 INTERSTATE ROUTE

199 U.S. ROUTE

20 STATE ROUTE

37 NATIONAL FOREST PRIMARY ROUTE

392 NATIONAL FOREST SECONDARY ROUTE

PAVED ROAD

ALL WEATHER ROAD

DIRT ROAD

See map 29

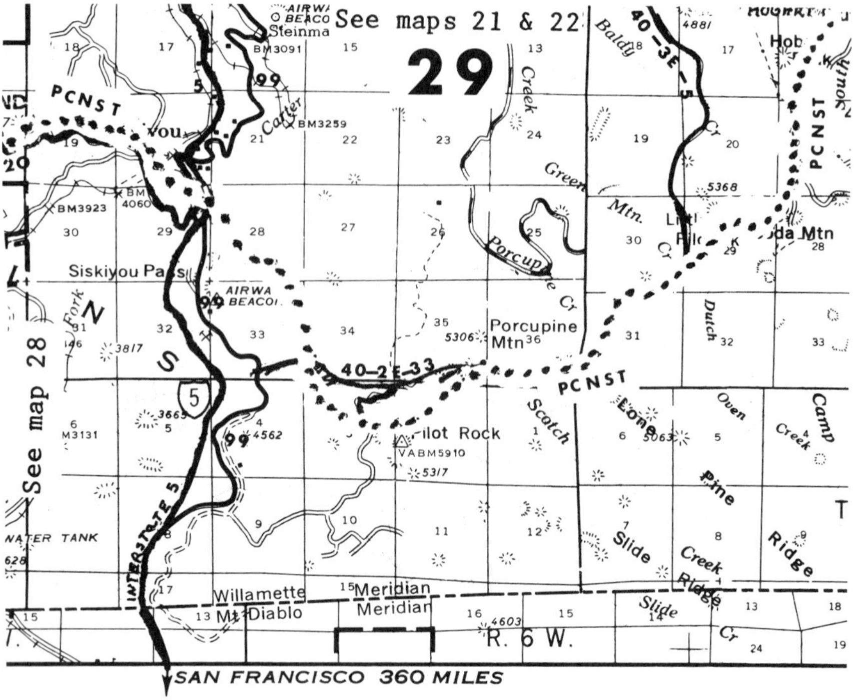

IVER National Forest

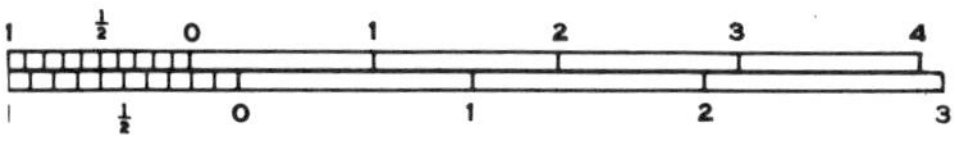

LEGEND

ROGUE RIVER NATIONAL FOREST	CAMPGROUND
ADJACENT NATIONAL FOREST	PICNIC AREA
BUREAU OF LAND MANAGEMENT	FISHING
STATE LANDS	LAUNCHING RAMP
FOREST SUPERVISOR HEADQUARTERS	WINTER RECREATION
RANGER STATION	NATURE TRAIL
FOREST SERVICE STATION	TRAIL SHELTER
PACIFIC CREST NATIONAL SCENIC TRAIL (Closed to Motorized Vehicles)	WINTER PARKING (FEE AT SOME AREAS)
	POINT OF INTEREST

See Map 28